CONFESSIONS OF A CONJUROR

www.**rbooks**.co.uk

DERREN BROWN

CONFESSIONS OF A CONJUROR

Books

TRANSWORLD PUBLISHERS
61–63 Uxbridge Road, London W5 5SA
A Random House Group Company
www.rbooks.co.uk

First published in Great Britain
in 2010 by Channel 4 Books
an imprint of Transworld Publishers

Copyright © Objective 2010

Derren Brown has asserted his right under the Copyright, Designs
and Patents Act 1988 to be identified as the author of this work.

This book is a work of non-fiction. In some cases names of people, places, dates, sequences or the detail of events have been changed solely to protect the privacy of others. The author has stated to the publishers that, except in such minor respects not affecting the substantial accuracy of the work, the contents of this book are true.

Photograph on p. 147 courtesy of Mary Evans Picture Library/Harry Price.
Line illustrations by Patrick Mulrey.

A CIP catalogue record for this book
is available from the British Library.

ISBNs 9781905026579 (cased)
9781905026586 (tpb)

Addresses for Random House Group Ltd companies outside the UK
can be found at: www.randomhouse.co.uk
The Random House Group Ltd Reg. No. 954009

The Random House Group Limited supports the Forest Stewardship
Council (FSC), the leading international forest-certification organization. All our
titles that are printed on Greenpeace-approved FSC-certified paper carry the FSC logo.
Our paper procurement policy can be found at
www.rbooks.co.uk/environment

Typeset in 12.75/17.5 pt Bembo by
Falcon Oast Graphic Art Ltd.
Printed and bound in Great Britain by
Clays Ltd, Bungay, Suffolk

2 4 6 8 10 9 7 5 3

Every effort has been made to obtain the necessary permissions with reference to copyright material, both illustrative and quoted. We apologize for any omissions in this respect and will be pleased to make the appropriate acknowledgements in any future edition.

Mixed Sources
Product group from well-managed
forests and other controlled sources
www.fsc.org Cert no. TF-COC-2139
© 1996 Forest Stewardship Council
FSC

For the Dolly

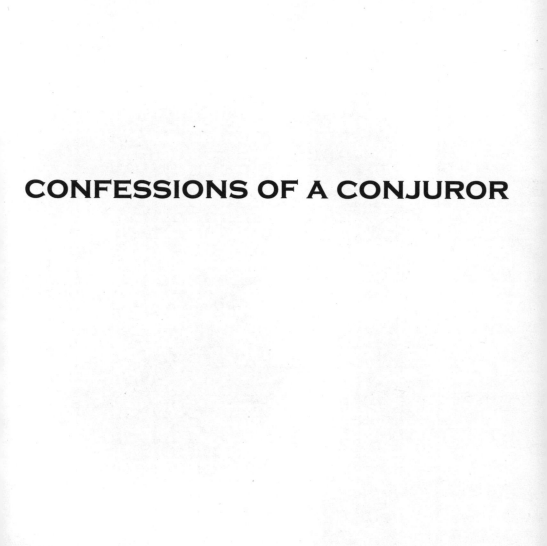

CONFESSIONS OF A CONJUROR

CHAPTER

1

I loathed myself again. My heart pounded beneath my *stupid blousy gay shirt*, and as ever, I found it absurd that I had done this a thousand times yet still battled with the same weary desire to be veiled in the shadows of a corner, to keep out of everyone's way and let them enjoy themselves in peace. I was conscious that the grey eyes of the French barman, who had now seen me emerge from the disabled toilet three times in the last fifteen minutes, were resting on me with an appropriately mixed signal of curiosity, admonishment and condescension. This glance, on reflection, may have simply been the natural look of a Frenchman abroad, but it struck me at the time as a recognition of my ludicrously transparent capacity for procrastination, and my self-hatred ratcheted up another notch, making it even more difficult to shake myself from the immobilising stupor.

For all he knows, I have to prepare mentally and take time to choose my spectators with care and precision. So with a serious expression I surveyed the restaurant for the hundredth time and flipped over the deck of cards in my hand.

The new deck of red-backed Bicycle-brand poker cards had that afternoon been worn in for the gig through bending and riffling and springing until the deck's spirit had been broken; in the way that a puppy, made to walk to heel, piss on the newspaper and not eat the roast, loses its bungling vigour and learns to behave. A brand-new Bike deck is, for a short while, wanton and precarious. For those first few minutes it may simply spread effortlessly in the hands, the cards riding the frictionless slivers of oily space that lie between each virgin surface and gliding on their own advertised 'air-cushioned finish'; absorbing and re-directing the pressure of the fingers into a beautiful, even spread at the slightest touch; each pasteboard fluidly moving along with its one-higher/one-lower neighbour. But as marvellous as this evenness of movement is, and as satisfying as it feels to see a ribbon of fifty-four perfectly spaced and ordered indices appear almost instantaneously between the hands with an apparent mastery of controlled pressure that could not likely be wielded upon grubbier cards after a career of practice, the new deck is at other times reckless and prone to belching itself without warning from the hand, leaving usually just two cards held: a circumstance caused by the natural moisture from the thumb and forefinger pads adhering to the back of the top card and face of the bottom respectively and holding them back while the others issue defiantly from one's grip towards the floor.

Idiot. In my velvet frock suit and ruffled cuffs, like some ludicrous hybrid of J. S. Bach and Martin Kemp back in the day. Around the bottom of my face a goatee like a seventies pubic bush, untouched by clippers since its first appearance as a student years before and which would remain so for another year still, reaching madly in all directions, until one morning, standing at the mirror in my freezing mezzanine bathroom just down the stairs from my flat, I would eventually cut into its sides with the bacon scissors with a view to divesting myself of it completely, and a pleasing Mephistophelean point would emerge.

I held the deck level in my hands and played at tilting and squeezing the slippery pile, almost but not quite enough to discharge it on to the flagstone tiles in the manner I found myself considering. I pictured them tumbling to the floor, myself bending over to gather them up, and the embarrassed derision of the silent diners as they watched me carry out the apologetic, uncomfortable process. I caught myself being distracted again, and tried to heave my attention back towards these covers I was being paid to entertain. Tried, but within seconds my focus returned obsessively to the shifting fifty-two pasteboards in my hands and the further preoccupation they offered.

Following the unstoppable spillage caused by the combination of pinching pressure and the merest accidental misalignment, the finger and thumb will instinctively continue their trajectory towards each other following the sudden disappearance of the remainder of the deck, and the top and bottom cards (in the case of a newly opened and unshuffled set of Bikes, these will always be the Joker and an advertising card offering a discount of fifty cents against further purchases from the US Playing Card Company) will be brought together in an action not unlike that of a belly-dancer's finger-cymbals, while

13

the balance of the cards lie scattered on the floor in a face-up/face-down slop. Here you are faced with two sources of annoyance, the greater being the anticipation of having to kneel down and begrudgingly assemble the cards into a disordered pile of single orientation, which involves not only upturning all the downturned cards (or vice versa, whichever set is smaller), but also the trickier task of neatly squaring up a near-deck of chaotically strewn playing cards into a single satisfying block. This is easier said than done, and is most easily achieved through a manoeuvre known to experienced card-players and magicians: grabbing the entire set of misaligned cards into one cluster and holding them perpendicular to the floor (or table), then *rolling* the messy stack back and forth along its side until all the corners have been brought into alliance. The secondary, lesser source of displeasure is the niggling sense that the deck has been soiled: it may never again be seen in manufacturer's order, and the patented air-cushion finish has most likely been forever lost following the intrusion of hairs, skin-flakes and other carpet debris into the spaces between the cards.

The barman was now busy dealing uninterestedly with a fat man wearing a thin, loose tie who was peering at the whiskies over the counter. The bar was pushing into the man's stomach as he heaved himself high enough to read the labels on the Glenmorangies, Laphroaigs and Macallans that authoritatively lined the raised shelf behind the brandies and cognacs. He was pushing up on to the balls of his feet and grasping with both hands a brass rail that ran along the front of the bar perhaps a foot below its edge. I wondered what he was feeling at that moment: the tension in his hamstrings, the cool brass, the push of the counter into his middle section, the straining of his eyes and jutting forward of his slack neck to recognise the labels on the bottles. I tried to recreate these sensations mentally, and considered, as I tensed and shifted in microcosm, that that was what he was feeling *right now*; that for him the experience of all life revolved in this instant around those sensations, and that I was (with my annoyance and self-hatred and reluctance to work) at most a blur in the corner of his vision.

As he pointed to a bottle and then, a beat later, happy that the barman knew which he required, hauled himself back to standing straight, I tried to lose myself in what I imagined his world to be. I tried to picture the bar and barman straight-on, to hear the buzz of the restaurant behind me rather than to one side, to imagine the feel of his meal inside me, his weight on my bones, the faint sensation of comfort following the loosening of shoe leather from across the bridge of my toes as he lowered himself back to the floor. I wondered whether he had picked a whisky he knew well – I imagined so, as the range was not especially adventurous and he seemed to care about which one he was given – and whether, in that case, he was at that moment imagining the walloping peaty taste he knew he was soon to enjoy. There was something in the showy ease of the barman and the assured way in which he set the glass upon the counter that had about it a hint of performance, a suggestion of the 'flair' that sometimes flamboyantly attends the preparation of cocktails; I presumed that the man was noticing this affectation too, with mild irritation at its pointlessness, and making quiet judgements accordingly. I did the same, following my own references: a blurry memory of a poster for the film *Cocktail*, and a repeated film-loop of a chess player planting a knight upon a square and firmly twisting it into place with that same defiance.

A woman passed by, having emerged from the ladies' toilet behind me, and the game ended. The sound of the refilling cistern within was bright and loud, and then abruptly muted as the door bumped closed. The fat man wobbled away from the bar and from me, a little inebriated, and my empathy with his thoughts and sensations was lost under the high ceilings of the wide, noisy lounge. The restaurant was again before me, and my hand again noted its grasp of the cards. I resented the severing of the connection, and wondered whether being privy to a person's meandering thoughts and gently tracing their dreamy associations was to really know them, at a level far deeper than answers provided by personality tests, school reports or the selective, retrospective narratives of traditional biography.

I watched the man manoeuvre himself to a low stone slab of a table in a far corner of the lounge, occupied by his chattering friends, who paid him no attention as he placed his glass down with a faint double *cli-clink* and remained standing to look round the room. His eyes trailed uncertainly in my direction while I observed, and passed me, still searching. Eventually they found the back of one of the slim, neat, white-clad downstairs waiters, who was taking bundled napkins and glasses (each containing an inch or so of part-melted ice, a citrus sliver and a long plastic stirrer) from an unoccupied table and placing them on a round, black, rubberised tray.

The fat man approached him unseen. The waiter began to walk towards the large carved wooden door that led to the small kitchen. I knew where the glasses and napkins would be put: I had seen the colossal dishwashers and machines inside the small downstairs kitchen where meticulously wrought cold starter platters were prepared for those who wished to nibble downstairs before moving upstairs for their main meal. The older, larger man was moving more slowly, but called something to the waiter before the latter had a chance to disappear into the back-room hive of steel and steam (and, usually, heavy-accented discussions of what stock might be needed for the next day). The waiter spun round to greet the man, eyebrows raised, suddenly alert and smiling. The smile remained as he almost imperceptibly jutted his head forward and narrowed his eyes to understand the gist of a lubricated glutton who did not speak his first language. Barely had the fat man begun to speak than the waiter looked towards me and pointed with a gesture made by flattening his free right hand, palm to the left, and tracing a full arc in the air. This full-handed point alighted almost directly upon me for a beat, and then, as one, his fingers levered quickly and neatly at the knuckles, signifying to the man the secondary, left-turn instruction that was necessary to locate the gents' toilet. The man mouthed an acknowledgement and started to walk towards me, slack-faced and lumbering, slightly sad and out of place, away from the enthralled and exuberant jabbering at his friends' table.

I watched him approach, nearly colliding with the blonde girl from Bolivia or Bulgaria who squirted mists of sweet-smelling liquid on to tables when the diners were gone, but who wore the black outfit instead of the white and whose English was as impenetrable as the joyless eyes that peered from the depths of her dark, grave sockets. I moved to my right to give him ample room to pass, and as he came close he saw that I was looking at him. We both dropped our gaze and, glancing indifferently at the cards in my hands, he shuffled past. I saw the shabby edges of his black soft-soled shoes, and his wristwatch, the brown leather strap tight around him like wire pulled around dough. My mind flashed back to the annoying band on the water-snake toy I had as a child. This was a green, endlessly rolling-in-on-itself water-filled balloon that would shoot from your hand when you tried to grip it, but which was encircled by a band of rubber: a band which not only disappointingly betrayed the edges of the infinite loop, but also, being slightly too tight for the toy, stuck it intermittently and upset its otherwise smooth, unholy operation. (It eventually emerged that the water inside these toys was contaminated, which motivated my mother to throw mine away despite my protestations that I would be extremely careful never to burst it.)

I turned my attention back to the cards undergoing the absent-minded and precarious manipulation in my hands. They were red-backed, as ever, because the other readily available colour, blue, had never appealed. Blue cards contrast less satisfyingly than red with the green baize of a card table or the jet black of the suit I wore when working, and red has the advantage of a certain new-world pizzazz over the duller blue. Blue-backed cards are stolid PCs to the lively Apple of reds; they are BT or BA to Virgin. Since leaving school I have had as much distaste for blue ink in fountain or rollerball pens as I have had a general fondness for the pens themselves. Blue was the prescribed ink colour at my primary and secondary schools, and I cannot use it to this day without feeling in my gut that I am again a student and should be handing in my work for marking. This is not dissimilar to the way the sight and smell of a particular cheap pink liquid soap, dispensed from a hand-operated sink-side pump in a favourite Italian restaurant near my apartment (and an Indian restaurant in Blackpool), fling me back, like Proust's *petite madeleine*, to ages five to ten and the vivid recollection of my primary school wash area, with its uneven green-painted cement floor and baking-parchment toilet paper and shoe bags and football boots. The smell of the soap quickly commingles with the earthy scent from the studded footwear and the chemical pong from the lavatories, and in this olfactory-led reverie I can recall details I haven't thought about in decades. In this proudly old-fashioned school we used dip-pens, and the ink from our Bakelite inkwells, full of sediment and finger-staining, was always blue.

School ink. Later, at a fine, leafy grammar school in Croydon, turquoise ink was a favourite of Mr Pattison, and is thus firmly associated in my mind with the affectations of much-admired and gently eccentric teachers. For many years during and after university I liked to use brown ink, and enjoyed the rather Victorian effect of the sepia-toned script that flowed unevenly from the tortoiseshell Parker I still own, and which, I note now after a brief search, is still crusty with the very same ink of which I speak, the barrel now firmly secured to the nib section through years of neglect following a shift in allegiance to the breathless peaks of Mont Blanc some time ago. I have since settled for black ink, following an urge to purge myself of what I felt to be the more obvious poses in my life: somehow with the ghost of my ambivalent feelings towards Mr Pattison's mannered turquoise notations still a faintly lingering presence, brown ink had to be replaced with something less showy.

To be swept back by an unconscious association to the muddy, soapy smell of the wash-and-change area of our primary schools by a restaurant's thrifty choice of hand-wash, and once in that sense-memory to recall the origins of a faint distaste for a particular ink, and from that aversion to understand why thirty years later we have chosen to buy hundreds of playing-card decks wholesale with one back-colour over another; to be thrown into that long-forgotten world and to remember details which a conscious effort would be unlikely to produce, is to connect to those years with a peculiar immediacy.

This happens in stark contrast to the discovery of old photographs of ourselves at the same age. The mental image we carry around of our classmates seems to age along with us, to the extent that when we as adults come across a photograph depicting us and our friends aged seven or eight, we are struck by how stupidly young we all appear. Could that really be J— whose collection of Star Wars figures I envied beyond words and with whom I argued over administrative aspects of the Worzel Gummidge Fan Club that we started together? And could that be P—, an older boy who I told my friends had bionic implants and was the subject of a very early crush? And dear Lord, surely that mop-haired taller girl cannot be M——, who my parents said was a bit 'slow' and who once showed her front bottom to a queue of us after a French lesson? The curly platinum-haired kid in shorts, who could draw excellent witches and was frequently congratulated on his handwriting, must be me. But we are all little kids there, with the same kid-hair and kid-faces that don't match with the mental pictures I make of us from memory – here inside my head I realise I have been trying to see older faces of my own age, struggling to depict firmer expressions and sharper lines, to remember us as something we never were (and when I recently met with an old classmate, G——, decades after receiving the slipper for sticking the nib of a dip-pen into his buttock, I didn't recognise him at all). Old photographs of ourselves are strange, for with them we see that our world really was a child's world of childish concerns.

Photographs offer the cold stare of limp reality, whereas the smell of pink soap shrinks us down like Alice and ushers us in through a side-door, where we now hate Mr White for shouting at us during football, where we are embarrassed not to know the price of a second-class stamp when Mrs Parker asks us and are furious to be sent to the headmistress to be called stupid (and end up getting the slipper again because we are caught lying when we only *pretend* to have reported to the terrifying blazered octogenarian lesbian, and therefore the punishment is increased. I can bring to mind the stinging slap of my plimsoll being brought down angrily on my outstretched hand in an instant; tears rolling down my face not so much from the pain but from the humiliation of having to walk into a class that she was giving and *ask* for the slipper; having to explain what I had done to deserve it; removing my regulation grey rubber gym-shoe in front of the silent, fascinated older children who were no doubt excited to be watching the rare treat of a naughty boy getting the worst form of punishment the school could offer; extending my hand palm-up and letting the old monster slam the plimsoll down, hoping that she didn't catch my fingers, which would hurt the most. I was slippered eleven times at that primary school: mainly for simple insolence, once for the pen-nib incident, once for pushing B— into the frog pond).

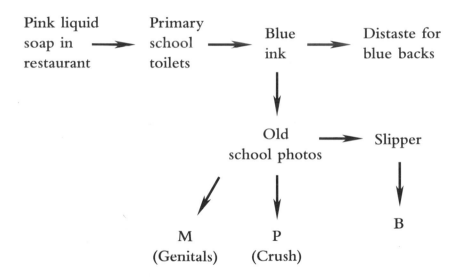

Holding the cards, complaining at the resurgence of the memory, that palm throbbed a little now.

The restaurant was split over two levels, and the downstairs was my domain on Thursday nights, for that is where diners enjoyed their *digestifs* and the post-dinner entertainment hired for the evening. I was such entertainment: a jobbing close-up magician based in Bristol, a few years before a lucky phone call brought me a TV break and a move away from that green city of artists and therapists and tramps to a grey metropolis of actors and wankers and hedge-fund traders. After performing at one of the owner's other restaurants I had been brought on board at the entertainment-planning stage of this sprawling new high-concept restaurant, and it had become my professional residency. A regular restaurant gig is priceless for a working magician. The clientele were also perfect for me: what the restaurant lacked in cosy corners it found in space for larger groups, so each Thursday I performed a few hours for corporate teams and groups of friends who sometimes booked me for their own private events, and in doing so supplemented my restaurant pay and allowed me to earn a comfortable enough living doing what I loved.

Loved, certainly, but there is an aspect to working as a table-hopper that is deeply excruciating to anyone other than the most repellently unselfconscious of us. I was lucky in that most of the diners expected an entertainer to be in their midst, but approaching a happily chatting group with the offer of magic tricks was a necessary embarrassment with which I never quite made my peace. The experienced table-magician will be sure not to interrupt a meal and will develop his own ways of ingratiating himself with a table of diners. Hopefully, once the other diners realise his presence, and perhaps call him over, his job becomes easier; and he can make sure that certain tricks are interesting enough when viewed from a distance in order to quickly engender a feeling of curiosity in the room and minimise the awkwardness of introducing himself again at the next table. But rarely is it so easy, and the potential for self-loathing is enormous. On a good night he might come away feeling like a performing monkey, beckoned hither and thither to impress drunken idiots he would hate to meet under any other circumstance; on a bad night (after a group has politely but firmly expressed its lack of interest upon his approach and others have been clearly only humouring him) he might crawl home hating himself quite considerably − or at least until that night's episode of *Friends*, recorded while he was out and now accompanied by a Highland malt, the chatter of his parakeet and a few chocolates, diverts his mind from such heavy concerns.

The potential for self-loathing comes from the unavoidable problem that one is engaging in a childish, fraudulent activity: although it has the capacity to delight and amaze, the performer is also a hair's breadth from being justifiably treated like a silly child. It is, after all, just tricks. Much upset and controversy can be triggered in the magical fraternity by such disgraces as revealing a method or performing another magician's effect ('effect' is the preferred word for 'trick', and comprises the plot that the audience should follow as opposed to the 'method' which explains it), and equally one may feel a quiet pride in using a method one has devised entirely for oneself, as opposed to one taken from a book drawn from the substantial secret library of the magical fraternity (annals that contain some of the most wonderful, obsessive and pointless texts we human beings have produced), but these considerations tend to seem absurd when viewed from a distance. Two old men arguing over bits of rope or who first shoved a card into his pocket in a certain way are the types of issues that can raise the temperature and lead to ungentlemanly behaviour at any magic hang-out anywhere in the world. It is perhaps the oddness and exclusiveness of the magic world that makes issues of perceived status so important to performers. Among fellow professionals, many have a huge reputation that is not reflected in the public arena outside the magic clubs and conventions, and which can lead to the most appalling bitterness. Even performers who enjoy wider success, not allowed to honestly express to their audience the joy of applying curious and unexplored psychology as well as of creating and employing deceptive methods, can be prone to aggrandising themselves to laughable proportions in a circular battle with their own guilty fear of being seen as a fraud.

A peculiar instance of the precariousness of the table-magician's self-imposed status can be seen at the unfortunate moment when a waiter approaches the table during a trick and interrupts the performance. The carefully controlled play of attention and relaxation which the performer has established is thrown into disarray, and, more frustratingly, the suspicion will arise (and remain) that the magician could have done *anything* while everyone else turned to look at the waiter. The up-until-then status-enjoying Svengali must defer to the restaurant employee and will probably freeze, feeling his anticipated climax slipping further away in direct proportion to the length of time it takes the waiter to carry out his task.

Waiting staff must live in a world of frequent freezes. The

arrival of a waiter has the same dramatic effect on conversation as the intrusion of a person into a lift already occupied by a nattering couple. There is at the table the curious 'Parmesan Moment' when the most animated chatter enters, sometimes mid-word, a cryogenic phase equal in length to the time it takes the waiter to shave hard cheese on to the plates of the erstwhile vivacious diners. No conversation is too mundane, no babble too banal for it to be suddenly classified as anything less than entirely confidential once the rotary grater invades the periphery. If I were a waiter (and I would like to imagine that this idea has already been put into action), I would rotate the utensil as slowly as I could for as long as possible, speeding up perhaps for brief moments here and there just to abate the frustration of the silent parties and keep their annoyance beneath a verbally expressed level. It would be satisfying to think that cooperating staff members might, using discreet stopwatches, time one another attempting to set a record for the longest sustained Parmesan Moment before the party resumes talking, the cheese cube is entirely dispersed or a diner, set to explode, screams for the infuriating process to be curtailed.

The oddness of the reverie that solemnly greets the cheese-bearing waiter is echoed by the strangeness of requesting a napkin and having it brought to the table with disproportionate reverence aboard its own tray, with much of the pomp and silver-service showmanship one might expect to be reserved for the arrival of the entrée. The curious presentation of the napkin is surely not necessitated by hygiene, as the waiter will handle the solitary cloth manually as he places it on the table with a final flourish, but rather by a delight in presentation that makes a white cloth on a tray rather more *special* than a white cloth flopped flaccidly in the hand. This is context; this is pointing the presence of the napkin by putting a clear space around it, rather like a picture, hung in a gallery, looks more special than the same picture propped or hung near other objects that interfere with its sacred periphery. The blurriest and most ill-composed of our personal photographs look quite passable in an album; indeed any one of these incompetent images could look like art if given centre stage on an otherwise empty page. The space around the subject seems to dictate its status (a perhaps counter-intuitive notion given the more familiar sight of celebrities and royalty surrounded by a swarming flurry of bodyguards, press-people and/or fans).

A friend once showed me photographs from his holiday in New York which had been dragged and dropped from a digital library to a virtual album on his computer, after which, following a modest online payment, the album had been printed, bound and sheathed, and sent to my friend in the post. The result was astonishing: these nice but modest family snaps, mounted in what felt like a commercially produced art book, looked like the work of a professional photographer. Here the space around the pictures was not an accidental result of sticking the latter into a shop-bought album, but instead was the product of design, inseparable from the printed and arranged images, and their status was thus raised even further. The same pictures would have seemed far less noteworthy had they been shown without the framing of each page, and merely been 'gone through' by my friend holding the pile of 4×6s in his hand and transferring individual pictures from front to back in a cyclical sequence immediately identifiable as the holiday-snap-showing action. Or at least immediately identifiable to those of us not brought up having viewed photographs only on a computer.

With the demise of the print photograph (and with the printing-out of sets of digital photographs, at least at time of writing, a sentimental throw-back we associate with mothers and the declining classes of the computer-illiterate), we have also lost a particular part of our mimetic repertoire: skipping from one photograph to another on a screen with a mouse-click does not provide us with a familiar gesture-set peculiar to the enjoyable activity of viewing our snaps and allow us to be transported back to fun or beautiful moments, and thus a modicum of charm is lost from the whole process. Inoffensive activities in which we can find the quality of charm because they involve unique and immediately identifiable actions include:

Riding a bicycle
Here a very particular set of actions is involved, used only when cycling; and given the fact that there are far more effort-less modes of transport available to a person who wishes to get from A to B, that set of cycling actions can be seen as peculiar to the point of an almost redundant indulgence. The pedalling action therefore gives this choice of transport mode a kind of quaintness. When bicycles become obsolete, we will have lost a source of charm (a fact to which the following will bear witness: anyone who makes a point of riding one will be seen as an eccentric).

Climbing stairs

Houses of two or more storeys have a particular charm that perfectly lovely bungalows and single-storey flats do not. This is in part due to the necessary architectural inclusion of stairs, and the fact that their presence invites a unique and immediately identifiable sequence of actions. A stair-lift is charmless, as sitting is a commonplace posture, and (perhaps literally) bypasses the stair-ness of stairs and therefore their inherent charisma.

Placing a stamp on an envelope

Written communication will become entirely charmless when no unique actions are involved and all communication happens electronically.

Preparing a tube of toothpaste

or other substance for first use by unscrewing the cap, then turning over the cap and screwing it back *on the other way round,* whereupon a pointed cone in the centre of said cap satisfyingly penetrates a small circle of foil covering the mouth of the tube. The minor charm of this activity is heightened by (a) the barely noticeable amount of suspense experienced as one twists the contrary crown towards the foil and awaits the moment of penetration, and (b) the almost completely imperceptible tactile feedback received as that instance is reached and the tiny silver disc is annihilated by the effortless and cruelly disproportionate force of your phys-ical might, channelled into the tiny, rotating, advancing cap.

Reading a book

Like a napkin borne with great ceremony upon a tray of unnecessary proportions (to make the diner feel that even his face-swab is deemed sacred by staff lost in fawning wonder at his decision to eat and wipe himself within their walls), a magician at a table will create physical or psychological space around an item he wishes you to treat as important. At the same time, the genuinely important item – the fake coin, the special card, the hand that conceals a palmed card – is apparently ignored by the deceiver and where possible pushed to the side among clutter, as he knows that if he does not give it status you will probably not think to do so yourself.

Perhaps the magician wishes to create the illusion of a knife passing through a twenty-pound note, and will achieve this by using an ordinary note but a special knife bought from a magic-shop or built to his own design, which creates the illusion of penetration but in fact causes no harm to the note through which it apparently moves. He could borrow the note to prove to all that it is unfaked, but the better magician might, after moving aside cutlery and crockery from the table, purposefully cast suspicion over this innocent element by producing the twenty from a special pocket in his own wallet (a special pocket is the note's own special space), and then placing it flat on the table, the clear space around it signifying its importance. The knife, meanwhile, has been casually sneaked in among the other cutlery as he swept the objects aside, and lies surrounded by table objects, denied the space, the display and therefore the significance bestowed upon the entirely blameless currency. Keeping his gaze fixed upon the money as he picks it up, the magician takes the knife with his other hand (as if it were any suitably pointed object from the table) and thrusts it through the note. He appears to withdraw the blade, and the small audience see that the paper has remained unharmed. They are incredulous, and stare at where the hole should be in the centre of the note. The magician keeps their attention focused by slowly placing the twenty again on the table before them, returning it to the space he has cleared for it, a designated table-top performance area from which it would be rude for the spectators to remove the money they wish to examine. The cleared region around it has made it the primary object of focus, and without saying anything the performer has allowed all their suspicion to be directed towards an innocent item.

In the same gesture of placing the note back on the cleared table area, the knife has been replaced to the side, and without pause the magician's hand casually slides across and hovers above a different, similar, nearby knife. This small move is missed as the note is the centre of attention and the spectators are waiting to be allowed to examine what they now suspect is a special note. He then gestures for the money to be examined, which they grab willingly; and as he sits back, he lifts the second, guiltless knife, which is under his hand, and places it in the space previously occupied by the note. So now he is using the same space to give a (but not actually *the*) knife importance, and moments later when they realise that there is nothing for them to find in the note, they turn their attention to what they presume is the knife used in the trick, snatch it, and examine it thoroughly to no avail. A trick knife might be the rather disappointing physical solution to the beautiful illusion, but without the magician's deft use of space to focus attention and manipulate status at a wordless level, it would be far less likely to create an effective mystery.

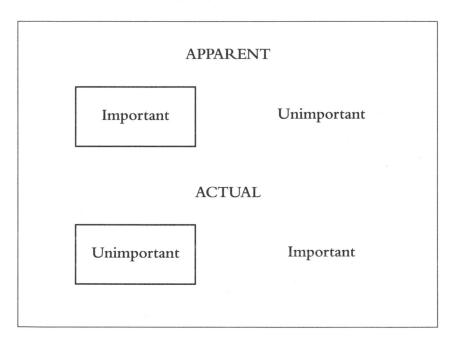

The pristine, white-linen-covered tables that constituted this restaurant work area and which caused my heart to hang heavy were echoed by the coffee-ringed, cheap pine or melamine café tables that populated much of my playtime. The slopes of Bristol host a thriving café industry, and like any arty type with his days free, I was usually sat in one of them. Something in the limp, camp, damp aesthetic of the tea-sipping flâneur appealed, and still does, although the dandyish tea-houses of my graduate years have given way to the Starbucks of my professional period. There is a particular joy, well worth mentioning, of having one's favourite table in such regular haunts. Today, though my time is largely filled with work, I still seek out and jealously guard favourite tables in favourite cafés around London. I hope it does not sound too preposterously flaccid to say that there is a singular bliss in settling down at one of them for a day's reading or writing at the start of a free weekend. Such pleasures I find self-affirming and oddly moving, most probably because they bring with them a wash of nostalgia for those years in Bristol.

Like most people, I prefer tables by the window, and my favourite local table is in a modest Starbucks overlooking a high street from just around a corner in a side-alley. This fortu-itous positioning offers both a bright and busy view of passing London life and a discreet vantage point that means only those few people using the side-alley would be aware of me at all. The fact that I love a bustling backdrop when reading or working in such a place confirms for me that I am very much a city rather than a country type; to gaze out of one's window at a lonely pastoral panorama would be to deny oneself the joy of periodically observing the masses and would not provide the regular, intermittent distractions necessary to keep working for an afternoon. From inside a warm café, through a picture window, we can view pedestrians across the road for far longer than they think (they may be aware of being seen from inside shops and eating-houses on *their* side of the road, but rarely do they consider whether they are being watched from the other). Our eyes can settle unsympathetically upon walloping fatties and then dart to crack-heads and on to toddlers and well-dressed elderly couples. We can judge them all as clichéd and ridiculous or feel a warm glow of love for them, depending on our sentimental state at the time or what we are reading. Alternatively, we can play the private game of if-you-had-to-shag-one-person-on-the-street-who-would-it-be. All options are open to us.

Meanwhile, if we wish, we can enjoy a direct and more scrupulous scrutiny of fellow patrons seated inside the café and the delightful tension that comes from knowing that they might look up and catch our eye at any time. In the café, we can observe more delicate and private behaviours: we can see with what combination of sugars, sugar-substitutes and/or flavoured dustings people prefer to drink their coffee; how they deal with becoming entangled inelegantly as they try to remove coat, scarf and headphones in the wrong sequence and suddenly become self-conscious; what exaggerated expression of exhaustion rolls across their face after reaching their table and realising that they have forgotten to take a stirrer from the dustings bar, and, knowing that they must now cross the length of the café to fetch one (in front of everyone else who has just watched them pimp their beverage with assorted peripherals at the very bar they must now return to), the signal they provide that they themselves find their return just as annoying as it must appear untoward or amusing to the other patrons.

This tutting, eye-rolling signal is related to the gesture we might make on the street after realising that we are walking in the wrong direction from that where we wish to head. Wanting to turn round but fearing the attention we will attract by breaking rank and turning one-hundred-and-eighty degrees for no clear reason, we decide to use a cartoon-gesture that denotes 'Having Forgotten Something': we raise a forefinger slightly to make a minimal 'A-ha!' point, raise our eyebrows, stop in our tracks and provide a visible motivation for the very public rotation we are about to perform. 'Look,' we imagine people will think, 'that guy has realised he has forgotten something; how sensible that he should now turn round and attend to it. What sound judgement on his part.' If we were alone, we would not make that cartoon-gesture of sudden remembrance.

I like to catch myself and others acting out such brief self-conscious thought processes because they remind me of what I have come to think of as 'In a Play' moments: reliable actions one encounters only in actors on stage and never in the real life they are failing at that moment to depict convincingly. Here are some 'In a Play' moments I have mentally collected:

Sitting like a king in a play
Kings in Shakespeare relax back in their chairs and slouch to one side, allowing the hand on the side to which they are leaning to be comfortably raised to the face for beard-stroking or waving things away.

Sitting like a prince in a play
A prince, on the other hand, sits jauntily forward in the chair, legs spryly and widely apart, leaning to one side as if telling an imagined neighbour something in confidence, with an elbow resting dashingly on the knee towards the side he is leaning.

Entering a room for the first time in a play
Here, one should clearly look at each of the walls and especially

the imagined ceiling, twisting the head up and round to take in the whole of the space with a gentle, wide-eyed display of wonder.

Approaching a lover in a play

Lovers approaching each other, especially if singing, should lean back a little and extend both arms forward at an angle of forty-five degrees to the floor, with hands extended. The lady's palms should be facing down, the man's up, so that when they meet they can clasp their hands together in one bundle, bring them up to the centre of the chest and gaze unconvincingly into each other's eyes.

Looking at something far away in a play

When checking if one can see a person or thing that is so far away that it resides well off-stage, the sense of distance is magically created by looking into the wings and stepping up on to the ball of the forward foot as if one were looking over a fence that was a little higher than one's eye-level.

Telling a story in a play

When person A describes an event to person B, both A and B should face forward so that A can move his hand to paint a picture in the air and B can follow that hand in order to build the same mental picture for himself. B should be engrossed in the gestures made by A, and if at any point A wishes to ensure that B is entirely infected with his own enthusiasm for the tale, A can simply bat B on the chest with the back of his hand. I have to say that while I have never known human beings to communicate in this way, or in any that resembles it, this is both one of the most bizarre and yet blindly accepted 'In a Play' moments of which I am aware.

Flirting in a play

If you are a lady wishing to secure the attention of a handsome but shy male, a surefire route is to clasp your hands behind your back and walk round him in that coquettish, pointy-toed, one-foot-directly-in-front-of-the-other, shoulder-swinging style that handsome but shy men read as sexually attractive (as opposed to a sign of mental illness). If this fails, laugh a lot over your shoulder, pull at his tie a little or do walky-fingers up the front of his shirt before laughing again and running off. No handsome but shy male should be able to resist.

Delivering sexual innuendos in a play

An audience at a Shakespeare play are not usually a clever lot, so it is best to clarify any sexual double-entendre in a line by thrusting the right forearm into the air (like a phallus) while gripping the bicep with the left hand. Characters who use sexual innuendo are usually fun-loving and spirited, and tend to say things that are 'tongue-in-cheek'. This can be clarified by actually poking the tongue clearly into the cheek just after a line has been delivered.

Experiencing loss of a loved one in Shakespeare's time in a play

Sixteenth-century ladies would always place one forearm across the stomach and bend forward, extending the other arm before them in the gesture of 'I'm trying to reach but simultaneously stopping myself with my own arm' that we so commonly associate with loss.

Noticing people when wandering outdoors in a play
When approaching people on a beach or in a forest, do not notice them until you are close enough to be seen on stage yourself. Even though you would have seen them from miles off, it is best to save being startled by their presence until very close.

Being a lady working in a guest-house in a play
By the end of the day you have had enough of hard work and time-wasters, so it would be correct to slam a pitcher down on the table and sigh loudly into an uncomfortably lopsided both-hands-on-hips position to let us know that. If you are particularly salt-of-the-earth, you can certainly take the towel used for wiping the table clean and throw it heartily over the shoulder, before standing like that to show your rustic exhaustion, just like in real life.

Squaring the cards in my hands, and then rotating the deck to enjoy the cool texture of their flush edges, I scanned the wide sweep of the restaurant interior to locate a table appropriate to approach. A fresh wave of reluctance twisted through my gut at the thought of interrupting happily chatting groups or risking a dead atmosphere at a quiet table. In the restaurant's toilet I had assembled a few magical aids among and under my clothing that I would use later in the evening. It was a comfort to think that all over the world, close-up magicians at the top of their game had to find moments to lock themselves in cubicles and sort out their pockets while peering into a toilet bowl. This is the wonderful, sad human reality behind the mystery of much of magic. The hobbyist conjuror who suddenly produces a bottle of champagne from a handkerchief for his friends has been carrying that bottle around all evening, cold and wet and heavy against his thigh, and while keeping up a pretence of conversation has been thinking of little other than when there might be a suitable moment to do his trick and rid himself of the weight that pulls him down on one side. For the professional and the amateur, the toilet cubicle is the only place to hide, perhaps several times an evening, to ensure that the more fiddly tricks are all set up. Given that some tricks demand apparatus to be worn under the clothes, it is a common and humbling thing to be stood in the disabled toilet/storage-room, velvet trousers around one's ankles, trying to feed near-invisible thread into some hidden mechanism for the eighth time, angry and impatient; and easy to understand why magicians tend to pretend to be more important than they really are.

And for now I had to pretend. By holding the deck with pressure from my right thumb and ring-finger at diagonally opposed corners and my forefinger curled on top, I sprang the cards into my left palm and stepped out of the gloom to begin a stroll around the restaurant floor – a promenade designed to achieve two separate but important aims:

1. Draw attention to myself as a magician.
2. Stall.

I could meander like this, building up the courage to approach a table, for a very long time.

The restaurant, converted from one of the many warehouses around the dock area of Bristol, was stylishly decorated with a North African theme: a grey flagstone floor and warm, rough, orange walls formed a backdrop to Byzantine fixtures and heavy stone-topped tables covered with white cloths. It combined the grand visual splendour appropriate for a restaurant of its calibre with the ethnic affectation adopted by the white middle classes who were evidently feeling guilty about being white and middle class during the nineties.* As an undergraduate at that time, I had seen the first 'ethnic' trinkets appear in student shops in Bristol, and start to spread and flourish as art students with stupid hats and impressionist postcards looked to decorate their rooms and find places to stash their stash and stick their sticks of heady incense. Soon, stalls dedicated to naively fashioned fish and boxes made of fret-worked dark wood and brass filled the harbour walkways and offered all ages of arty, velvety people a hand-carved opportunity to create a Moroccan souk in their own rented accommodation. I, being such a person, bought these things enthusiastically; I even asked

---

* Post-colonial guilt had reached its height in the exhausting relativism of post-modern hermeneutics. Language and meaning had become the new oppressors: X cannot claim to understand a thing's true meaning, as that would oppress poor Y, who thinks differently, and what would we be then? The disgrace of one's Western past seems to have led to a fanatical embrace of all things Eastern, particularly in the realm of interior decor where a pose of *esprit de corps* with the suffering East could be easily, sentimentally and indiscriminately adopted at the safest, most ornamental level.

my Aunty Jan, visiting for the day, to buy me a large, colourful wooden fish for my twenty-first birthday present. Now, a couple of decades later, the fringe appeal has dwindled and 'ethnic' is the received term for a style of interior decor available at John Lewis for home delivery. And how charming to imagine those impoverished workers making cabinets and towers for our extensive DVD and CD collections – really quite touching.

I had begun my card-springing/strolling action by the bar; now I allowed it to take me in between the babbling, noisy tables. I looked for signs of friendliness and of possible hostility from the guests sipping at their brandies and coffees. This was a preferable set-up to working tables when people were having a full dinner: the team behind the restaurant had, thankfully, decided to restrict entertainment to the relaxed ground floor, and offer an uninterrupted main course and dessert upstairs.

Understandably, responses to a magician can be hostile. I am tempted to think that the responsibility for this should generally lie with the magician in question, but clearly, when an entertainer at your table is far from what you were hoping for during a romantic meal out, you'd be justifiably surprised to be bothered even if the performer was rather good. Once, and only once, I performed a card trick that involved a card disappearing from the deck and appearing in a lady's zipped-up handbag under her chair. The woman in question, far from being enchanted by the impossibility, immediately accused me of having had my hand in her bag without her consent. There was no answer to this, certainly no way of pretending that I had not violated that privacy, despite the fact that the bag appeared to have been inaccessible to me. Furthermore, the same witless witch then decided that twenty pounds had gone missing from her purse (the purse, of course, had been kept in the bag), and insisted to the restaurant that I had stolen it. All this on the first night I had been booked to appear in that particular restaurant. The second week at the restaurant brought a customer complaining that I had damaged his watch during a trick in which I had caused it to stop on command. This was a more likely assertion. It was a miserable start.

Quite commonly, a man dining with women will respond with hostility to a magician's approach, as the latter is seen as a threat to the former's role as alpha male of his group. This will be the man who interrupts the magic with sarcastic comments, until eventually shushed into submission by his friends, which makes him sulk. Sat back, arms folded, refusing to be impressed, he becomes the child of the group and must be handled as one. The most professional response by the magician is to direct the performance to make this individual look good: this man can be made to correctly divine cards against all odds, and the magician can position himself as a clear non-threat. My own response was rarely as honourable. I would compliment him on his jacket and steal his wallet while making a point of feeling the cloth. On a good day I would return to the table and purposefully lose a bet to this same customer, and while he gloated I'd hand him his winnings, which he did not know had come from his own wallet. He might not search for his wallet to put the money away for some time, and the longer it took before he realised I must have it, the better. On a bad day, if the individual in question was just intolerable, I would silently drag his wallet under the table across a very powerful magnet I had strapped to my knee for other purposes and in doing so wipe all his credit cards, before returning the wallet with its useless plastic invisibly to his pocket.

A still unwelcome though well-meant response from a family is to have the adults turn to their child and say, 'Look, a magician!' Children's magicians form a thankless band of their own in the world of magic, and unless he is a brightly jacketed, horn-carrying member of that dedicated rank and file, and has so far managed to circumvent police arrest, the chances of a magician being able to competently perform anything for a child are minimal. Children are the worst audience for grown-up conjuring: the knowledge of interpersonal psychology held by the performer which is so important for the success of the tricks is wasted upon the very young, who have not learnt to respond automatically to social cues. Relax and ask an adult a question during a trick and he will look you in the eye; do the same with a child and he would have no compunction about ignoring the query and grabbing the props from your hand to inspect them.

In the same way that the diners, some of whom were now looking over at me, were making snap (and, I always presumed, somewhat unfavourable) judgements about me, I was engaged in similar acts of societal pigeonholing as I decided whom I should approach. We have evolved enormously efficient ways of telling if a person is a threat to us or to our group, and each time I approached a table I was on the receiving end of this human ability that we have honed over hundreds of thousands of years, and had to make sure that I radiated only signs of friendliness. But equally my own need was to see whether a particular table would be a welcoming or threatening place, so I too became hyper-aware of relevant signals and learnt to make quick judgements to protect myself. In constantly sizing people up, I was of course necessarily reducing them to stereotypes. Friendly young couples were a happy bet, and always a relief to find. Corporate parties, easy enough to spot, were generally good value until the combination of excess alcohol and their lack of awareness of anyone else in the restaurant made them unbearable to be around.

There is something I find strangely reassuring in our ability to quickly assess people and form snap judgements about them (accurate or otherwise), for it allows us to know that we are just as susceptible to instant classification ourselves. Rather than see this as insulting stereotyping, I like the fact it can make our own worries seem much smaller from the outside, indeed sometimes no more than predictable symptoms of the cliché that we present to the world through our choices of clothes and language and posture. The overbearing mother who expresses her unnecessary concern over aspects of her children's lives would do well to hear how she sounds to her average listener, and could take comfort in appreciating the unnecessarily high level of her anxiety. The ease with which we can usually offer productive advice to worried people (precisely because we draw simple conclusions about their troubles) is usually masked by our empathic noises and desire to appear sensitive, and the worrier is sometimes denied a possibly very helpful chance to see her problem as much smaller and simpler. In the same way that the old school photograph shows us how ludicrous our all-encompassing concerns were at that age, the knowledge that we are the only ones to take our tribulations so seriously and that the rest of the world would find our little anxieties silly if we spoke them out loud, is to me at least a relief. As much as we all believe we are far more fascinating than we at first – or perhaps ever – appear, I like to hang on to the idea that I might present something of a banal stereotype to those I meet, and am happy to receive from others more perspicacious opinions about my life than I can provide myself.* This is why I find it comforting to visit my parents in my childhood home and be struck by the fact that the shelves in the living room are much smaller and lower than

---

* As a parallel to this reductionist self-view that I sometimes adopt, I also note an enjoyment of the clichéd behaviour of glimpsed, unknown others seen through shop windows, viewed at their table from mine, or watched as they pass by the glass front of some café when I, inside, have just looked up to find some dislocated thought. Ambling past a hairdresser's today, I looked in, and for two seconds I saw this: three young members of staff, assembled at the reception desk, dressed in black T-shirts, the two wide-eyed coiffeuses listening to their flamboyant, tanned, spindle-shanked male colleague report some scandalous event to them, rolling his eyes, running a bony hand through his profuse, meticulously disarranged hair. It seemed a ludicrously hackneyed vignette, more the product of lazy character-writing and unimaginative casting than a glimpse of real people. Quickly one is surrounded by other background extras, crossing the set: here, the businessman barking into his Bluetooth headset; there, the eager charity fund-raiser and the ragged pack of schoolboys, shirts hanging and ties loose, laughing at something on one of their mobile phones. The clichés seem too obvious, too broadly sketched. One is faintly appalled and

I remember them as a child. Time passes, and the concerns of the moment will make us smile further down the road.

My concern of the moment was that I wished to be seen by my employers to be working. To overcome the cowardice that was becoming stifling I decided I would begin with a table of three men, two of them in their late forties or early fifties and, at a guess, treating the third member of the group to dinner after giving him a job in their legal firm: the new employee was younger, and his thick-soled shoes, high-street suit and nervously chosen tie placed him lower on the corporate ladder than the other two, one of whom looked like he had been born in the three-piece pinstripe cloth that was moulded around his lawful corporate gut, silver watch-chain grinning smugly across his front.

But as I stepped forward, a man's voice, loud behind me – 'Hey, show us a card trick!' – made me stop, smile, and turn to face a table near the door that I had not yet considered.

---

comforted by such predictable classifications, and for a moment entertains the grandiose delusion that one is the subject of some enormous hidden-camera reality show, in the same way that, on visiting Germany on a school exchange, I was convinced that the locals must revert to English when out of my earshot.

CHAPTER

2

'Hello, I'm Derren.'

Two men and one woman sat on low sofas round the table. I greeted the first, the man who had called me over. Benedict. Early forties with strikingly grey hair, firm handshake, slightly Steve Martin appearance, ruddy, overweight, in a good-quality suit. Looked me right in the eye in a practised manner. Next to him, Charlotte: a sumptuous, messy crop of reddish-brown hair high upon and around her head in which every movement from below was amplified and expressed in lively jiggles and shudders that made it appear to move at quite an independent pace to the woman beneath. Tortoiseshell glasses, about thirty years old, pale-skinned, sexy, open, twinkly, bright, a little curvy. Handshake firmly planted but held still, holding my gaze too but with more playfulness than Benedict's authoritative statement. *She definitely works with people, is practised at making them feel at ease.* Across from them was Joel: mid to late twenties, dark, funky, spiky hair, green eyes, svelte, feline but not effeminate, attractive, American, *could be Canadian – listen for 'ou' sounds.* (Canadians make 'ou' sounds like Bristolians, stands out a mile, worth waiting to find out, many points scored for correctly asking what part of Canada a person is from.) *Could be Charlotte's boyfriend?*

Good. Great.

Benedict's small eyes were flitting between the cards and mine. I guessed he had probably learnt a few tricks when he was younger. I performed a 'pass' while he was looking at the deck – a potentially invisible cut that few magicians, including me, can get exactly right but which to a certain extent separates the amateurs from the pros – and he didn't register it, even though I purposefully made it a little heavy-handed. That was good: *not a knowledgeable magician, maybe just knows a couple of tricks.*

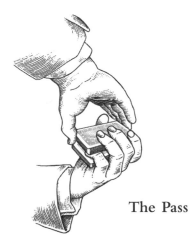

The Pass

I asked if I might join them and gestured at the vacant side of the table nearest me. Joel was sat opposite Charlotte and Benedict, which made the shorter sides of the table ideal positions from which to perform. I needed a chair; a few were dotted around among the sofas. Behind me at a nearby table a tall woman and a short man were sat with a boy of about thirteen, who was very smartly dressed. I smiled, feeling a pang of bittersweet reminiscence as I recalled being taken for grown-up dinners at about the same age, and I bowed and wished him an exaggeratedly formal good evening. There was a weak ripple of amusement from this group; all eyes turned to the kid. I asked the lady if she could spare the chair that had been left at the end of the low table, and after her invitation to take it, I did so, knowing that I had secured an easy approach for later. I transferred the black, slender, Mackintoshesque furniture to my group's table and sat down with them.

Aiming to ingratiate myself, I complimented Benedict on his shirt, which was clearly brand new: a ghost of a steam-pressed line was still visible around his ribs where he had not fully ironed it after unpacking it that day. Probably lived on his own: it looked like man-ironing. He accepted the compliment silently, so I extended it into making the semi-honest observation that they were a stylish and attractive group.

At that point, Benedict picked up a half-full bottle of Merlot from the table and topped up Charlotte's glass – unnecessarily, for her glass was already almost full. After pouring her wine he lifted the bottle, affectedly turning it as he did so, and repeated the same action for himself, emptying the vessel. Joel was not drinking red, so Benedict replaced the bottle in front of himself. Because the wine had been in front of him at the start of this process, this was, seemingly, at least twice in a row that he had poured wine for her. It seemed he was drinking it faster than Charlotte and his judgement was likely to be a little softer than hers. Importantly, the wine-pouring seemed to be a move to distance himself from the flattery he was sensing: a means of stepping out of the situation for a second to assemble his internal response to it. It reminded me of the way in which the fluster caused by hearing terrible news or suddenly, self-consciously, speaking up in company over dinner often finds us needlessly straightening our cutlery as we fight our internal agitation, rearranging objects on the table, smoothing out a tablecloth or the folds of our trousers: these are controlling, placating actions that allow us to take charge of and impose order on a seemingly important little something at a time when we feel threatened.

As he poured, he caught Charlotte's eye and widened his own for a second. She looked from him to the wine, failing to return the sentiment he was trying to communicate. The wine-pouring, then, was also a blocking gesture: a means of cutting me off from the group for a second to re-establish authority himself. The look from Benedict presumably was meant to communicate a weary 'Who's this guy?' attitude, which he wished to be shared and returned by his group.

The other unexpected conclusion from this action on his part was that Charlotte also did not respond when he poured the wine for her. She had laughed when I mentioned the group's attractiveness, and her laugh had been unaffected and generous. Immediately afterwards she had lowered her eyelids, assumed a comically exaggerated smouldering pout and released a honeyed, husky 'Really?' through the vampish sponginess of her lips. To confirm that this flirtatious display was not to be taken seriously, Charlotte curtailed it with a second chuckle, and as if to reiterate, her hair quivered a moment later in agreement. She had been smiling in the wake of her own mellifluous tease when Benedict poured the wine for her, and the lack of a 'thank you' told me that these two were a couple, or at least had been recently intimate. I had imagined that Joel and Charlotte, opposite each other, were the romantic pairing in the group, but this proved me wrong. Friends thank each other for top-ups; this absence of response was the silent expression of a closeness that does not feel the need for politeness or pleasantries. Perhaps an appeal of love is to extend one's sense of self to include part of another's, and an enjoyable by-product of this conjoining is that much of everyday verbal courtesy becomes unnecessary.

Involuntarily, the memory came to mind of a retired couple I had seen sat at a table in a Chinese restaurant near my home. The place was busy and buzzy apart from two tables: mine and that of the couple in question. I had glanced up from reading, or rather across, as I had not rested my book flat on the table but was holding it propped up at eye-level in my left hand, resting my elbow next to my meal, freeing my right to turn the pages between collecting food on my fork and delivering it to my mouth. For such a restaurant where plates and side portions abound and space is valuable, the smaller footprint of this reading posture serves well, unless the book is a heavy one. It must also be said that it confers, too, a distinctly poetic air that echoes, to my memory, the posture of Helen Mirren's ill-fated lover in the Peter Greenaway classic *The Cook, The Thief, His Wife and Her Lover*, when we first see him sat reading at his table — an image which had lingered in my formative years as *the* way to read a book in a restaurant.

My eyes had drifted from the book and were scanning the smart environment, which resembled, as do so many better Chinese restaurants, a 1970s roller-disco. It is hard to move one's eyes across such a place without looking to see how many or few Chinese patrons have chosen to eat there: I was feeling the satisfaction of being part of a small British minority who had found an Authentic Place, and wondering to what extent even a better restaurant like this *really* reflected genuine Chinese cuisine for the families and business groups around me who were tucking into extraordinary dishes with absolute familiarity.

As I considered whether my predictable order of crispy duck pancakes had caused groans in the kitchen and flagged up the presence of a limp, ignorant Western diner, I caught the bluish Caucasian eye of a pale, elderly Brit who was also surveying the room and perhaps thinking similar thoughts. I involuntarily looked away, then drifted back, to see him blandly observing a large, lumbering lobster indifferently nudge at the rear of another with an impotent blue-banded claw in the murky water of a tank close by. Across from this man, and with her back towards me, was slumped the blanched hump of his wife, a mound of knitwear supporting a tangle of creamy curls; her cheek, well matted and dusted with old-lady beige, was turned away from the tank just enough for me to see that she was staring across his shoulder and out of the large window at the evening's to-ings and fro-ings on the rainy street. They neither looked at each other nor spoke.

So they sat, having booked and travelled to a good restau-rant where they were paying for the pleasure of having their dinner feel special, opposite each other as plates of plain rice and chicken came and went, conversation as foreign and odd to them as the untouched pairs of chopsticks resting neatly upon the table. When they did mumble something to each other, it seemed each time drab and inconsequential. I could not hear clearly but she appeared to make a comment about the restaurant, which was responded to with an eyebrow raise and a faint nod; and then, some time later, she might have enquired as to what somebody they knew had said previously over the telephone.

I wondered just how they, like so many other couples, had reached this point, and where along the line that traced the familiarity they shared (which started with them as youngsters, accepting a top-up of wine without the need for thanks) things had given way to this dreary resignation that seemed to touch on contempt. I considered how rarely we remember to retain an interest in our partners' secret motives and barely remem-bered desires that once burned and crackled in the same way as our early romantic passions. I made a note to remember this point in future years as I resumed my reading in a restaurant that had suddenly become chilly and uninviting.

Some years after that I was first told 'I love you' by a new partner, and the generous statement produced a curious para-noia by virtue of me not having been the first to say it. My thought process ran like this:

1. X loves me. Do I love X in return?

2. What does it mean to love X?

3. I sometimes think I might love X. Is that enough?

4. X has declared a binary position: love or not love. I am to take a clear position on either side.

5. If I do not state that I do love X, some time soon, then my position will be taken as not loving X.

6. Now I am going to have to say I love X in order not to cause this relationship to become very tricky by X feeling unloved.

7. Instead we will progress with X loving me and me uncertain about loving X but certainly pretending to do so.

8. What a terrible thing for X to say.

Once this eight-part sequence had run its course, two clear images rapidly passed through my mind. The first was that of a flamboyantly dressed twelfth-century minstrel, one of the feather-hatted troubadours who discovered the tantalising appeal of courtly romance and so began the extraordinary public-relations exercise on love that still leaves us with an oppressively idealised sense of what we are supposed to feel when in its presumed grip. Secondly, I considered all humanity for a fleeting instant as four-legged, two-headed creatures whom, according to Aristophanes, the gods jealously divided, leaving each of us to search the Earth for our estranged, once-conjoined remainder who, when found, will make us whole again. This was an image of love less tyrannical than the first: simply that of looking for a complementing self, a person who completes us.

These images faded and were replaced by warm, sepia-toned close-ups of a black couple embracing: vaguely formed, dim snapshots created by the memory of the lyrics to a smooth, smoky song I had heard called 'I Love You Forever, Right Now' by Joi, and which now ran through my head:

If I could make time stand still
I'd be happy in your arms.
Love without end, drowning and overwhelmed by your
    fire and charms.
It's hard to explain, really don't know how, but
I love you forever right now, right now.

The sentiment had struck me as important: that love changes, hides, soars and reinvents itself from one moment to the next according to the caprices of our fitful states of mind. An *I love you*, therefore, is a statement of feeling *right now* even if it feels like it should be a *forever*. An *I love you right now* admits that feelings change on both sides. It does not demand reciprocation, it need not leave the other panicked. I had been so struck by the notion that I sought out the album, certain that I had stumbled across an artist who would connect with the feelings I had at the time. It was perhaps quite fitting that the rest of the album was not something I enjoyed at all.

As if on cue, Charlotte reached her hand out to Benedict's thigh and gave the soft, full flesh a squeeze through his already over-accommodated, taut, shiny trouser. It was not a gesture of gratitude for the wine, rather an offered assurance to Benedict that her previous light-hearted coquetry was not meant. His small eyes darted down to her hand, then looked across at me. He raised his chin.

I returned his gaze and placed the deck of cards on the table before him. The empty card box was in my right trouser pocket. I removed it, closed the flap and placed it on the table to my left with apparent disregard; the flap was positioned towards me with the cut-out half-moon downwards. Returning to the cards, I gave them an overhand shuffle – the simplest, most popular means of shuffling. The deck is held in the right hand which makes a repeated chopping motion into the left hand and away; but each time it pulls up from the latter, the left thumb catches a clump of cards from the top edge of the deck and causes them to be pulled down into its hand as the right moves away, each new group of cards falling on top of the last group, beneath which they had until then sat. The overhand shuffle is modest and familiar; it does not ask for attention and therefore allows for a journey towards flashier displays of skill as the trick progresses.

I sometimes used a different shuffle, particularly with an Asian audience. It is not known to many that Asian people typically have a way of shuffling cards which is rather different from the way the rest of us set about it. In magic, it is known as the 'Hindu shuffle', though I am unsure why. Magic does rather enjoy using names that attempt to conjure up – pun emphatically intended though unimaginatively employed – an Old Empire world of far-off, geographically blurred, culturally confused but fundamentally exotic lands to which unashamed references often seem bewilderingly racist to today's ears. The popular Asian way of shuffling cards is referred to as 'Hindu' perhaps because a travelling Western magician once saw an Indian (one hopes at least it was an Indian) mix his cards in a new manner, and regardless of whether the local prestidigitator was Hindu, Sikh, Jain or Buddhist decided that the 'Hindu' moniker would appeal most easily to his impressionable and largely ignorant British countrymen back home, for whom a bejewelled turban and an imposing disposition were enough to convey all the mysteries of the East.

The Hindu Shuffle

Or at least one East. The other East, meanwhile, is still occasionally and touchingly celebrated by magicians through the portrayal of the fawning, curly-slippered, pointy-hatted laundry worker or comedy mystic, shuffling and bowing inter-mittently with hands clasped to opposite forearms inside voluminous silk sleeves, who moves on to produce an endless washing-line of flags or undies to the tune of (of course) an Egyptian Sand Dance. Velly solly indeed. Far more extraordi-nary than any of the illusions these tired and insulting acts can produce is the fact that they can still find employment at all, since magic has now developed a younger, darker, cooler face quite at odds with this painfully outdated yet oddly watchable litter still dredged up for barely sentient audiences at magic 'gala' nights occasionally advertised on theatre hoardings along our tired coastlines. Nothing of the glamour and allure suggested by the word 'gala' is to be found in the spectacularly low-rent (if bizarrely charming) awfulness of the average magic show. Great acts of course exist – the Edinburgh Fringe hosts a handful of magicians of exceptional talent and originality – but to have a genuine love for magic and wish to be transported by a conjuror is to be almost always disappointed. Imagine if comedy followed the same route: that the tone of stand-up had not changed since 1973, and that everybody told roughly the same jokes.

And women! Since the 1920s, grand illusion on stage has been synonymous with the restraint and mutilation of female assistants, as if the first act a lucky mortal, newly endowed with the ability to overturn the laws of the universe, would wish to carry out would be the casual torture of the fairer sex for our entertainment. Modern cinema is as familiar with this cliché as the conjuring fraternity, and sometimes with a similar capacity for witless mawkishness, but film usually approaches the custom with a dramatic sensibility unknown to most magicians who strap up and stick swords through their frozen-smiling victims purely because questionable convention dictates such unimaginative behaviour. What became an unhappy tradition began rather more spectacularly, in January 1921, with the first Sawing in Half, performed by the conjuror P. T. Selbit, an entrepreneurial giant of magical history who can fairly claim to have been responsible for this most grisly, popular and oft-imitated mise-en-scène of all magic, and to have had the real surname Tibbles, which he sensibly reversed so as not to sound stupid. His flair for the theatrical was the key to his enormous success: when performing his Sawing in Half during a run at a theatre, the publicity-savvy Selbit would rather brilliantly have his assistants slosh out buckets of what appeared to be blood into the gutters outside the playhouse.

Consider those sloshing buckets, for in them resides much of that which is exciting and unique about magic. It was the time of Grand Guignol, a gory form of popular theatre which had become famous for its highly visceral, bloodthirsty visuals. This new French theatre had opened in London a few months before, and presumably appealed to an appetite for naturalistic horror that the real-life bloodshed of the First World War managed to strengthen. But the joy in the buckets of blood has nothing to do with schlock tactics: it resides in the magician's sensibility towards creating an *effect*, in his knowing that the buzz created by such a simple but bold bit of business outside the theatre would greatly amplify the spectators' preparedness to believe events that transpired on stage.

The magician knows that all magic happens in the perception of the audience member; there is no necessary connection between the greatness of a magical piece and either the technical demands or the cleverness of the method behind it. A successful magical career will begin with learning sleights and buying endless tricks, but as he matures, having absorbed many years' worth of technical knowledge in order to establish a mental encyclopedia of possible means to achieve impossible ends, the performer is likely to eschew tricky and pedantic methods in favour of more gleefully audacious modi operandi. To create a powerful piece of magic through the simplest, boldest method is one of the sweetest pleasures of the craft. Generally, the success of an otherwise childishly simple method relies upon a deception taking place at a level that the audience, when attempting to unravel the means by which the miracle was accomplished, simply wouldn't even think to question. These are methods that may be considered insulting by the average spectator if he or she were to find them out, yet which succeed as some of the finest methods known to magicians by virtue of the same fact. The best methods are the ones that would never be dreamt of by an audience, and a magician knows that his spectators are more likely to suspect clever and complex methods than brilliantly effortless ones. The method should therefore be the simplest possible, and create the greatest, most disproportionate effect. It may be a crushing disappointment to an enlightened audience member to find out that she had been thinking on an entirely different level, but that is the unavoidable concomitant of such a gorgeously daring subterfuge. Its status as a superior means of achieving the effect is secured by the fact that it consists of the least, and does the most.

As in magic, in science. The finest theories are the simplest ones that explain the most. Evolutionary theory, as Richard Dawkins points out, immediately reads as a better conjecture than Creationism because natural selection is a very simple idea that easily explains a huge amount, namely all of life, whereas a posited supernatural Creator would take far more explanation than the life He is supposed to have created, rendering the latter theory rather unhelpful and topsy-turvy when looked at on its own merits.

Sometimes a bold method may be employed not to create the effect itself, but as a 'convincer' – the name given by magicians to describe sub-tricks that act as proofs of the validity of the primary effect. For example, a hoop might be passed over a floating assistant to prove that she is really unsupported. What appears to be a casual demonstration of 'Look, nothing holding her up!' may in reality be a very complex procedure and every bit as fascinating in method as the trick itself. It is a secondary piece of conjuring, not presented as a trick, but necessary to convince the audience that the trick they think they are watching (the levitation) is really occurring. Because it is not seen as anything that in itself presents a puzzle to be solved, it usually goes by unquestioned, and the principal piece of magic is made to seem all the more impossible. The audience rarely suspects that a complex, second subterfuge has occurred.

In fact, the history of levitation gives us a great example of one such bold convincer, as described by Jim Steinmeyer in his very enjoyable book *Hiding the Elephant*. At the start of the twentieth century, a great magician of the golden era, Howard Thurston, performed a levitation that he had bought along with the rest of his act from Harry Kellar, a hugely successful but recently retired fellow American performer. A female assistant was made to float above the stage, and the levitation was contextualised by the type of exotic framing we have already mentioned: it was explained that in certain Indian Temples of Love, such a floating goddess could be seen, and that it was possible for visitors to come and touch her magical bejewelled ring to cast a spell over those they loved. This romantic fairy-tale scene setting made the levitation all the more mysterious, but Thurston would have been aware that, of course, the audience would suspect some unseen means of support. He developed, therefore, one of the boldest 'convincers' I have come across. He would ask a boy to come up from the audience, bring him right upstage and lift him to kiss the ring of the enchanted assistant as his fairy-tale patter reached a touching peak. The child would gape with astonishment, the audience were convinced there were no wires to be seen from any perspective, and magicians were absolutely dumbfounded.

It remained a mystery. Or it did until recently, reports Steinmeyer, when a well-respected magician friend of his began chatting with a fellow diner about magic in a Los Angeles restaurant. This neighbour, as a child, had himself once been invited on stage by Thurston and held up in the magician's arms to view the floating woman, elegantly proving that there could be no wires. Thurston's thinking as a showman was revealed as the man described what had happened. He had been lifted right into a fan of wires which were perfectly obvious to him. But before the boy could react to the supports, the urbane magician, who moments before had been weaving a spellbindingly exotic tale of eternal love, whispered in his ear, 'If you touch those fucking wires, I'll kill you.' The boy had never heard language like it, his mouth dropped open in shock, and the audience, taking his expression to be one of wonder at an improbably airborne female, applauded loudly at the confirmed miracle. The child was far too terrified to repeat to his parents what Thurston had said. And so the miracle was achieved, and achieved every night.

Finishing my brief mix of the cards, I offered them to Joel with a raised-eyebrow expression, thereby wordlessly asking him if he wished to shuffle them too. Happy to help, he took them and shuffled – an encouraging sign of a desire to cooperate playfully. Had I asked out loud whether or not he would like to mix them, I would have interpreted his taking of the cards as a move to establish control of the situation – a potentially tricky customer. The expected and polite response to a verbal offer to shuffle would be a word or gesture that communicated 'No thank you, I trust they're real cards and mixed'; to resist that urge and actually demand to shuffle them further is a sign of distrust. However, to take the cards in response to a *silent* signal from me suggested the opposite: that he and I had an easy rapport, that he understood and would follow subtle cues, and may have a fairly suggestible personality. I imagined that he would perform all the necessary exaggeration in his memory of the trick, which after I had left would turn it into a miracle. At least half of any trick happens after it is over, when the applause has long died and the magician has packed his case and arrived home and is winding down to sitcom, conure and confectionery. This finishing process occurs as the spectator reconstructs the trick, ready to tell his friends; as he edits and deletes all the errors and bias of personal memory; as he ensures the trick sounds impressive enough to enthuse others and save him sounding too easily duped. The magician plants all the seeds needed to ensure that this inevitable process works in favour of a true miracle.

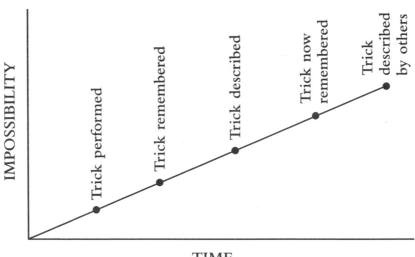

IMPOSSIBILITY

Trick performed

Trick remembered

Trick described

Trick now remembered

Trick described by others

TIME

Joel was a good punter. He mixed the cards in the same overhand way, not with particular skill but nonetheless with a deliberate air and a shaky stab at confidence. His efforts caused a silence to hang over the table for a moment, a tension broken by Charlotte whispering a deathly serious 'Shit, you're good', making both Joel and me laugh. His face crumpled and he mimed a retarded, hopeless, clumsy mix with accompanying hapless moans that caused Charlotte to guffaw deeply, then clasp a hand to her mouth in embarrassment at the unexpected timbre of her own sound. This spurred Joel to continue with his unlovely portrayal of mental and physical disability, and to drop his voice two octaves to incorporate an equally cruel impersonation of Charlotte's mannish laugh. This in turn caused Charlotte to emit the same involuntary sound, which incited more convulsions from us and therefore fuller breathless bellows from her, until she doubled over, both hands thrust between her upper thighs through fear of sudden percolation, which only seemed to amplify her paroxysms and punctuate them with louder, more viraginous and fuller-bellied eruptions.

Meanwhile, Joel's choice of overhand technique was another sign of rapport and a desire to enjoy the whole experience. Some people, if able, will take the cards and attempt a fancier mix: they cut the deck into two, place the two halves end to end on the table and riffle the short ends together with the thumbs, the cards of each packet (the magician's term for a group of cards in a pile when not constituting a full deck) neatly interweaving. When this is clearly done to impress, the magician normally makes a mental note that the spectator is not necessarily going to enjoy being fooled and may prove to be a pain. Luckily, having this heads-up at such an early stage allows a deft performer to utilise that challenging nature for the good of the show.

For example, if you were me and were faced with a 'challenger' in this way, you might confidently – even arrogantly – tell him that if he were to concentrate on a letter of the alphabet, you would be able to tell him what it is. He should jump at the chance to prove you wrong, and at that point he'll become every bit as predictable as he is determined not to be. A non-challenging type would think of any letter quite fairly at this point, making your chances of guessing correctly precisely one in twenty-six. The chap (and it is sadly almost always a man) who is determined to catch you out, however, is going to scan the alphabet and, if you have convincingly set it up to feel competitive, settle on Q or Z. He'll consider these to be the least probable ones anyone would choose.

Now you stand a vastly improved chance of guessing correctly.

To cover both options, pick up a pen and paper, and as you stare him in the eye, appear to privately draw his thought. Actually you write a large 'Z', without making it clear that you're doing so.

After this, act as if you are having difficulty reading his mind, then casually screw up the paper and drop it on the table. The feigned uncertainty serves not only a dramatic purpose (by introducing suspense), it also allows for the following ruse, which will bring the trick to a convincing climax.

Say these words: 'It's not Q, is it?' Using an old linguistic trick much employed by psychics ('He didn't die in an accident, did he?'), you have covered yourself either way. A negative or affirmative response can be framed as a success. If the answer is a dumbfounded 'Yes', then congratulate him on being a good subject as you pick up the discarded paper and put it in your pocket (abandoning your former arrogance here is important, as the success of the effect is meaningless if you are unlikeable with it). If he shakes his head, answer, 'No, I didn't think so, but I nearly wrote a Q.' Push the ball of paper towards him and ask him what letter he chose. Presuming he says 'Z', you can still claim an unequivocal success.

If, due to lack of practice on your part or finding yourself with a rare customer, *neither* is correct,[*] then apologise and

---

[*] Note, though, your original statement that 'if he were to *concentrate* on a letter of the alphabet, you would be able to tell him what it is'. Notice that this statement ascribes some weight to the process of concentration. This is important: not because his concentrating plays any role in reality,

congratulate him on outwitting you. Tickle his ego and plan a greater victory. Or if you prefer, flamboyantly climb upon the table, denounce those watching as the worst sorts of scoundrels, and urinate upon them mercilessly.

---

but because him *thinking* he has to concentrate, distracts his attention from whether or not his choice will be predictable. If you merely told him you could foretell any letter he might think of, he might consider things more carefully and come to the conclusion that Q or Z would be a little predictable after all. The distracting business of concentration, which can be played up, is misdirection: he should hopefully think enough about which letter to choose to pick one of those two, but, occupied then by the second issue of having to concentrate, consider the choice of letter no more carefully than that. Such are the things I lie awake at night considering, while my clock radio blinks away the seconds and eventually the hours in the darkness.

CHAPTER

3

Three. The magic number. Three gives us beginning, middle, end; three can give us a story; three can give us drama. Three has power, and the magician knows this well.

Imagine this: the magician takes a card, rubs it on the table, and – hey presto! It reappears on top of the deck that has been sitting to the side. Your reaction to this single event? 'I must have missed something. Do that again.'

You had not known to watch the deck, you were caught unawares, a repeat performance would only be fair.

So, *One* does not satisfy.

The magician takes the card again and repeats the trick, this time taking it more slowly and explaining the things you may wish to look out for. But now he uses a different method, as you, knowing no better, watch so pointlessly for what you missed the first time. The weak and strong points of the first method are balanced by strengths and weaknesses in the second, and you, misled into believing you are seeing exactly the same trick and now paying attention to all the wrong places, are fooled more powerfully than the first time.

Despite the shift in method, *Two* is mere repetition; it still does not quite fulfil. In fact, having been granted one repetition, we might even expect to be able to ask for another: seemingly it is a challenge-trick that we are being offered as a puzzle to work out. It may be a puzzle, but it is not gratifying magic.

So the magician offers to replicate the effect, only this time blindfolded. Now the stakes are higher. He dons the blindfold, then takes the card and rubs it on the table. Again it disappears. He turns over the top card of the deck . . . but this time it is not there either. He spreads the deck: it has gone entirely. You look, for the first time in a long time, away from his hands to his face for an explanation . . . and see the card peeping out the top of the blindfold.

That is *Three*. Now there has been magic. There has been beginning, middle and end, and there are no demands for repetition.

This has been the structure behind almost every routine I have performed to create the greatest possible impact from the material to hand:

One – to establish

Two – to invite greater attention; perhaps by raising stakes

Three – to surprise*

---

* Sadly, time constraints have often meant that a trick written and performed in three phases has been edited down to two for the television

Three allows a finale, and flair, and a final 'no more'. Even the card-to-blindfold third stage has its own dramatic threefold structure:

One – the card is rubbed and has vanished (we expect it to be back on the deck)

Two – the card is not where it should be! Our expectations have not been met: there is a crisis

Three – the card is found, in an unexpected place, and we have ended up somewhere greater and more resonant than where we expected to be

This is the elemental structure of drama that takes us explicitly back to Aristotle in the West, but deeper into the mental processes of all struggling human beings throughout our history. Wherever and whenever we have seen ourselves as the protagonists in the dramas of our own lives, beset with conflicts but with a desire to satisfyingly overcome them; ever since we have told stories that reflect that drive, and enjoyed tales of adventure, this structure (reflected in the final card-to-blindfold plot of this trick's third stage) has been our guide:

---

viewing public. This is a necessary but sometimes frustrating evil. Of course it can add variety to an episode: if everything followed the same structure it would become too obvious, and the subtle pleasures of light and shade would be sacrificed.

One – protagonist sets out to achieve a goal (or the magician sets out to transport the card to the top of the deck)

Two – his expectations are not met, and difficulties beset him (the card is not where it should be)

Three – conflict is resolved, he achieves an unexpected final position that resonates more than the one he set out to achieve (card is found somewhere even more unlikely)

Three creates story, and allows for struggle and resolution. In magic, *One* is empty. *Two* is repetitive and pedestrian. *Three* is dramatic, stylish, and rhythmical.*

When Joel had finished shuffling, I took back the cards into my left hand and complimented him on his skill, asking him if he had played cards professionally. He clearly hadn't (all but the most modest professional player probably *would* use a riffle shuffle, maybe even in the hands rather than on the table, and would have checked the deck for abnormalities upon taking it), but this flattering question led the group to look across at him, empathically feeling his gentle embar-rassment and anticipating his answer with a slight communal smile.

---

* Jean-Eugène Robert-Houdin, the extraordinary father of modern conjuring, made the salient point that 'a magician is an actor playing the part of a magician'. This is a very good description. However, an actor takes for granted how to create drama in every word, movement and look. The average magician is barely aware of its existence.

As they looked away from me, I took the deck from above with my right hand, and in the action of bringing the deck forward and on to the table in order to spread the cards for the necessary selection I quickly ran my thumb up the short edge nearest me. I applied just enough pressure to make the cards quickly and lightly snap off my thumb, until I felt, midway through the deck, the location of the Queen of Hearts, from whose length I had shaved an otherwise imperceptible half a millimetre that afternoon while working in the deck for use. The absent sliver caused the modified court card to miss the thumb-pad and fall with the card beneath it, creating a slight tactile inconsistency. Having found this card, I slightly raised the upper half of the pack at this point, enough for the tip of my left little finger to enter just above it (hidden under the cover of my right hand, arched over the whole deck), and lifted the top section, held between the shiny curve of my left little fingernail and the middle two fingers of the same hand, while my right shifted its grip to wedge the bottom half against my left thumb. In this position I performed the previously mentioned 'pass', better than before but still sadly far from perfect, more or less imperceptibly reversing the two halves of the deck to bring the shortened Queen to the top, the larger forward-movement of my hands to the table hiding the smaller action of transposing the two packets.

The deck arrived at the table with my one altered card in a position where I could make sure it wasn't chosen. This single, unremarkably doctored, indiscernibly deficient card, lying otherwise flush with and directly above its fifty-one fellow pasteboards, able to be located among a shuffled deck and controlled in an instant due to this diminutive discrepancy, was to be a mole in the ranks; a spy to signal the movements and positions of other cards; one small but vital part of ensuring the hoped-for successful conclusion to the trick that had now commenced. With my right hand I swept the deck across the table in a wide arc, releasing cards evenly to form a crescent of card-backs: white borders alternating with flashes of the white-on-red rococo filigree that wrought itself into the ornamented Bicycle back design.

'Joel, Charlotte, Benedict, perhaps you'd pick a card each.'

I turned away to my right, bringing my gesturing left hand casually around to hover over the few cards that now lay at the far right of the sweep. The rightmost of these was the short-ened Queen, and this seemingly accidental blocking of those cards ensured it wouldn't be selected. I enjoyed the feeling of a trick commencing, and this one in particular: it comprised a long series of effects, each more baffling than the last. It was not of my devising,* though I had adapted and altered it for my own use and made it a staple of my repertoire.

Pick a card. In those words resides everything tiresome about conjuring: the geeky kid at the party; the irksome enthu-siast with his pockets full of props; the promise of a gently embarrassing few minutes while someone else's fatuous friend fumbles to find a card unconvincingly lost in a fingered, filthy deck. Magic has both feet planted in cheap vaudeville and childish posturing; in dishonesty and therefore not in art. The

---

* I had learnt it in its original form from a favourite conjuror of mine, Tom Mullica.

magician *cheats*, and this truth runs cold through the craft's bloodless veins. Because he cheats, and because tricks are not tricks unless they are inherently impressive, it is hard for anyone other than another magician to tell whether he is really any good or not. The typical novice magician is regularly told by startled spectators that he is of a suitably amazing standard to, say, appear regularly on television, when that can logically only be the case for a very small number. (This is an encouraging illusion but an illusion nonetheless, rather like the way most men believe themselves to be better than averagely endowed, and most people believe themselves to have a better than average sense of humour. It is a difficult exercise to imagine *most* people having a more than average anything.) Therefore magicians starting out are prone to falling victim to a rather convincing trick being played on them: that they are better than they are. Compare them to people starting out in stand-up comedy. A comedian is not a comedian unless he is on stage telling jokes. If people don't laugh, then he isn't any good, and it's a painful, self-evident truth when that occurs. In magic, anyone with a shop-bought trick deck is a magician, and if people aren't fooled they usually pretend to be, and they are understandably likely to mistake being fooled as a sign of being in the presence of an excellent magician. Comedians starting out do also tend to think up their own jokes, whereas it takes a long time for conjurors to work out tricks and methods for themselves.

Those – and I have seen a few – who elevate magic to something artistic are those who overcome the innate puerility that besets the craft, and bring to it a performance personality that an audience would feel is almost enchanting enough on its own. The best magicians, or at least those I most like, do not merely do one trick after another at you, appreciating instead the value of light, shade, and even understatement. In the best performances, the trick itself is often not the primary pleasure: the finest pieces soar not necessarily because they are the most bamboozling in and of themselves, but because they are performed by an utterly captivating character, or imbued with a theatrical sensibility that turns a puzzle with a disappointing solution into an experience of genuine drama, fun or enchantment. These are not qualities synonymous with glitz and sensational production values. For what it's worth, I most readily identify such exemplary magic with Chan Canasta, David Berglas, Mac King and Penn and Teller. Not all of these names may be known to the reader and none has embraced the Vegas aesthetic, even though King and P&T are must-sees for visitors to that extraordinary, sweltering city of confection.

Although personality plays a huge role in stand-up comedy, a joke can work well enough written out in a joke book or shared online, separate from any voice other than the reader's. Perhaps this is because a naked joke can still tell a story, or at least make us laugh; we are engrossed, surprised, and made to feel good. A bare trick, on the other hand, may surprise us but is unlikely to engross or delight without a performer and a thought-through presentation. This means that better tricks do not for a moment make a better magician.

For a successful magician, beneath the huge amount of attention paid to presentation, and the attempt to create something theatrically powerful, there may exist an embarrassment about the unavoidable presence of deception that binds it all together. Many bright and talented magicians (spurred on by a misjudged desire to show themselves to be knowledgeable performers), treat the notion of cheating as a great leveller when in the company of those more successful than themselves. I dined with a veteran and true genius of magic who compared this point to a kid bearing holiday snaps approaching a famous photographer to give critical notes on the latter's work. This discourteous self-regard typifies a certain type of amateur conjuror and of course exists in other arts – a very famous actor once told me that earlier that day a drama student had confessed she felt he was 'struggling to find the character' during a rehearsal to which her class had been invited – but the singular problem of cheating makes this impertinence very common within magic. (Being now in the position of the successful performer, I meet any number of otherwise perfectly lovely hobbyist magicians who, upon meeting me at the stage door, are only too happy to give unsolicited notes and launch into criticism of the show – a strange business that I am sure happens with far less frequency in the roughly parallel world of the touring comic. The peculiar mists of magic can severely obscure the judgement of how to ingratiate oneself socially, which is, touchingly, what these magicians at the stage door are most likely seeking to do.)

All too aware of my own excruciating personality as a young magician, it is clear to me that a craft that is largely about designing quick, fraudulent routes to impressing one's peers is unlikely to encourage much in the way of genuine likeability.

The desire to impress is an efficient means of bringing out one's least impressive qualities. It is related to a phenomenon known as negative suggestion, and many people with a fear of heights know a common example: that of struggling with the desire to throw oneself into the abyss. The panic or paralysis of a sufferer is normally not so much caused by the height itself but by an internal battle with a ludicrous, powerful temptation to leap into it. It is classic negative suggestion, encapsulated in the instruction 'Don't think of a green elephant': the trying *not* to do some particular thing flusters the mind and leads one towards doing exactly that.

I have no particular fear of heights, but in a similar way to that described above I seem to perversely enjoy the profound disorientation and panic induced by carrying out the following exercise when faced with a balcony railing overlooking some panorama, particularly at night. I recommend imagining this sequence rather than actually trying it out:

1. Sit on the railing but face inwards, towards the building.

2. Lock your legs into the vertical struts of the ironwork.

3. Start to lean backwards, keeping your eyes open, rolling your eyes upwards.

4. Arch back as far as you can, watching as the ceiling of the balcony opens into the vast starry sky, and then (if you can keep going as your centre of gravity shifts to the wrong side of your support and threatens to pull you over) feel the horizon dizzily

swing inverted into view from the furthest reaches of your vision as, struggling against every impulse to pull yourself back to safety, you strain your head back to take in the swooping-up ground beneath you.

This nauseating vertiginous experience, usually effective by the early stages of number four but woozily and effectively recreated here in a comfortable reclining library chair as I act out the process in microcosm by means of reference, is bizarrely addictive. The very knowledge that it is idiotic, transparently dangerous and gut-heavingly repellent to lean backwards as far as I can over a balcony edge only has me all the more eager to try it whenever I find a suitably precipitous balustrade. And it is that impulse to perform the act one knows one should avoid that not only makes smoking so hard to give up but also has us fail miserably on social occasions with our peers. The deadly formula 'I must not . . .' puts the prohibited act foremost in our minds and allows the idea of its execution to quietly blossom and flourish until we concede defeat and let the proscribed word slip from our mouths, or, through frantic over-compensation, achieve for ourselves the exact end we had wished so dearly to avoid.

I am acutely aware of this happening in company. This is partly because I sometimes find people acting oddly when meeting me, and also because I am aware of my own tendencies to over-compensate for my weaknesses. Returning for a moment to the theatre stage doors, it is not uncommon to meet there a small band of truly devoted people who follow me from show to show. Among this group are numbered an even smaller handful who, having stood in the rain and cold with many other patient and delightful people awaiting my arrival, usher everyone else forward before them so that they themselves can spend more time with me after the others have left, as if they and I enjoy an exclusive relationship not extended to ordinary 'fans'; and then, out of this same eagerness not to appear obsessive (as if the other people were being anything other than entirely flattering), they finally feign indifference and exaggerated nonchalance to the point of actual rudeness, wordlessly thrusting across photographs to sign and then looking away with a grand display of apathy while I accede to their requests. They are kind enough to have spent their money on several shows, sufficiently sweet to follow me from city to city and queue in unfavourable conditions when they should be getting home, yet in a misjudged effort not to seem like a loony, they act exactly like one. I have spoken about this with many performers, and it seems a very common occurrence – a wonderful, predictable glitch in our natures that makes us behave quite antithetically to how we would like to appear.

I have, of course, made the same mistake. A few years ago I met Hugh Grant at a party. It was, as can be imagined, quite an occasion: a huge marquee with glittering chandeliers, fifty beautifully set tables, and the guest list enough to leave you standing motionless, in awe of the people in whose midst you have found yourself.* Thus I found myself mingling with the great

---

* At one such party I saw Baroness Thatcher talking to a small group of guests. It was all I could do not to eavesdrop: I could not imagine *what* one discusses with Mrs Thatcher when one meets her at a party. The traffic on

and the good. Knowing his then girlfriend, I was introduced, and of course I asked the only question I could think of: was he enjoying the party? His answer made me laugh: 'I think it's a complete disaster.' It was a brilliant response, and although we barely spoke after that, it left the impression of a liking for inappropriate humour, which of course was very endearing.

Some months later I was dining on my own in London after a show when Grant came in, along with the lady I knew, and a second couple. They spied me and invited me to join them. Imagining at that point that my life would never be visited by a finer or prouder moment, I took few pains to insist that I would be interrupting their evening and bounded over like a drooling Labrador.

I was introduced to the other couple and offered a glass of wine. It was a charming gathering, and it was lovely to see the lady with whom I was already on friendly terms. However, seeing as it was only my second encounter with Grant, I wanted to impress him. I decided that the best way to do so would be to make an inappropriate comment.

Now, upon reflection, I understand the impulse. I have on a number of occasions listened to people trying to ingratiate themselves to me by telling me how fascinated they are by some aspect of interpersonal psychology. I can see why they might imagine such topics would appeal, even as I try to steer them away as quickly as I can from such well-trodden ground.

---

the way down? The quality of the canapés? I was desperate to know what was being said. I was not brave enough to listen, so I cannot tell you. I merely note my intense curiosity.

Of course we all imagine what might appeal to another person based on the limited knowledge we have – or imagine we have – of his character, and seek rapport in the way that seems to make sense. What made sense to me as I sat next to Hugh Grant was that if I made some rude comment I would endear myself to him. I'd make him think, *Hey, this guy's like me. Maybe we shall become friends.*

I seized the opportunity as soon as it was presented. Until the moment in question I had been speaking mainly to our mutual friend. We were discussing the show I had given that night close by, in which I had walked upon and ground my face into broken glass. Hugh, kindly, said he could not imagine doing such a thing.

Aha! The chance to make a new friend has presented itself!

'Well,' I said, 'with the company you're in tonight, glass in your face would be preferable.'

I had, lacking confidence at the vital moment, mumbled a little, so his response was 'Hmm?'

I think at this point I already hated myself entirely, but still held on to the faint possibility that the comment might work as a joke so startling that he would sense a kindred spirit in me. So I repeated the line, all joy or irony now absent from my voice: 'I said, with the company you're in tonight, it's probably preferable.'

I do not remember if the rest of the party heard these words. The incident blends into a single stinging moment of self-loathing that pains me deeply to this day. I believe he offered, after a moment, a courteous laugh, to politely show that he at least *hoped* I was joking.

I excused myself shortly after that and returned to my table, all appetite lost.

On other occasions I find it hard to bring out the best in myself when around people with huge, domineering personalities. As the more single-mindedly successful celebrities generally fall into this category, I watch myself, as if from afar, shrivel up into a dull, vacuous shadow when I occasionally find myself hopeless in their overwhelming company. I emerge appalled at what I perceive as my own incapacity to contribute interestingly to a conversation. After all, I am perfectly capable of being the life and soul of a gathering, as long as . . . what? That I'm the most impressive person in the room? Hateful.*

---

* On a few occasions I have had the opportunity to meet a hero of mine, and have since learnt to avoid such situations where possible. It is not just that these people are inevitably disappointing when encountered in the real world; more dispiritingly, to find oneself recoiling from a figure one has privately held in such high esteem is to be left unable to enjoy his or her work to the same degree, and therefore with a life a little less pleasant than before. This is especially treacherous in the case of writers. We take such pleasure from particular authors' works, hunt down their old titles or eagerly anticipate new ones for the private delight of immersing ourselves in their worlds; we have been inspired and moved by their great ideas or turns of phrase which made our lives richer in an instant. As inspiration from such sources normally comes not so much from our discovery of a powerful new idea but instead from a lucid and eloquent confirmation of something we already knew but had never found such perfect words for, there is a tendency to develop a strong feeling of rapport with the author – to believe that he must be the same as us, and that because we share one idea, other aspects of his personality will also echo ours.

The crushing reality tends to be that this leap is a huge misjudgement, and that he is more likely to seem a regrettably predictable embodiment of

Those rare colossi aside, most people who enjoy some mid-level fame through their work are likely to be looking out on the world no differently from before they became known, and will be just as bewildered by strange behaviour as anyone else. And irrespective of what type of people we meet, famous or otherwise, it is comforting to know that we all warm to largely the same qualities in people. Typically those qualities boil down to one main quality: one single character trait which we all possess to one extent or another; one attribute which is a pleasure to foster and the greatest pleasure for others to feel in us. This was the simple point that I missed, in all my

---

the peculiarity of his writing style. An author who is endearingly detached and pedantic in his work is likely to be boringly so in real life. One who writes with unforgiving, unapologetic single-mindedness that thrills on the page will most probably seem merely cold and charmless in the flesh. Equally, the much admired but neurotic artist seems plain rude when we are introduced at a party, and the flamboyant musical genius reveals himself to be a dull, self-obsessed show-off when away from the stage.

Therefore we find them disappointing for all the same reasons we had loved their work. Now we read those words or listen to those lyrics and can only remember the more pedestrian character we met, and we interpret the once adored idiosyncrasies as symptoms of social ineptitude. We may struggle to banish such thoughts from our minds and view the person as quite separate from the work, but we cannot rid ourselves of the associations, and the work is forever tarnished. Who, after all, could love an author's works with the same self-abandonment after being blanked by him at a party?

A luminary at Channel 4 once declined an invitation to dine with Woody Allen, a hero of his, anticipating this disappointment. And I'm sure he continues to enjoy Allen's films more than if he had attended and been struck by the prosaic humanity of his idol.

excitement, when I found myself sat with Hugh Grant in that restaurant. This is the quality which has been missed in all the generations of self-help books and get-what-you-want volumes and seminars; the single most valuable element of character which is most likely to win us friends, influence people and leave us untroubled as we consider our lives at three a.m., yet which has been routinely ignored by the industries devoted to improving our lives with quick-fire magical techniques. For those of us who feel a little uneasy when we hear the rhetoric of self-improvement courses, and more so when we meet those whose selves have been improved by them, recognising the absence of this one quality is the answer to understanding why such courses so often don't quite seem to achieve their goals.

The single most valuable human trait, the one quality every schoolchild and adult should be taught to nurture, is, quite simply, kindness.

Kindness. If you prefer, *compassion.* Even *benevolence.* It is the quality that makes people *lovely.* If that sounds rather anaemic, it's because it is the opposite of setting goals and learning how to persuade and close deals; the antithesis of self-reliance and get-what-you-want thinking which form the backbone of modern self-improvement. Its simplicity and obviousness mean that we forget it constantly when we try to impress people, yet it is the most impressive trait we can ever show. It has nothing to do with intelligence or witty banter. We make the mistake of thinking we have to be funny and clever among the ranks of the funny and clever, or match the more obvious qualities of people we would like to like us, when in fact few of us seek out in others those outward aspects of personality we ourselves emanate. In fact, we tend to be sceptical of others with similar noticeable qualities to ourselves. That clever person will not like us more if we appear clever ourselves. He will like us more if we are kind, and lovely, and personable, and not trying to be anything else. In an attempt to be socially striking, and in all the contrived effort we go to in order to make ourselves remark-able, we miss how simple the answer really is. Meanwhile, we all know people who possess those qualities we wish we had more of – intelligence or wit, for example – yet if they are not also lovely, we struggle to really like them.

So many of the self-help, persuasion and communication industries could be swept away with the single mantra 'just be nice'. If you are nice to others, they will be nice to you, and they will like you. If you are nice, you are more likely to be happy, both because it makes for a cheerful conscience and because you will enjoy more friends, which have been (unsur-prisingly) shown to rank among the principal factors of a deeply contented life. If you are likeable and kind, without merely being a pushover, you may not necessarily be on the fast-track route to millionaire status, but you are more likely to glide forward through life with less effort and find comfortable success. Once you are kind, everything else falls into place.

I have seen people who previously lacked confidence absorb the high-powered idiom of modern self-help gurus, turn their lives around and become, at first glance, the no-nonsense professional powerhouses they admired in other people. I've seen them model themselves on those they wanted most to emulate, as they were taught to do, and I have on the one hand been amazed by the transformation and felt happy for the beneficiaries, and on the other felt unconvinced by the soulless and uncomfortable imitation they have managed to pull off. They have always emulated the most telegraphed and obvious characteristics of their unwitting mentors, evolving into more striking but less pleasant versions of themselves, only to be once again delightful when the straightforward old self accidentally glimmers through for a moment. The high self-help dosage can achieve slim, particular ends, which may be of enormous value to a person's self-esteem, but it is forging a difficult uphill path to a possibly far less worthwhile destination. Naturally there is worth in developing specific skill-sets that make you an excellent salesman or able to face a room of strangers in a way you previously never thought possible; chronic shyness and miserable self-esteem are terribly debilitating conditions. But while it is important to overcome such troubles, the internal gauge that tells us when the goal has been reached (or how to reach it) is skewed by the very lack of self-belief that led to the problem. Hence the achieved result may feel like a solution to the poor soul in question, but it may also achieve a forced, unpleasant type of confidence that has no room for humility, leaving him therefore less attractive than his previous incarnation, and the 'improvement' therefore fails, at least in part and as far as the outside world goes. There has been, in that case, no external guide to gently assist with finding a balance, just a pathologically driven need to achieve a fetishised form of fantasy confidence, warped through the perspective of one who has felt he would never achieve it. Soon perspective is lost, the control becomes addictive, and, in a pattern known in a more monstrous form to gym addicts and those with eating disorders, a destructive momentum kicks in.*

Be kind. It is a richer project than may at first be obvious. For example, it can involve stepping out of what is emotionally immediate, and realising in moments of everyday conflict that those with whom we're arguing are most likely taking a standpoint equally as justifiable (to themselves) as ours. Kindness may involve preferring to understand the other's one-sided view in such situations rather than blindly pushing our own. If we are prepared not to concern ourselves with the immediate blow to our pride that comes from conceding in this way, we can enjoy the warm glow later when we feel like the greater man or woman, rather than lying awake in bed fuming with rage, replaying arguments and running imaginary conversations with ourselves that make us even more livid. Ideally, this ability to detach emotionally when approaching conflict, and to look for connections rather than stand aghast at someone else's apparent bloody-mindedness, is to be combined

---

* This is the same impulse that drives women to pay for extensive and unnecessary plastic surgery. They do not achieve their goal of looking more attractive, in the same way that those intent on improving themselves through dedicated courses also miss their ambition of becoming improved people. The women instead achieve the familiar look of one who has 'had work done', and in parallel, the self-improved are rewarded with a similarly unconvincing, somewhat caricatured version of what they had hoped for. At least the woman of a certain age who has chosen to greet her world with an unchanging mien of tense astonishment has a curious status about her; typically the person who has been taught how to have a loud, 'motivated' personality is simply an embarrassment.

with an otherwise emotionally open and empathising personality. That is where the perfect balance is struck, where we would be best positioned to have a pleasant effect on others.

There are those who are undoubtedly lovely, but lovely to the point of flaccid, vapid futility. They have developed their own wearying addiction to selflessness; cannot themselves receive; feed off the broken; and perhaps even live through a string of abusive relationships as they attract those who exploit them. There are those damaged souls who live out an ostentatious display of masquerading kindness born only from desperate, toxic neediness. Balance is all. I would not dream of suggesting how the right sort of kindness can be achieved, as it is quite enough trying to attend privately to one's own life. It needs perhaps to be driven by a desire to be liked, maybe the teensiest proneness to paranoia, and a possession of all the little insecurities that drive us to pay attention to what others think of us and the effect that we have on them – probably the first stirrings of the same neuroses which plague the truly tragic.

Lest it sound like I am proposing a vacuous, smiling, endlessly giving approach to life that shrieks in horror at the mention of personal gain, I would draw the reader tentatively back to the lessons learnt from persuasion research and the skills of powerfully charismatic leaders. So often we heard during and after the Bill Clinton era that the eternally charming President would speak to you as if you were the only person in the room. Princess Diana, we hear, was a flirt. In Robert Cialdini's seminal book *Influence: The Science of Persuasion*, we learn how US President Lyndon B. Johnson's surprising ability to get a very large number of laws passed through a non-partisan Congress in his early years seems to be explained in part by the huge number of favours he was able to call in, after he himself had bestowed so many favours during his previous career as a Congressman and Senator. Cialdini compares his case to that of Jimmy Carter, who ran very much on an 'outsider' ticket and who had tremendous difficulty passing laws, even through a much more sympathetic Congress, as he was unknown to the law-makers and therefore was unable to benefit from owed favours.

Cialdini is describing 'reciprocity', one of the more powerful elements of persuasive technique. It is not the same as kindness, but it is born of it, and points in its own way to one value of being kind. If you wish to find a self-serving reason to embrace kindness, the law of reciprocity is your rationale. In a well-established experiment, you (a naive participant) find yourself paired off with John (who is posing as another partic-ipant but in fact is in on the trick) and you are given a task to carry out, such as a word test or a memory exercise, which you mistakenly believe is the purpose of the experiment. At some point during the proceedings, John leaves the room for a few minutes. When he returns, he has bought himself a can of Cola, and, thoughtfully, another one for you. The faux experiment continues, and after it appears to be all over John mentions that he has some raffle tickets to sell, and asks if you would be happy to buy some. This enlightening test showed that when he brings us the unrequested drink we are far more likely to help John out and buy his tickets than when no drink is forth-coming. Moreover, it does not significantly affect how much we like John when we emerge from the room; it is simply that when someone has done something nice for us, we have a very powerful urge to reciprocate. The lesson: if you want someone to do something for you, do something nice for them first. In a perverse way, this is one of the true values of being kind.

Ah, I hear you smugly pronounce, that's it, isn't it? There is no genuine, selfless kindness: we are all selfish creatures, and what may appear generous or benevolent is in fact self-serving.

Witness the hugely expensive pot of Crème de la Mer moisturiser I included amongst the gifts I gave my mother last Christmas. The 60ml tub cost an extraordinary *one hundred and fifty-six pounds*, an amount she (nor anyone else, I'm sure) could never truly justify spending on a pot of face-cream, even if she had read the blurb on their site:

Do You Believe in Miracles?
If miracles are unique events that seem hard to explain, then surely the discovery of Crème de la Mer can be described as a miracle.

Despite my uncertainty over their lax definition of 'miracles', which should surely involve a suspension of the normal laws of the universe, I was seduced by the extravagant price, the promise of a 'Miracle Broth™', and enthusiastic recommendations from those who know about such things. I bought some for Mum and perhaps a pot as well for myself – not that it's any of your business. A lovely gift, I thought. The brand, I was assured, was legendary, and I expected excitement from its lucky recipient when she unwrapped this gift on Christmas Day.

But when the family was gathered for present-opening at my younger brother's house – after an excellent turkey and just before a moving duet of 'Something Stupid' on *Singstar* by me and the mother in question – no gasp of recognition greeted the name on the tub as the gift was revealed; no 'you shouldn't have!' escaped her lips to suggest a lady presented at last with the astonishing cosmetic indulgence she had always felt herself lacking. Instead she, with due maternal gratitude, acted in a way appropriate for one receiving a gift of some quite ordinary moisturiser, and of a brand she did not seem to recognise.

A flash of disappointment was triggered in my gut. I asked if she knew the make. No, she didn't. I rapidly considered my options:

Make no comment and trust that she'd soon realise the superior quality of the product.
This involved an extraordinary trust in the product and a level of modesty I was unable to find in myself.

Remark that it was a highly regarded brand and that I hoped it lived up to the hype.
This sounded like the correct response, but it would leave the expenditure of £156 irritatingly unbalanced by a lack of acknowledgement of my generosity.

Jokingly point out that it was very expensive.
But aside from how gauche this would undeniably sound, her idea of 'very expensive' would be unlikely to be as high as

£156, so I would not only be faced with regret at making the comment about cost, but this would also be exacerbated by a frustrated desire to blurt out the exact amount, just so I would know that my bounteousness had been fully appreciated.

Remark that it was a highly regarded brand and suggest that she Google the product to find out about how it was made.
The curious online mother would find the Crème de la Mer website and stumble across the price-tag herself.

Considering this last the most elegant of the options, I took it.

Upon reflection, I wonder if the desire for her to have a sense of the price-tag was more about wanting to fuel her with the same excitement and anticipation I had for the product than merely to point out that I had spent more than she might have imagined on this particular gift. I think this might be the case, for if I now imagine that I had somehow acquired the tub for free, I would be more than happy for her to know that, but *still* want her to appreciate its price in the hope it would raise her enjoyment of the product and hopefully her expectations of its effectiveness.

On this latter subject, it has been shown that a potent method of selling an item is to *raise* its price dramatically rather than lower it, as we associate a higher price with superior quality. I write as someone pathetically influenced by such tactics. Only yesterday I was nonchalantly browsing Amazon for a particular DVD with no strong intention of buying it, only to find that for whatever reasons of scarcity, it was on sale for around £80. I immediately bought it. What an arse.

Even if I had only desired my mother to be as excited as possible about the gift rather than impressed with my munificence, we are still left with the fact that I probably wanted that appreciation and excitement to be associated with *me*. The thought exercise necessary to test this is simple: would I have been happy giving the gift anonymously? Would I have felt a sting of jealousy or disappointment had my brother given her the same product in the larger-size tub? The answers are Not Entirely and At Some Level Yes Probably. So do we not seek to direct that warm glow of kindness back upon ourselves from the first moment we consider the kind act?

Well, if this is selfishness, then bring it on. It is not, in these times, a mark of the publicly admired personality to be particularly kind (and if it were, there would be no need to recommend it), and we are told to be wary of kindness as if it only masked weakness or a desire to manipulate. Our ambivalent relationship with this most admirable trait seems to be due to our distrust of it in our natures. In the fifth century, the once-rowdy teenager and erstwhile lover of concubines Augustine of Hippo, one of the most influential figures in the development of Christianity, unforgivably burdened us all with the first clear outlining of the doctrine of original sin. With it came the notion that only through self-sacrifice can we transcend our bestial natures to achieve 'caritas', the Christian understanding of kindness, achievable only through God's grace. This answered, in its day, the question of how man, created in God's image, could be so unpleasant and cruel. Without hard work and suppression, it was explained, we are violent and merciless.

Augustine was Catholic, but the sixteenth-century Protestant Reformation took his unforgiving view of our natures and made it far bleaker. Luther, the leader of the Reformation, and his disciple John Calvin, the French theologian, painted a deeply anti-human picture of us as driven to evil and deserving to burn for eternity. This aspect of Christianity, which vilifies humanity (without its God) and denies the pleasure of this life in favour of a posited hereafter, was particularly loathed by Friedrich Nietzsche, the ruthless moustachioed champion of human potential. The Protestants were a business-savvy bunch, and as Adam Phillips' and Barbara Taylor's charming book *On Kindness* tells us, they swiftly demoted 'caritas' to institutionalised 'charity', and the very notion of brotherly love was lost beneath the new commercial spirit and religious conflicts.

John Calvin gave us lofty metaphysics; Thomas Hobbes gave us a dim, cynical view of human nature, and thus boys and tigers are named. Hobbes, a seventeenth-century English philosopher reacting to the after-effects of the Reformation and religious vainglory, saw us as ego-driven power-machines where all seeming good intentions mask entirely self-serving motives. Hobbes' profoundly disheartening view of our natures remains with us today. His toxic impact was so strong that even with the Enlightenment's reaction against his pessimism and the new celebration of a human 'fellow-feeling' unshackled by torturous theology, we still find it very hard to think that motives are ever genuinely altruistic.

These ghosts of Hobbes, and more substantially of Freud, still haunt us, and have us read into our kindness ulterior motives and even veiled aggression.* This is a shame, for a simpler view to take is that there is a genuine and important pleasure to be taken in kindness; in giving gifts, buying dinners and treating others generously.

Buying dinner! To any of you who always split the bill or have dinner bought for you by others, you are missing out on a pleasure far richer than that of a free meal. Try paying the bill next time and see what I mean. A few months before Harold Pinter died, I found myself dining a few tables from him and

---

* I sometimes wonder if Freud killed Dickens. Once the vague notion has filtered down to us that acts of true love and self-sacrifice disguise selfish unconscious desires, we are left to scoff at the florid chronicles of such noble behaviour that form much of Dickens' heart-tugging, orphan-laden tales, treating them as sadly improbable and two-dimensional. We would be more convinced now by a complex alternative drama of motherless Oliver Twist's psychosexual development than by Dickens' broader characterisation of his eponymous hero.

We may now find the depictions of these do-gooders simplistic and unfashionable, but we flock instead to the uncomplicated narratives of uplifting television programmes – *Oprah Winfrey*, *Secret Millionaire*, and so on – to warm our hearts in the same way. And it is a beautiful thing to weep with happiness at the openly engineered scenes of selflessness that frequently play out in this medium, and to be willingly manipulated by superficial, pared-down tales of rewarded goodness, all our cynicism suspended.

Scientists have studied the particular soul-soaring sensation of elevation we derive from watching these 'real-life' events unfold within the far-from-real-life frame of the small screen. It seems that something called the 'vagus nerve' may be affected by such experiences, which affects the heart rate and works with a hormone called oxytocin to provide feelings of calmness and a desire for bonding. Interestingly, oxytocin also happens to regulate lactation: in one test worth mentioning, it was found that nursing mothers

his wife in a reputed London restaurant. The classic film version of *The Birthday Party* had made a great impression on me as a schoolboy, and I had come to find him fascinating and frightening as I grew up: undoubtedly his performance in that film and the eerie oppressiveness of his dialogue set a tone which only my later appreciation of his political views and intellectual rigour allowed to mature into a fuller awareness of his particular iconic magnificence. My image of him as a physical being, however, drawn from that film and the few grainy

---

shown a particularly uplifting episode of *The Oprah Winfrey Show* produced far more breast-milk than a control group watching comedy clips. I was pleased, when reading of this eccentric experiment, to observe that the scientists in question had had their conclusions poetically prefigured by Lady Macbeth centuries before, in her 'milk of human kindness' soliloquy. I wonder if faint memories of early English lessons, shapeless and shifting but nigglingly poignant, stirred within these lab-coated researchers as they collected and measured the warm, watery cupfuls.

When we witness others being kind and in turn feel this elation, we are surprisingly *not* especially moved to replicate it. As this hormone produces such calming emotions, we are not prone to be driven to action by its release, despite how much the kind acts otherwise move us.

In Dickens, as in television, we are thankfully spared the pedestrian layer of meddlesome real life, which would throw the clear variables of a crafted tale into chaos and leave us cold. It takes the careful removal of this unpredictable stratum (and all the unhelpful conflicts and distractions it contains) to create a coherent contrivance upon which we can intuitively hang our feelings.

The distinction between fiction-story and real-life-story was brought home to me by an incident related by a friend, L—. He was on a train, returning to London after attending the funeral of his closest friend. His soul-mate, a young man in his early twenties, had lived a richly spiritual life, which he had himself ended in a tragic act of self-destruction.

black-and-white photographs I had seen, remained as fore-
boding as his heavy-set face, black hair and eternally sixties
sideburns.

Then, as an adult, though still a few years before the
evening in question, I saw him for the first time in the flesh,
dining out a few days after his Nobel Prize speech. He was far
older, frail, and had recently taken a fall. It was the first time I
had seen him as a living human being, let alone one so delicate,
and I was mesmerised. Later, he had to walk right behind me

Travelling home, L— was deeply lost in that peculiar wretched reverie
which we can imagine the mixed emotions of the service had produced in
him. Sat in the carriage, oblivious to the other passengers and the trundling
of the train, his mind dwelt on the significance of the loss of his friend; his
soul ached within him, and his thoughts and yearnings grew grand and
melancholy as his heavy heart reached out across dark expanses.

And then, at that moment, before him in the air, coloured gold by the
soft light from a low London sun which now revealed itself through the
window, there appeared a tiny, dancing airborne feather. Impossibly light,
it hovered, somehow held, six inches or so from L—'s face, by turns
motionless, then spirited into coaxing, winking whirls and pirouettes by
the warm air; and far beyond it the silent carriage had slipped into some
timeless golden world and nothing moved save for this floating, fleeting
apparition.

L—'s heart surged and lifted; his darkness fell away before the unlikely
feather that seemed to have found him there, a token from another dimen-
sion. He smiled and went to blow it, playfully, in order to watch it rise and
spin and fall before him. His intention, at least, was to blow; but as he drew
a preparatory breath he unintentionally sucked the feather into his mouth
and, with the full force of floor-fluff flying into the nozzle of a vacuum
cleaner, it shot to the back wall of his throat and clung there. A sudden,
violent fit of rasping coughing ensued as his body tried to dislodge the
intruder. Eyes streaming, he began to gag, and as the other passengers

to leave, and as he limped past I froze over my meal, feeling a giddy graze with greatness.

This was not the only time I was to see him at dinner: favouring, as we seemed to, the same group of restaurants, it happened again and again. By the fifth time, which was the occasion with which we are concerned, and having by this point overcome the instinctive motor and digestive shut-down that our proximity seemed to evoke in me, I wondered if it might not cause offence to anonymously and discreetly pick up the tab at his table.

Once before I had tried this ploy and been discouraged. I had found myself sat not far from Michael Winner in one of said restaurants, and the extraordinary man had come over to say hello. I had enjoyed his company so much that when I came to pay for my meal, I asked the maître-d' if I might quietly cover Michael's too; but after some discussion among the staff I was advised that it was a terrible idea: he was, it was tactfully and professionally explained, a generous and proud soul and such a gesture might cause umbrage. Here, clearly, is a man who well knows the pleasure of buying dinner for others. I might have insisted, but upon being cleverly informed that his caviar course alone had come to around ten times my own bill, I quickly acceded to their professional wisdom.

However, I was assured by an equally knowledgeable staff member that Harold Pinter would not be upset, and I arranged

---

recoiled, he reached into his mouth and tried to scrape it from his throat wall with a fingernail, retching on to his fingers, convulsing spastically as the train heaved into Waterloo.

to pick up the playwright's tab anonymously as I gathered my book and coat to leave. I say 'anonymously': I cannot for a second imagine that my name would have meant anything to either him or Lady Antonia, but the last thing I wanted was to provoke the urge of reciprocity and therefore any courteous concern on their part that they should have to respond in some way. The point is only that I left warmed by a happy glow that evening, and that glow was unavoidably a selfish one: for the possibility that this great man might be touched by the gesture – and that therefore I had made some infinitesimal, unattributed impact upon him – was enough to leave me reeling.

From most kind acts there may stem the potential for reciprocal favours, and intertwined with them a desire for the other person to like us more, but rather than these being embarrassing and confusing truths to torture those seeking purity, they can also teach us a very valuable lesson. Of course it does rather defeat the purpose of being kind if our motives are selfish. But to understand that kindness can genuinely be of benefit to the person *being* kind, quite aside from any reciprocation, as much as to the person having the benevolence conferred upon him, is to appreciate that it is a richer approach to life than its sickly-sweet overtones may at first suggest. Kindness makes us all happier.

Since the start of the twentieth century, as Freud's remarkable ideas seeped into the mainstream, the field of clinical psychology has been far more concerned with the question of how things go wrong, and how problems should be fixed, than with taking the initiative to teach how we can be happier. Until very recently, in the absence of hard research, this task was left to the self-help industry, which is largely content with short-term, quick-fix solutions to life's problems. This general lack of lasting efficacy is hidden among proud rhetoric, sarcasm towards clinical testing, and an overwhelming reliance on anecdote as evidence – barely different from the alternative health industry. For many, such techniques can be enlightening and useful in the short term, but for the searcher after a longer-term antidote, the only route offered seemed to be one of joining the cult: buying the books, attending the courses, and talking the right language.

In very recent times, a new movement known as 'Positive Psychology' has arisen to fill the gap left by the lack of grown-up empirical research and plastered over by self-help fads. It is a serious move to find out what really makes us happy, and then to teach real techniques and approaches to life that make an unfeigned long-term difference. It is also very challenging reading, for the results are often counter-intuitive, or uncomfortably close to home. And there in the middle of it all we find kindness.

Most of what we think will make us happier does exactly that for a little while, and then loses its power. A bigger house, a new car or any other conspicuous acquirement does give us a buzz of pleasure, but it is a fleeting enough sensation which, once it has subsided, leaves us no happier than we were before. And that place we return to is our default setting: a plateau of general happiness, our state of general contentment. A major key to achieving a fulfilled and happy existence, it would seem, is in raising that plateau by adopting behaviours that continue to generate happiness and make our default level higher. This is, however, an easy point to miss when we are densely surrounded by advertising media that insist we shamefully lack all the things that will, according to their glossy insinuations, make us feel complete. And what are those practices and habits we should seek to put in place? Kindness emerges as one of the most effective. Again and again, experimenters realised that the feeling of pleasure derived from committing an act of altruism far outlasts the pleasure caused by treating oneself. While we quickly adapt to acquiring nice things in our lives, we do not acclimatise to the pleasure of helping others. It raises that default setting of happiness to which we revert when the initial joy of a new toy has passed.

I write this while eagerly awaiting (and disappointed by the very late arrival of) two new digital cameras ordered online. Both of them – a Canon 5D Mark II SLR and a Panasonic LX3 Lyca-lensed pocket beauty – are currently at the cutting edge of their respective worlds, and in my eagerness to receive them I resemble a child waiting to run into my parents' bedroom at four a.m. on Christmas morning to bounce on the bed and empty my bladder on to their chests with excitement. I am also extending my apartment by conjoining it with the flat next door, and while the immediate exhilaration is not as charged as that created by the much-anticipated and belated Amazon package, I do imagine I shall enjoy a vastly improved existence welcoming over-awed visitors to my monstrous London *über*-pad. I delight in new technology on the one hand, and on the other have loved the idea of a sprawling living space ever since seeing the beautifully tangled result of knocking through from one apartment to another when, as a student, I visited the labyrinthine home of Dominic LeFoe, a charismatically anachronistic music-hall impresario who embodied exactly the white-goateed, bejewelled-cane-and-waistcoated Dickensian aesthetic I privately had in mind for myself at that preposterously precocious age.

I am very aware that neither camera nor expanded flat will really make me happier than I am now. Doubtless by the time I have finished writing this chapter the cameras will have arrived, the flat will be as cluttered with debris as it is now, and I shall realise that, perversely, the most enjoyable aspect of their entry into my life was the anticipation of their arrival.* On the

---

* Ordering from Amazon, which I do several times a week, brings with it several instances of enjoyment that far outweigh the supposedly delightful but in actuality rather crowded, noisy and disappointing experience of browsing through real objects on real shelves in real shops. These three moments are:

Finding the item immediately
Much as the successful online retail revolution is supposed to have us rueing the declining practice of browsing through bookshops for desired titles, there is a deep joy in entering the name of an obscure book into a rectangular box on the screen, at an equally obscure hour of the night, and near-instantaneously being faced with a long list showing every edition available from anywhere in the world. In a second, my computer has connected with the records of bookshops all over the globe, as well as the gargantuan storage units of Amazon itself that are sometimes passed in the car, yielding extraordinary glimpses of minute, innumerable DVDs and books on endless shelves through their tall windows – an image reminiscent of the final scene of *Indiana Jones and the Raiders of the Lost Ark*. It has found the records, searched through them to see who has the title I'm after, and then has presented them to me along with dinky images of their covers and an option to flick through a few pages. And it will do this whenever I want it to, apart from when my internet is down. Life is astonishing.

one hand I know these types of acquisitions will do nothing for me after the initial excitement has lapsed; on the other I cannot resist them. Meanwhile, the findings of the Positive Psychologists are a comfort, for if the cameras break or the flat purchase falls through, I shan't feel that I have seriously lost out.

Although one likes to imagine that success brings with it a need for, or even a presumption of, social skills, it is a sad truth that the wealthy tend to be among the least kind of us. Witness the successful executive who charms the bespoke pants off his dinner colleague in a restaurant, but treats the waiter with

---

Ordering the item

Unlike in a bookshop, online ordering allows us to enjoy the purchasing of a desired book, DVD or gadget as a quite separate joy-moment from when we first grasped it in our hands. We can experience the delight in securing the item as our own, and then, a day or two later, when it has slipped from our mind, the even greater glee of opening the package and finally handling it. Two joys for the price of one. As if this were not wonderful enough, there is also the extraordinarily appealing 'one-click' method of buying, which still makes me slightly giddy with delight each time I use it. Minor celebrity may bring with it an ever-present flurry of talented individuals devoted to keeping one happy, well groomed and topped up with coffee and sushi, but I don't think anything makes me feel quite as pampered as causing a book to be selected from a shelf, wrapped up and posted to me with a single mouse-click. I barely even have to press a button: my finger is *already on* the mouse.

Receiving the item

DVD covers can now be read, and books can be smelt, before being put on the shelf and forgotten about entirely. On occasion I have known cellophane wraps, never removed, to entirely biodegrade on my shelf before the DVD inside has been watched.

dismissive contempt. Unfortunately, for those of us who live in a world where a personal assistant and similar luxuries are necessary to function productively, an unfair expectation can arise of how easily life should fall into place, and therefore when it doesn't, a revolting tendency to blame others for not doing their job properly is a common reaction. A diner having a row with a waiter in a swanky restaurant chills the blood in a way that a quarrel over a pizza order elsewhere would never do. Compassion is rarely the custom of the privileged. How different things would be if that were not the case.

A poet I knew once suggested, while addressing a group of students, that the would-be versifiers improve their skills by writing a poem first thing each morning. When one of the students complained that it took her weeks to write a poem that she was happy with, and that the idea of writing one every morning seemed an impossibility, his answer was brilliant: 'Lower your standards.' This is also one answer recommended by the Roman philosopher and statesman Annaeus Seneca: if you have high expectations of how smoothly life will glide forward every day, you will be routinely disappointed and therefore prone to anger. Lower those expectations, and the world becomes a less frustrating and therefore more delightful place.

When we are customarily annoyed by what we see as the failings of others, we are judging them by a ludicrous standard: we are assuming that they fully understand our desires, quite possibly better than we do, and that they have nothing to do but arrange things to fall seamlessly into place around our probably ill-communicated wishes. Part of kindness therefore involves a more realistic appraisal of our impact upon other people, and being aware of our tendency to cast them as cameo roles in the fascinating epic of our own lives. This in turn reminds us of the elusively obvious fact that those we meet are already leading lives as complicated as our own; that people very rarely act or talk in a way that to them seems stupid, cruel or unjustified, and that therefore in arguments with anyone other than the most painfully slow-witted we would benefit far more from understanding and incorporating the viewpoint we find so inconceivable than being outraged at its unreasonableness. Each of us is leading a difficult life, and when we meet people we are seeing only a tiny part of the thinnest veneer of their complex, troubled existences. To practise anything other than kindness towards them, to treat them in any way save generously, is to quietly deny their humanity.

CHAPTER

4

*P*ick a card.

Joel, Benedict and Charlotte reached forward, while I faced away to my right.

'Should we take them right out?' Joel asked, and, thankfully, the more common pronunciation of 'out' answered the tricky Canadian question – here in the negative. Definitely American.

'Please do,' I answered, and noticed in my peripheral vision that he waited for Benedict and Charlotte to withdraw their own cards first. Benedict let out an involuntary sigh as he pulled himself forward. I noticed that he again looked for the gaze of the other two as he reached across. He was fiddling, I could tell, with a few cards before pulling one out. His girlfriend would have had the more uncomfortable reach down the length of the table. I could also check, from this angle, that none of them touched the Queen of Hearts on the far right, nearest Joel.

'What part of the States are you from?' I posed as I turned back round to face them.

'Upstate New York originally, but I live in California.'

'Where upstate? Near Rochester? Please, do look at your cards.'

Each looked at his or her card. Joel, as I was facing him, was most guarded, covering the back of his card like a gambler. Benedict checked his by lifting the index corner from the table with his fat thumb and middle finger, betraying again in that action a familiarity with cards: most likely he was a poker player.

'Kinda. I have friends in Rochester though.'

An image flashed through my mind of my week in Rochester, an unremarkable city in my memory but for Park Avenue Books and Espresso, where I had spent every afternoon while my host friend was studying, and where I had enjoyed the noble pairing of the modest institution's twin offerings in one of four or five comfy armchairs, listening to the jazz records played by the owner, whom I can still faintly picture as a smiley, jumpered blur, maybe called Bob. There was an old pony-tailed artist who looked like a country and western singer – I believe he was a photographer – who came in most days with his dog, with whom he travelled everywhere in a pick-up truck. I would have been a precocious twenty-one-year-old, and I'm not sure what we would have spoken about, but I remember now him saying I should visit his studio, and in the same breath, portentously, that he didn't worry about the 'whole man or woman thing' when it came to sex. I remember hoping he drew a line before involving his dog. I didn't, thankfully, visit his studio. Instead I listened to jazz I didn't know and read and drank unusually good coffee for an American outlet.

Those were the days before the Starbucks revolution here in the UK, and I came home missing the casual, intelligent mingling of laptops, literature and lattes; of hanging out and browsing shelves and no one being concerned you were going to stay too long or get coffee on the books.

The back of Joel's card was still concealed by his cupped hand, a little like how a schoolboy hides his work from a neighbour he suspects might cheat. I used to cheat something rotten in exams. I would steal paper from one exam, take it home and write on it notes for a second, then arrive with the illegitimately annotated sheet flat against my stomach inside a zip-up cardigan. A little while into the exam I would unfasten, take a few papers from the table and lift them flat against myself as I pretended to be looking at something on a sheet underneath, and then, as I placed them back down again, I would bring with them the extra sheet from its hiding place. The notes were scribbled to look like I had made them openly during the exam, and the ploy was convincing.

For a while I studied Law in Germany, which was, as might be imagined from the combination, a densely turgid time. I was required at one point to attend an examination in the form of a spoken test in a lecturer's office and cheated by having the textbook open on my lap as I sat opposite him at his desk. Moreover, there were two other foreign students accompanying me in the assessment, Chloe and Giuseppe,* who were reading from the same book, though it was my task to try to

---

* Those are their real names. I implicate them here in case I get into trouble.

turn the pages unnoticed and signal the answers from beneath the edge of the desk. At one point the examiner asked if any of us had the textbook to hand him, in order for him to check some aspect of what we had been required to learn. I like to think, on reflection, that he had sensed our ploy and some innate Teutonic *Schadenfreude* encouraged him to toy with us by asking for the very book he knew resided illegally on my lap. If this was the case, he also displayed a kindness in not reporting us or even mentioning it. In fact, if I remember, he gave each of us a good mark. I grabbed the book in one hand and my satchel-bag in the other, held the book behind the bag and brought them both up with the bag in view of our assessor, and in pretending to reach into the bag to remove the book I actually pulled up the latter from behind, with what may have been an unnecessary magical flourish. Giuseppe, to my right, started giggling and couldn't stop for some time. I seem to recall he had to stifle himself, in Italian fashion, with a handkerchief.*

---

* It was while living in Germany that I learnt to stop using handkerchiefs. Until then they had seemed to me to be the preferred gentlemanly option to the simple tissue: somehow innately elegant and unable to dissolve into tissue-fluff in the pocket. Upon blowing my nose into my cotton pocket square one day in Nuremberg while among friends, I was treated to a round condemnation from the natives who strongly expressed their disgust with square-jawed, purple-clothed, exhaustingly joyless German indignation. They were revolted by the idea of me evacuating my sinuses into a piece of cloth that would then sit heavy and full in my pocket to act as a receptacle for further explosions of mucus as need or comfort dictated; horrified by the notion that it would need to be brought out and audibly peeled apart for a clean spot to be found; that this cloth would, rather than

I reassembled the deck with a sweep from right to left, and snapped it into a fan. Reaching for Benedict's card, on my far left, I caused him to retract his hand a little, seemingly not wanting me to take the card. I hesitated and looked at him. He laughed a snort through his nose, and then almost tossed it at me, looking away to share his lingering smile with his girl-friend and Joel.

I took his card and placed it into the fan, near the bottom of the deck, with half of the card still extended. I repeated these actions with the others, inserting each one partway into the fan. I tilted the fan to show the faces of the cards, then brought it flat again, closing it with the three cards still protruding from the front of the deck. Then, in a well-oiled move, I appeared to push the cards flush into the deck, lose them in the process, and then cut the deck on to the table. This sleight was invented by one Dai Vernon, a Canadian magician known and revered in magic circles as The Professor; an extraordinary magician,

---

be thrown away, be kept as something precious, to be washed with clothes and used again. What perverse, retentive impulse would cause Englishmen to do anything other than expel waste into a tissue and throw it away? I saw their point, could offer no defence, and have not used one since without guilt and self-disgust. I was reminded of a boy at school known for his adventurous approach to personal hygiene, who boasted of carrying two handkerchiefs with him, one in each trouser pocket: he would use the first until he had filled it with his dense snot, before changing pockets and moving on to the second. By the time the latter was also glutted with nose-gloop, the first would have dried to a crust, and therefore was deemed useable once more. And so this cycle of drying and filling would continue, for up to a week, without either handkerchief being replaced. We really hated him.

sleight-of-hand artist and thinker. This efficient and elegant move resulted in all three cards being stripped from the deck and then brought to the top in the action of the cut.*

As it is impossible to spot the deceit when it is carried out with fluidity, the satisfying conclusion was reached whereby the cards were presumed by the trio to be lost, but in fact were right under their noses. This was my participants' first major false presumption. And an interesting one at that: clearly a second's thought would suggest that I would not really lose track of those cards and make things so difficult for myself. But an action had taken place that perfectly resembled losing them, and the casual nature in which it had been carried out made it seem even more guiltless. This is, perhaps, where the suspension of disbelief starts; an interior monologue begins, and the spectator's guard is first nudged awake. *The cards are lost in the deck. Are they, though? He must somehow know where they are. But OK . . . let's work on the presumption that they're lost and see where that takes us.* After all, I didn't let them shuffle the cards themselves. Why not? If I really wanted them lost, it would have made sense to have them do it. Maybe the neatness of the move provided a reason for why I took it upon myself. *If we had*

---

* There is an anecdote attached to Vernon, which runs accurately or otherwise as follows. He was showing a card trick to some fellow magicians one evening when the phone rang. The owner of the place (I suspect it was a back-room in a magic shop) answered the call, which turned out to be from the local hospital, bearing news that Vernon's wife had just given birth. Vernon, who we might like to imagine would have made a point of being at the birth, did not take the call: instead he finished the trick before calling the hospital back.

shuffled them into the deck ourselves, we'd have made a mess. He can do it better than we can, that's why he did it. This guard is now alert, and it is the magician's task to keep him occupied with menial tasks while the thieves slip by unnoticed.

With the placing of the deck upon the table before them, seemingly containing their three chosen cards at random locations, their attention was hopefully secured. I would only lose those cards in the deck if I were going to find, produce or identify them. The game we were now playing rested upon the hope that the seeming unlikelihood of being able to fulfil this unspoken promise would amplify their sense of curiosity as to how this might be nonetheless achieved.

Three cards: each brought secretly to the top of the deck. Most simple card tricks involve either this sort of control of a card to a particular position, or alternatively may rely on the *force* of a particular card, which once imposed upon the unwitting spectator might then be safely lost. In more complex diversions, the combination of force and control may achieve the desired aim.

A card can be forced to match a hidden duplicate or a prediction; much of the efficacy of such a trick depends upon how subtly and deftly the coercion takes place. The novice magician asks you to call 'stop' as he riffles awkwardly through a too-tightly-gripped deck: even if you do not spot the precise subterfuge, you can sniff the unmistakable odour of unnaturalness and deception. The experienced performer develops delicately invisible ways of having you arrive at a predetermined card, through a combination of psychological and physical means. You are asked to choose one of a small handful of seemingly random cards face-up in a line on the table. Eager not to pick anything too obvious, you avoid the cards at the end; the card right in the middle; the Ace; the only picture card; the only black card; the only card slightly misaligned; the only card mentioned by the magician as he laid them out; and you are left with only one card, which you happily choose, confident that you have picked the *only* card that is unpredictable. Which of course you were supposed to do. Or a deck is spread for selection, and you reach forward to take one, unaware that the spreading (and therefore the position of the force card) is being timed perfectly with your approaching fingertips: in effect you are bringing the inevitable pasteboard into an irresistible position through the naturalness of your own innocent movements. The finest forces are things of real beauty.

They are beautiful because they deftly play with aspects of

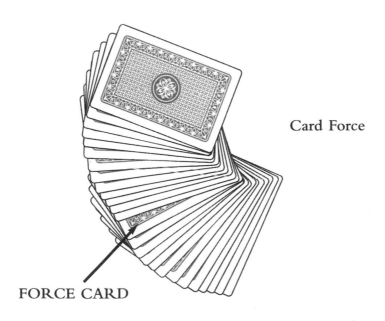

Card Force

FORCE CARD

our psychology with which we are not consciously familiar; because they use invisible skill and suggestion, and take place in a no-man's land between free will and automation where the hypnotist carries out his work; because they speak of us as human beings, fallible and surprising. The force may be more beautiful than the trick that follows, which is likely to be showy and flawed in comparison. A card is beautifully, perfectly forced and shuffled back into the deck; then, after suitable gestures, the magician reveals a duplicate of the forced card, which resides far from the deck, across the room, in the pages of a book. An impossible flight of a chosen card, and the magician has done his job. The fairy-flight of an Ace to an unfeasible destination may intrigue the spectator for some moments, but the unavoidable triviality of the event means it will soon be dismissed with a laugh, or a request to 'do another one'. The way in which the card was forced, never discussed, was of far more interest than the reason why it was forced.

In a similar way, the appeal of a psychic's reading, which holds our attention by playing on our self-interest, and which promises magic and impossible realms, is of far less value than the curious psychological forces and controls that are being used, knowingly or otherwise, during that reading to convince us. There is a cheat, like a card force, behind it, and magic methods may seem disappointingly prosaic alternatives to the supernatural, but a closer look reveals that the explanation of the psychic can be genuinely more fascinating than the effect. This is surely because it holds the ordinary and human up to the light and finds something extraordinary inside, rather than dealing in empty, misleading promises of other worlds.

Take the following exchange, a simple bit of standard stage cold-reading:

STAGE MEDIUM: I'm getting the name Jean, very clearly.

AUDIENCE MEMBER: That's me.

MEDIUM: And this was someone connected with your mother's side that passed.

AUDIENCE MEMBER: Yes, my aunt.

MEDIUM: That's right, she's saying, 'Hello there, luv.' She's quite a wild one, had a side that was very bubbly, but she had a lovely heart, didn't she?

AUDIENCE MEMBER: Yes.

MEDIUM: She's showing me the hospital . . . something about a hospital.

AUDIENCE MEMBER [*THINKS*]: My husband is in hospital.

MEDIUM: That's right, she's saying it's nothing too serious, you shouldn't be worried. You've been concerned, haven't you? Who is Paul?

AUDIENCE MEMBER: A friend of my husband.

MEDIUM: Yes, she's showing me Paul, his friend, as proof for you that it's her that's coming through. She's saying, 'The house will get sold' – what's that about?

AUDIENCE MEMBER: Don't know . . . [*thinks hard*]

MEDIUM: Well, give it some thought, because she's telling me it's a house being sold, quite clearly, and she's showing me a green or a blue door.

I have sat and watched mediums give this sort of information to people desperate to hear it, and been shocked by how well it tends to be received. The medium follows a pattern of throwing something out, letting the bereaved find a connection, then feeding it back as his own success. He can sound very specific in his declarations, for if the poor soul in the audience cannot find a link, she is blamed for not trying hard enough, left to work it out for herself, and then soon forgotten about. The pressure on the audience member to make the statements fit, in order not to have her connection with a loved one curtailed, is enormous. But most extraordinary to me is that there is *nothing* in what the medium is saying that is remotely extraordinary or even hard to explain, yet it will serve as proof for many of an afterlife, of psychic ability, and of the validity of such highly suspect performances. Of course this is due in the main to the eagerness of the bereaved to hear what they want to, and sometimes a show can be made more convincing by the medium ensuring that he already knows information about some audience members ('hot' rather than 'cold' reading), but for the most part people are ready to believe without asking for unbiased evidence.

Issues about the morality of mediumship aside, it is quite fascinating that a conversation such as the above, transparent when read through a couple of times at most, can convince a mature and educated person that the dead are able to communicate with us from beyond the grave. The work we must put into our side of that dialogue to make the medium's words appear convincing; the ease with which we can trick ourselves into finding substance in thin air − such things are far more fascinating and important in their beautiful, undeniable humanness than vapid non-sequiturs from the Happy Summerland. 'Human' is somehow always more interesting than 'super-human'.

There is a common response from people when they hear that in the absence of evidence to convince me otherwise I don't have any particular belief in ghosts, psychic powers or an afterlife. It normally runs something along the lines of 'So you think we just live, die and *that's it*? Come on . . .' There's a clear implication there that this earthly life − the wonder of being human − is somehow worthless. That it's cheap and disappointing enough to warrant that 'just' and the accompanying incredulous tone, which are usually reserved for sentences like 'After all that it was just a little spider? Come on . . .' I live, I am sure, in a fairly narrow band of life, and make an embarrassingly pitiful attempt to explore the world I find myself upon. I ache with guilt and conflict when I hear of people living as adventurers, abandoning mainstream lives and living each day with abandon. But I really hope I have a brighter vision for this life and a greater curiosity for its richness than one who can say, and mean, 'You think we just live, die and *that's it?*'

Until a single medium or psychic shows under controlled conditions (and that naturally means conditions agreed by the scientist *and* the psychic) that they are doing something paranormal – at which point I shall squeal with delight and devote myself energetically to such studies – I shall work on the sensible assumption that the rational explanations for supernatural phenomena are probably the correct ones. Given that, here is a list of some quirks of our nature that are far more fascinating in their implications and deceptive simplicity than the purported paranormal phenomena they can explain.

Useful and fascinating facts	Less useful and fascinating phenomena which they explain
We pay more attention to things that confirm our existing beliefs than those that don't.	Misjudged lucky streaks in gambling. Deciding that someone, or God, must love/hate us when they don't. Seeing evidence of supernatural design in nature. Spiralling depression.

When we are desperate, we will grasp at anything.	A booming industry of alternative remedies that aren't tested and don't do any particular good. Stage mediums. Health and diet fads.
We do our best to make patterns, especially human patterns, out of randomness.	Hearing ghosts talk on tape. Bible codes. Satanic messages hidden in music. Mistaking shadows for a burglar at night (but not vice versa). Divining images in vegetable cross-sections. Roulette systems for gamblers. Thinking we're psychic when a friend rings just after we've thought about them.
We like to think we are more in control of random events than we are.	Using good-luck charms. Walking around ladders to engineer good luck.
We are more likely to believe ideas that represent themselves vividly to us.	Being taken in by media scare stories.
We are scared by the unknown, and hate to lose those we love.	Believing in an afterlife rather than accepting our mortality.

If we're asked a question, we will look into the eyes of the questioner.	The success of a magician's simple trick.
Sometimes during REM sleep, our eyes open and our brains wake up, but we remain paralysed, and prone to hallucinations.	We think we have been visited by a ghost. We think we have been abducted by aliens.
Certain frequencies, caused by fans, rumbling motors or wind through a window, can make our eyeballs vibrate in our sockets and make brief dark patches appear in our peripheral vision.	Dark shapes in the corner of our eye that disappear when we try to look at them, and are taken to be ghosts.
We think we're far more unusual than we are.	Astrological and psychic readings that seem to tell us all about ourselves (but which could apply to anyone).

The cards returned and controlled to their required positions at the top, I picked up the deck from the table and asked Joel, 'Do you believe that the spirits know what your card is?'

The question was of course ludicrous, but asked seriously, it moved him to look me in the eye as he considered what tone to take with his answer. That sustained moment of eye contact, and the knowledge that the others at the table would also be looking at him, enjoying his mildly amusing micro-predicament, was my cue (see table above) to swiftly rearrange the deck with another 'pass', under the guise of a playful riffle from hand to hand. He opted for the safer answer of 'No, I don't think so . . .' and the others chuckled as the minor discomfort caused by the question was relieved with a response.

Inviting him to pay particular attention, I placed the deck on my outstretched left palm. With only partly feigned concentration, and a subtle tensing of my arm, I allowed the top half of the deck above the now central chosen cards to slide eerily forward, as if guided by some spirit hand. (A bending of the top half of the deck during the pass allowed for this movement to occur.) I removed the seemingly possessed top half and showed Joel that our unearthly companions had indeed cut the deck at his card, displaying its face, and he was suitably impressed. The strange movement of the deck had caused him to lean right forward; the reveal of his card, which I now saw was the Jack of Hearts, was his signal to react with surrender and delight, then to relax back into his seat. Naturally his friends' eyes followed him, before the three remembered that other cards were to follow and leant forward again in anticipation.

'What was your card?' I asked Benedict, placing the Jack of Hearts face-down before them.

'The Ten of Diamonds.'

I showed my palm empty, placed it flat over Joel's card on the table, and rubbed it gently. I lifted my arm, displayed my bare hand again, then asked Benedict to turn the card over. It had become his Ten of Diamonds.

Benedict paused for a second, looking at the card, then

raised his eyebrows as he looked away to something else – his wine glass – letting out a high-pitched 'hmmm!' of surprise.

I knew the change of the card was a strong moment. The finding of the Jack through the ghostly separation of the deck was light-hearted and curious, but the transformation of the first card to the second was magical. Knowing that they would fool themselves very convincingly, it meant that they were now being rewarded for their involvement, and hopefully would shed the lingering fear of the trick, or the magician, being an embarrassment. They – Benedict and Joel at least – were now *involved*.

Trivial as it may be by any other measure, this moment, seemingly impossible and fairly observed, would have created for Joel, Benedict and Charlotte a sudden intensifying of reality, a sense of being entirely in that moment. Their internal representations of the immediate world would have momentarily become brighter, more colourful, and more vivid. Searching for explanation, they could not afford to miss a thing; suddenly they were mentally replaying my act of rubbing the card, desperately trying to backtrack to find a solution. This is our response to bewilderment: taking the lifeless memory of the immediate past, to which we realise we have not paid enough attention, and rapidly scanning it, enlarging it and zooming in and out, searching for something we may have missed. This bewilderment is placed into an entertaining frame by a magician, so that while we are offered the experience of finding ourselves confronted with an impossibility, we are also spared the panic usually caused by our environment suddenly appearing to conspire against us. If the footstool before me now were to suddenly change into a fish tank, I should feel only alarm: to doubt my own senses without the promise of perceptual reconciliation from a tuxedoed magus would engender only rising dread and frightened confusion.*

This moment of reconsidering reality is valuable: we light up our present by reappraising our immediate past. Perhaps this enlivens us because it nudges at some unconscious primal threat response. If we have misjudged reality in relation to this pack of cards, perhaps we have also overlooked

---

* I remember three occasions in my life when I have experienced moments of absolute private bewilderment; when in some private way the forces of nature seemed to have been suspended and, had I been filmed at the time, you would have seen the background woozily pull away as in a 'contra zoom' shot, your author gaping in the foreground like Roy Scheider standing on the beach in *Jaws*.

The first was staring at a quarter-drunk mug of tea in my parents' kitchen, aged perhaps fourteen, and seeing *bubbles* rise to the surface for no reason that I could understand. It appeared to have suddenly started to boil, or alternatively some unholy amorphous entity had emerged into primitive life beneath the surface of my Tetley's. I stared, incredulous, my teenage mind unable to fathom what could be suddenly causing movement within the drink. On reflection, I imagine that bubbles of air had trapped themselves around imperfections on the inside surface of the mug and were now dislodging themselves following movement from the drink, but at the time I was both transfixed on the seeming impossibility, and simultaneously running what checks I could that I was awake, sane, and not the victim of some elaborate prank.

The second occasion happened only a little while after that and was also refreshment-related: I touched a teaspoon to another teaspoon on a dinner-table and found a slight magnetic attraction between the two. I was able to lift the handle of the second spoon a tiny way off the table by letting it cling to the bowl of the other before the effect wore off. This was

something lurking, sabre-toothed and predatory. So we widen our eyes and heighten our senses and try not to miss a thing.

Because it is a likely presumption that we have been holding a mistaken belief about our environment (that the card was what we thought it was; that the footstool was a footstool and not already a fish tank), we find ourselves picking through our memory of the event looking for those beliefs that maybe won't hold up on reflection. Did we see the card first? If he switched the cards under his hand, where might the first card

---

extraordinary, as it whispered to me of strange psychic abilities within myself. After the few seconds of magic, I could not repeat the effect, and was utterly baffled, believing I had witnessed − or created − something inexplicable. I have since been told that metal can gain magnetic qualities if beaten or treated in a particular way, and perhaps some by-product of the dishwashing process had lent it these mild, temporary qualities. When we do not understand some piece of science (to paraphrase Hume), it becomes indistinguishable from magic.

The third occurrence was a little different. I was younger, perhaps ten, lying on the grass in some field near the south coast, accompanied by my parents and a picnic we had taken with us. The car was parked nearby, so we may have come from visiting my grandparents, who spent their summers in a caravan in Wittering. I was, as I recall it, sprawled on my stomach in a red T-shirt, supporting my head in my hands, feeling the summer grass along the length of my upper arms, my sandalled feet swinging above me in a clichéd posture of childhood insouciance. I asked my mother for a ham sandwich (of which I was very fond, and still am. To this day, a tray of limp, triangular, white/yellow/pink/yellow/white heavily buttered and crustless ham sandwiches − especially if the filling in question is the thinnest possible sliver of miserable processed substance more aqueous than porcine in its composition − brings sweet flooding memories of early birthday parties, packed lunches and Salt'N'Shake crisps), but there were none left. I turned back to the grass, looked down into its

be? Was the hand really empty afterwards? It is rather like Descartes' barrel of apples.

René Descartes' great work *Meditations* was concerned with the theory of knowledge, and an attempt to ascertain what you could know for sure to be true. Which is an interesting question to concern yourself with, considering that you have no way of knowing that you're not currently just a brain kept alive in a vat, wired up to a machine run by a mischievous demon, being fed electrical impulses that create the illusion of,

---

blades, and saw two black ants, shiny and strong, busily exploring. I saw one climb a long green shoot, change its mind, turn and descend. I watched the two walk the earth between the grass, constantly changing direction as they searched for crumbs and other ant treasures, turning and searching, all with a relentless urgency and unstoppable sense of purpose; they moved with the light, accelerated velocity of characters in a silent movie, yet with the meandering tenacity and uniform pace of miniature sci-fi robots. Then I noticed a third ant, and a fourth, trundling silently and with similar steadfastness, enlarging the pattern; then ten more came into view, then twenty, which opened into a hundred, a thousand, as the moving, shifting, living pattern beneath me expanded, and I was floating on this undulating carpet of moving black-brown bodies, all proceeding at the same speed, shifting noiselessly between the grass blades, and somehow I was seeing them all, the entire pattern, not individual ants but the *whole*.

And then I was suddenly alone and ten and my parents were gone and there was just me and an empty picnicless field. I could see them nowhere. I got up and headed back to the car and found them there, annoyed. They said that they had several times told me to get up and come with them, before giving up and leaving me to sulk (as they had seen it) over an unavailable ham sandwich. They were unaware that I had neither heard their calls nor thought again of food because I was in the grip of some experience of auto-hypnosis, entranced by the surprising sight of so many insects, seemingly for twenty minutes or more. I excitedly tried to explain

for example, having a body, being seated in a room reading a book written by a guy on television (televisions, guys appearing on them and rooms to contain you also do not exist of course; the experience of all these things has been invented by our cackling sprite controlling your every thought and feeling). Descartes' famous conclusion, when all else is stripped away, is that the very fact that you are thinking at all means that at least *you* exist in one form or another. The demon may trick you about what you are doing and all sorts of other things, but the one thing he cannot trick you about is your existence. You may not exist in the form you imagine, but you can assume that you are a *thinking thing* and therefore must exist. This is encapsulated in his famous 'Cogito ergo sum', which is generally translated as 'I think, therefore I am'.[†]

---

to my mother, who, still feeling angry, was not interested. I did not comprehend what had happened, but I remember the return to the white Chrysler in the lay-by, the dismissive reaction, and the warm drive back home as I wondered about ants and the loss of twenty minutes.

[†] Some months ago I was at a local gym, being trained personally by D—, my personal trainer. My motivation during such sessions is low, and my awareness of motivational techniques high, so I always enjoy my trainer's transparent and ineffectual attempts to boost my stamina and make the whole business of lifting heavy objects and placing them back down again seem like great fun. At one misjudged moment, when I was lying on the bench holding up a metal bar with each end inserted into a pitifully petite circular weight, and while I was expressing the usual combination of exhaustion and resentment with him and the entire charade and pooh-poohing the number of 'reps' he intended for me, he offered the following spur to prick the sides of my intent: 'Come on! Remember – *I think, therefore I am.*'

Descartes' process of deciding what could be known to be real, as opposed to illusion, was to go through every belief he held and cast the bad ones out, like bad apples. In order to ensure that you have only good apples in your barrel, you are required to tip them all out then check each one in turn before returning it to the barrel or discarding it. With this approach he aimed to discern possible illusion from reality. The Cartesian apples approach is, for this reason, the most sensible way of trying to work out a magic trick. By tipping out all your beliefs that have led to this sudden collision, they can be examined individually:

I believe it is impossible for a card to change like that on the table. Perhaps – but could it not also be a mechanical card that, as it

---

The sudden realisation that this exquisite epistemological axiom had, through simple miscomprehension, been reduced to a vacuous motivational slogan had quite the wrong impact upon my reluctant iron-pumping, and I had to hand the weight to D— to avoid a possible health and safety incident.

After my revolting burst of intellectual smugness had dwindled, I was left intrigued by the unsettling question of whether the phrase was of more use with this misunderstood meaning than it was as intended by Descartes. What was more beneficial, self-help or philosophy? Immediate personal fulfilment or grand intellectual exercises? The obsession with self, or the shedding of self to gain a clearer perspective? Of course there is no need to place the two into an opposing either/or: there is plenty of self-improvement to be found in philosophy: to live a better life has always been a goal implicit in much of philosophical thought. But somehow the fact that I was considering this question on the way home from a gym, which I was attending for what felt like intellectually embarrassing reasons of improving my self-image, made the question more pertinent.

is rubbed, allows hidden pips to slide across and replace the design previously seen? Unlikely, but possible. If this were true, it would be highly unlikely that the card could be examined afterwards. Was it shown fairly?

I believe the card definitely re-emerged from under his hand transformed into the Ten of Diamonds.
Most likely, but could it be that the card hadn't changed at all, and some obfuscation or skill could have simply made it *appear* to have been different?

The magician's hand was definitely empty before and after rubbing the card.
Possibly he has some way of showing a hand empty and still concealing a card, but this seems less likely than a simple exchange at an opportune moment when our guard was down, prior to the moment of directed attention (the rubbing on the table).

I believe that it was the Jack of Hearts when his hand covered it.
Ah! The whole illusion depends upon this, for if the face-down card had been secretly exchanged *before* it was rubbed, the trick would be solved. Are we merely presuming that Joel's Jack of Hearts, just produced from the deck a moment before, was the same card rubbed on the table? Was there a moment when it could have been switched? Were we off-guard?

After this process is complete, memory is the only enemy, and a good magician will have planted seeds through deceptive language and little 'convincers' to ensure that the path his audience's memory takes is predetermined – well-greased and safely steered away from moments and places where the method took place. Here, the magician performing close up or theatrically without television cameras has a huge advantage over the TV conjuror: manipulating the memory of modern television viewers is largely redundant in an age when they can rewind or watch online, correct their first false impressions, and even examine the performance frame by frame.

For a second time I transformed the card by covering it and rubbing it against the table. Upon removing my hand, the card had changed again, this time to the Two of Hearts, and Charlotte squealed to have her card seemingly identified, located and mysteriously introduced in one moment. She brought her hand briefly to her mouth as she let an 'Oh!' escape, looking at Benedict first, then Joel, to share her amazement. Only Joel returned a look of delight, enjoying her reaction.

I have worked for years as a magician, and rarely do I experience the pleasure of being surprised by a good trick. When those lovely moments do occur, I am transported back to watching *The Paul Daniels Magic Show* on my parents' portable black-and-white television, upstairs in their bedroom, while downstairs on the big TV they watched something like *Juliet Bravo* or *The Gentle Touch* or another show for parents whose very theme tune would cause a sudden rising of distaste that I still, at thirty-eight, feel instantaneously upon hearing: a faint nostalgic repulsion triggered by a sense of alienation caused in turn by a private grown-up world of entertainment that held no appeal for me as a child. I still have the same reaction to hearing the theme tune for *Ski Sunday* or *Crown Court* or any other show from my childhood that I would hate, and hate because it meant Mum would put on her glasses and be absorbed for long hours while I — off school ill, reaching the end of summer holidays, or otherwise kicking around the house — found myself jaded and fidgety. But Daniels was a fantastic treat: I enjoyed the *Bunco Booth* as much as I was fascinated by his displays of *Extra-Sensory Deception*. The delight of watching his show during childhood has stored in me a sense-memory pleasantly roused when I am shocked and mystified by a beautifully performed piece of magic. Plenty of times I watch a trick and do not know the method — this is not as rare among magicians as you might think — but to be *transported*, to *care* about it: this is the exceptional prize. The last time it happened was when I was watching Teller produce coins from a fish tank during the Penn & Teller show at the Rio, Vegas. Conjuring at its best has an aesthetic quality generally lacking in mind-reading performances. A handful of coins plucked from clear water is beautiful; a man on stage convincingly plucking thoughts from someone's mind may be baffling or even frightening but there is not that sting of touching exquisiteness that comes from a perfect visual moment.

Yet the pleasure Charlotte had taken in a card transformation — which had I seen it myself would have probably left me unaffected — may have been every bit as beautiful to her as Teller's reworking of *The Miser's Dream* was for me. Equally, and far more interestingly, in *that moment* of surprise and delight, when all else was forgotten and the change of the card entirely occupied her mind, Charlotte's experience may have been just as surprising and delightful as any other moment she may encounter in life. The trivial nature of the variables (a playing card changing during a magic trick) is irrelevant: the experience does not limit itself to the lowest rung on the ladder of enchantment purely because the moment in question is so unimportant.

For example, I find it very hard to leave my apartment without a frantic search for pens. Enjoying the use of quality fountain pens and expensive instruments of scripture as I do, I have a small collection of such items at home. Pens, by their nature, are carried around in pockets, placed on tables and clipped to the back covers of books and pads; thus my enthusiasm for these objects grew alongside my frustration at how easily I would lose them. To remedy this, I decided to buy two sets of pens – a set to remain indoors, and a set from which I could select one to take out with me. Those that accompany me to meetings and restaurants and so on tend to be my favourites, and those of which I am feeling less fond remain in designated spaces and holders near my writing desk or library chair at home. Or sometimes vice versa. Either way, I had imagined that this two-sets ploy would make it easier to keep track of pens: I would never need to search for a pen on leaving for the day, for it would always be in my jacket by the door or in the little pen-box close by in the hallway. This has turned out not to be true. The moment one has two pens, one need never keep track of either. If a pen has been absorbed into the upholstered cleavage of a matronly sofa, it will not be looked for with any urgency when another pen is available to replace it. Soon, it is entirely forgotten; and when remembered, it is too late to recall the details of where it might have been lost. Equally, with a larger number of pens, it is harder to keep track of where they all are, whether all the correct outdoor pens are in the hallway box or jacket pockets as they should be, as opposed to illegally residing in desk drawers or on the floor, having rolled in the latter case under cabinets. I have attempted to stick to a rigorous system of removing pens from pockets and placing them into this convenient little hallway box upon my return, but I must look again at this routine, for it clearly fails, and jackets have a habit of moving deeper into the apartment as changing weather or whimsy suggests alternative outdoor sheathing.

Having spent the money on the pens, I am angry when I cannot find, for example, my new mock turtle-shell* Visconti this morning. The anger is composed of various factors, which perfectly combine to form a raging fury directed both at myself and everything in the world around me:

The pen isn't where it should be
That's fine; there are a couple of other places where it might understandably be without recourse to annoyance. Shall I just grab a biro and take it with me? No, no, I have committed myself to the aesthetic of having finer pens and paid through the nose for them, so I shall make a point of finding the desired

---

* Made, of course, from the armour of Lewis Carroll's unlikely chimera.

instrument before leaving. Anger when not found: 25% – weary, familiar frustration.

Go through coat pockets

Not easy: I have a lot of coats and the cupboard in which they hang is also used for storing a mop along with some other long batons and thin poles left over from work done in the flat. These swing and poke among the coats and make the futile job of searching for pens (in pockets of garments I haven't worn recently but feel obliged to look through) even more irritating. Anger when not found: 70% – genuine annoyance: why does this always happen, why does the pen system not work, etc.

Fucking cleaner

Once it's established that the pen is not to be found, there is the automatic response of blaming my (blameless) housekeeper for moving it, tidying it away, or otherwise upsetting my delicate system, which I have never remembered to explain to her. So now I embark on hunting through a search of locations where she may have stashed it, placing myself, like an eighties homicide detective, into the mind of a proud and talkative Ecuadorian, thinking and feeling *as* her, letting my instincts guide me. Anger when not found: 90% – she always hides stuff, I must talk to her, now I'm late.

Where's my brown jacket?

Thinking it might be in the corduroy (*Cor du Roy* = Cloth of Kings) jacket that I wore a few nights ago, I look for that, but now this jacket is not to be found either. The jacket is not in the coat cupboard where it should be, so I look all over the apartment for it, and it's nowhere. How can I lose a jacket? Eventually I find it, in the coat cupboard after all. Pen not in pocket. Anger: 98% – oh for Christ's sake . . .

I loathe myself
Why do I always do this? I gave myself plenty of time and now I'm properly late. I can't just buy another pen – I keep doing that and it's just revolting to spend that much on replacing pens that I lose so readily. I'll be late again and that means I'm the guy who's generally late. Late not because I'm lazy but because I can never find things when I want to leave. But if I was better organised I would sort this out earlier or have a system that works and I wouldn't lose the pens and then I wouldn't be late and look like some crapping starry wanker who thinks he can keep everyone waiting and just roll in when he wants to. I want to be the guy who's always a bit early. Anger: 112%. (Pen invariably in pocket of trousers I'm wearing.)

The fury and loathing I feel towards myself and anyone else in my flat at such times is disastrously out of proportion to the offending grievance of a mislaid roller-ball or wayward fibre-tip. There are acts of genocide and unspeakable cruelty happening on this planet right now that I am appalled to say don't bother me at all in comparison. I cannot bring myself to feel anything like the same kind of furious rage towards such reported atrocities as that to which I involuntarily submit in the mocking face of a missing biro. It seems as if my entire environment – the pen, my jackets, my cleaner, my meeting –

have conspired against me to reveal what an insultingly ill-organised shirker I am and always will be. The fuming, flaming ire boils my blood, and I leave the flat in a proper stink.

Charlotte, at least, if not the others, was hopefully experiencing genuine astonishment at the transformed card, despite the moment's lack of gravitas from any other perspective. In this case, the reason why the transformations of the card from one to another to another had been hopefully *magical*, as opposed to merely *puzzling*, was above all due to a single important detail: the covering of the card with my hand while the change seemingly took place.

In the mid-nineteenth century, after the wave of Spiritualism had taken grip of America, Ira and William Davenport became well known as the Davenport Brothers, astounding audiences with supernatural feats on stage. This was the grand age of the stage medium, of ectoplasm, floating ghosts and tambourines thrown in the dark, of screaming audiences and hysteria. One aspect of the demise of such fraudulent histrionics, following relentless exposure from magicians, is that we have lost the showman's vision for séance and mediumship and replaced it with camp, anaemic cold-reading demonstrations, which do nothing but witlessly fool those eager to believe.

The highlight of the Davenports' act was the 'Spirit Cabinet'. A large wooden cupboard of sorts was introduced, and the brothers were tied into it in such a way that they appeared quite restrained and certainly unable to move their hands. Musical instruments were also placed in the box, seemingly out of the reach of the brothers, and the door of the box was closed. The audience would then hear the sounds of the instruments, blowing and clattering and scraping inside; yet when the box was opened, the brothers were still tied and clearly unable to reach anything that could have made those noises. The spirits had played the instruments, the audience was told. There seemed to be no other explanation.

The Spirit Cabinet is still presented, albeit in a modern form attributed to Glen Faulkenstein and his wife Frances Willard: the wooden box has been replaced with a red curtain on a frame, which can be pulled open or closed by the stage performer while the medium is tied within; and rather than instruments being played, tambourines, plates and other noisy items are thrown impossibly from the cabinet, despite the fact that the only living entity in there, namely Frances, is

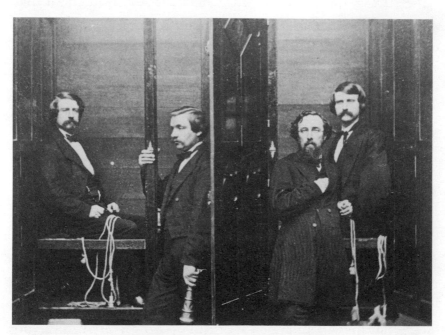

The Davenport Brothers' Spirit Cabinet

restrained quite securely. Faulkenstein and Willard set the bar; now various magicians have their take on this classic. Some of you may have seen my own Spirit Cabinet routine included in the *Séance* programme or *Enigma* stage show. Although nowadays we are arguably not expected seriously to attribute the noisy goings-on inside the cabinet to actual ghosts, the cabinet still retains its eldritch appeal for a simple tantalising reason.

The Davenports had appreciated the value of the darkness in the séances they had attended, and, unable to create such pitch blackness every night on stage, created a controlled area of darkness to work in on stage. In the domestic dark séance, the blackness was necessary for two reasons: firstly, for the medium to cheat without being seen; and secondly, for the sitters to fall prey to their own imaginations and believe they had experienced things that had in fact never happened. Again, allow me to refer you to my own televised *Séance* special: the pitch-black finale produced a wave of screaming terror among the group that we can more accurately attribute to their over-active imaginations than the occurrence of anything especially threatening. This blind, hysterical aspect of the séance is lost with the Spirit Cabinet, as the audience sits in only the half-darkness offered by the dimmed house-lights of the auditorium. Yet the Cabinet offered the tied mediums inside the same cover to free themselves and create the pandemonium, and more interestingly, by closing the door (or, later, the curtain), the audience are still allowed free rein to imagine what might be happening inside. The result is less of a visceral scare, but there is an undeniable chill to be felt when clattering objects are thrown from the top of the cabinet and Faulkenstein whips back the curtain a second later to reveal scattered debris and the beautiful, black-clad, hypnotised Frances still securely tied to her chair, sleeping soundly, not having moved an inch.

The true impact of the Cabinet does not come from an instrument playing on its own or an object being thrown over a curtain. It is the power of *cover* that makes it remarkable. A magician could easily enough create the illusion of an object picking itself up, playing itself or being thrown into the air, and an audience would perhaps be amused but no doubt presume wires or the usual trickery. Far more unnerving is to be denied the ability to see the animation, and instead only to hear it: now our imagination plays with us; we imagine the impossible. The closing of the curtain may be the only way of hiding the prosaic method of the trick from the audience, but it also, conversely, can create the necessary magic for it to be unforgettable theatre. When the curtain closes, we are in the realm of The Unknown, and something primal stirs us. This taps into a truth missed by most magicians: that when we watch a magical performance, we are still hoping to relate to it on a human level, and that the presentation of *process* in one form or another is vital for us to connect with it. Process may be based in struggle (and therefore drama), or whimsy, or anything in between, but without it there are only puzzles offered for solution. The Cabinet is powerful because it pulls all focus towards the process at the same time as it hides it with the front curtain. It *flaunts* process, and forces the spectator to speculate madly from moment to moment what could be happening, and to watch, alert and wide-eyed, in case he spots anything that confirms the suspected culpability of the medium.

A playing card changing beneath a hand does not have these eerie undertones, but when the magician covers the card the participant is suddenly forced to imagine what may be happening beneath the palm – here, probably sleight of hand rather than machinations from beyond the grave. Thus, when the hand is removed (clearly empty) and the card on the table has changed, she mentally returns to that moment of cover and wonders what on earth could have happened to change the card. Of course, the cover played no part in the method (the card had already been secretly exchanged with a sleight before the cover happened), but was vital for the effect.

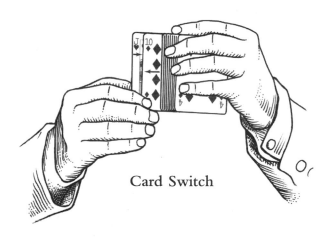

Card Switch

For me to have placed the card face-down on the table, looked at it for a moment, and then picked it up in its altered state would have only caused Charlotte and her friends to mentally rewind my actions back to before the point of placing it down, working on the presumption that the card put down had already been somehow substituted for another. The covering action says eloquently, 'It's happening *now*, whatever it is, and something fishy must be happening, otherwise I'd have no need to cover it up. There's something I don't want you to see that's happening now.' It curtails the post-trick rewinding process at a plausible but misleading moment.

Open cover, as we might think of it – of a card, or of a medium in a cabinet – is a coy move. It teases the audience and asks them to enter into a relationship where they are to enjoy being fooled. To insist on seeing the trick again but without the employment of cover misses the point: the magician is saying *I'm going to hide this, and something will change while you can't see it, and hiding it like this will frustrate you, but that's the game we're going to play.* This coquettish ploy of unavailability makes what is denied us (a view of a Jack of Hearts while it changes, or of the sounding instruments in a Spirit Cabinet) a source of potentially immense curiosity.

For this reason, while we happily love, we may still lust. Requited love is a wonderful prize, but the very ease with which our partner returns our interest denies us the particular pleasures of furtive obsession and fantasy. Meanwhile, the partners we cannot have – the prizes we are not allowed to touch – remain inevitably appealing and occupy a particular place in our minds, even though we may be content to devote ourselves to a single real-life individual. With happy love, the Spirit Cabinet door is flung open; no questions remain; we may still marvel at what the medium does now that we can see her clearly, but there is no dark mystery to invade our thoughts, no illusion left to weave its web. When we consider doing the most delightfully unforgivable things to a flawless but entirely unavailable specimen of humanity, or when we wonder about the hidden cabinet interior or covered Jack of Hearts, we are free to imagine such things as impossibly wondrous. The card, we decide, gently morphed from one to another; the instruments floated and were played by invisible hands; equally these imagined lovers are insatiable, sweet-breathed, and strangers to flatulence.

To make yourself unavailable is therefore to have the greatest potential of exciting this desire in those who seek you out. The opposite approach, that of the abundantly available prostitute, might provide the uninitiated with an initial guilty thrill, but her (or his) obligation not to withhold denies the client the pleasure of yearning. True, these Daughters of Joy (though rarely the Sons, tasty lot as they are) have frequently featured as romantically desired objects in bohemian songs and stories since *La Bohème* itself, but of course it is the fact that the courtesan in question is never quite available enough that provides the pathos: she will not truly love, and she has other clients to serve.

The most enticingly unavailable people are the celebrities who on the one hand daily trumpet their desirability in near-nude photographic spreads, and on the other are safely tucked away from the musty, sweaty reach of the admirers they taunt. Here we are consistently invited by the publicity machine to wonder what goes on behind the Cabinet curtain: we are given titbits and insights into private lives that act as clues, and once a tear has been spotted in the fabric of that curtain, and a celebrity becomes vulnerable, a frenzy of fascination begins.

It is entirely unfair, however, to blame the public's interest in celebrity for the stinking affront to kindness and dignity that pours from the bottom-hole of the modern media in the form of hateful stories or candid photographs of these celebrities at their early-morning worst. I, like almost all performers, can read a review of a performance I have given and be tormented by the one point of criticism otherwise lost in hundreds of words of glowing kindness, the latter entirely forgotten in favour of this lone negative comment. I can quote you every point of denigration I have read in a review but would be hard pushed to remember more flattering remarks. And these are from informed and professionally written reviews; the accessibility of online blogging and even Twitter (the mentioning of which I'm sure will date this book very quickly if the references to DVDs haven't already) has meant that truly witless spite is easier than ever to accidentally stumble across, even if one is very careful what one reads. Perhaps a flip-side to public adoration is inevitable, but I pity a sensitive performer who, having done nothing wrong but seek to entertain, opens *Heat* or a similar publication devoted to hurtful, hateful hearsay to find herself listed as number three in a list of the Top 10 Ugliest Celebrities, lampooned for looking imperfect in a bikini, or tarred with a fabricated, mean-spirited story.* Just imagine. The publications in question wrongly insist that the fault lies with the public, that they are merely catering to a demand for such sensational tales and cruel invasions of privacy; but this is the

---

* And I cannot see the word 'troubled' prefixing the name of some poor starlet who is being dragged through the mire of tabloid spite without vomiting directly into the newspaper. Troubled by whom? Troubled by *you*, you fuckwits.

equivalent of opening a sweet shop and then blaming children for flocking to it.

At the opening night of one of my stage shows I was honoured to have a particularly popular television actor among the guests. A few days later I read a clearly silly article in the *Sun* claiming that he had made a fuss about the price of the drinks at the theatre's VIP bar. It was an extraordinarily vapid non-story, accompanied by a picture of him clearly in a rage. Seemingly, he had cried 'How much?' when told the price for a drink, much to the alarm of some 'shocked bystanders' who said he 'grabbed his change and left the bar'. The story itself was so oddly limp, wholly flatulent and without interest or drama from any perspective that I teased the chap in question about it when we next spoke. Of course he had paid no attention to the story, accepting it as part of the strange symbiotic relationship between stars and the press, but what I found quite staggering was his revelation that the drinks at the VIP bar that night had been free. Free! We imagine that tabloid stories might exaggerate, even wildly, but for the paper to have entirely made this up in order to be able to mention his name and include a picture (even the close-up 'angry' image was taken not from life but from his television show) struck me as quite confounding, even after years of experience with the press.

I am neither famous nor interesting enough to have stories frequently invented about me, let alone one as bone-dissolvingly lurid as that of a man caught in the act of unashamedly thinking drinks were expensive and *literally* taking his change. I have been lucky with only one case of an entirely fabricated story in the press, but it happened to be so entertaining that I took no offence. It was clearly a publicity piece for a stripper hoping to push her career up a notch: the article, in which she 'revealed all', as we might expect, described her experience of me coming into the strip club where she worked and paying her for a private dance, and then how I caused her to have an orgasm, using only my mental powers. It also contained the quite brilliant sentence 'I bent over in front of him and he read my mind', which certainly clarified where this girl kept her brain.

I grumbled a little more heavily into my morning Raisin Wheats and Earl Grey a few years later after hearing of a *Sun* exclusive that had just run.

I had some months before 'come out of the lavatory' in an article for the *Independent* and clarified for those still in any doubt that, given the choice, I was a stickler for man-on-man action over the more mundane heterosexual variant still promoted in right-wing pamphlets and throughout the internet. Such declarations are a necessary evil: I was privileged enough to have met my beloved and had no desire to hide him away from public events for fear of people thinking they had happened upon a juicy story. So a little mention in a broadsheet article had elegantly 'got it out there', and I had walked through the more avant-garde streets of Soho on the morning of publication expecting a reaction from the lounging locals reminiscent of the last scene from *Dead Poets' Society*. I thought no more of it, and it all seemed rather tastefully done. Then, several months later, I was interviewed by the *Sun* about an upcoming series, and during our conversation the journalist asked me why I had felt I needed to make the whole dirty matter public. I explained that it was certainly not in my nature to 'feel the need' in the sense of wanting to make public anything that was personal, but it had been a required move on my part to ensure that it didn't become seen as a silly secret. The chap on the phone understood and seemed pleasant enough, and we moved on to other things.

A few days later, the (inspired) headline appeared in the *Sun*, EXCLUSIVE: I'M A MINDBENDER!, alongside a picture of me tagged with the line 'Ginger Beer . . . Derren Brown'. The article was written to heavily imply that I had myself chosen the ignoble mouthpiece of this iniquitous tabloid to proclaim 'exclusively' to the (presumably non-*Independent*-reading) world the nature of my fascinating private life. This was rather humiliating: the thought that people would think I had chosen such a crass route. And worse, the suggestion that I was ginger. I'm not. And I don't mind if other people are, as long as they keep it to themselves.

CHAPTER

5

Twice the card had changed: once from Joel's Jack to Benedict's Ten, and again to Charlotte's Two. But according to the rule of Three, a final stage was needed. A third act to the sequence could offer transformation with a surprise.

My left hand still held the deck, and now it picked up Charlotte's Two of Hearts at its fingertips, showed it for a moment, then seemingly slipped it face-down on to the table under my right, which immediately covered it. I rubbed it a little against the table as before, repeating the ritual; then, tensing my hand awkwardly as if it were palming the card, lifted my right hand a few inches. The card was gone from the table, but I knew it appeared to be held against the palm.

'I shall bring it back,' I added, and brought my hand back down.

Benedict had suddenly found his moment. 'You've just got it in your hand,' he declared, clearly rather pleased with himself.

I pretended not to hear. Charlotte was irritated and responded curtly with a 'Ben, don't.' Joel said nothing.

The card, of course, had never really been placed under my right hand. This was a stalling subterfuge: a point of *time misdirection*. I was soon going to show that the card had indeed disappeared, but for the moment I wanted them to think that I still had it palmed, and by delaying the reveal I was going to make it very hard for them to backtrack to the actual point of method.

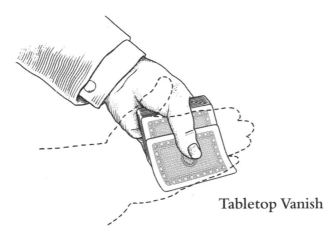

Tabletop Vanish

I enjoyed the tension between Charlotte and Benedict, and once again rubbed my flat hand on the table a little more as if I were still planning on producing the card . . . then spread my fingers to show only tabletop, and the sudden disappearance of the pasteboard. I turned over my hand to reveal the empty palm, feigned surprise at the complete vanish, and peripherally noted Benedict's confusion and displeasure at the dupe. Charlotte let out a squeal, leant forward and brought her hands to her cheeks, and Joel laughed out loud. It was so much more powerful for having led them to believe the card was still held there a moment before.

Benedict, feigning indifference, brought his left hand up on to the back of the sofa that held him and looked away, over his shoulder, at the metal artwork on the wall to his side. This arm movement pulled at his tailored, open suit jacket and exposed the liberal left side of his stomach, which lolled loosely over his trouser-top. A small triangle of shirt, I saw, had come untucked. Clearly the ill-ironed garment did not extend far enough to orbit the belly and remain entirely secured by the belt beneath it — at least not at the side, where the shirt-tail sweeps up to meet the edge of the front section, and where an upwards arm-swing from a tubby wearer might cause this section to emerge from above the belt and expose a small piece of fat flesh.

I remembered at that moment an interview with John Major conducted by Sue Lawley, just after (or perhaps just before) he had become Prime Minister. Despite the inter-viewee's status, the production team had seemingly not included a wardrobe assistant that day, or if it had, perhaps she had been too nervous to say something, for my lasting memory of that interview is not Major wriggling out of Lawley's ques-tioning about the poll tax, nor of any other aspect of the interview itself. Rather, I remember that Major sat with his legs crossed, a misjudged action which lifted the leg of his right-hand trouser to expose a pale, two-inch-thick strip of bare leg above his short socks. He remained in this position for the whole interview, mesmerising me and, I'm sure, many others with this unexpected semi-display of white English skin, bordered by grey sock and grey-green trouser, which swung a little hither and thither as he spoke words that I barely heard. Lawley, in her first on-screen high-profile political interview, was trying perhaps a little too hard to show her worth and was being (or so it seemed to me) unfairly aggressive with the new (or soon-to-be) PM. There was something rather lovely about her efforts to shine as a serious political interrogator being undermined by a distracting bit of ministerial shin. How blissful if Major, realising that Lawley was going to be trouble, had allowed his trouser-leg to rise that vital couple of inches on purpose.

The previous moment of lifting my flat, empty hand while keeping it tense (to suggest that the card was retained in a palm when in fact it had never even been placed on the table) was designed to provoke a certainty in the minds of Joel, Charlotte and Benedict that the card was still there. Mentally they could see it, held somehow against my palm, clipped perhaps at its corners between the fingers, and they would seize the opportunity to outfox the conjuror. This made the vanish that then followed far more striking, and importantly, allowed them to forget how fairly or otherwise the card had actually been placed on the table to start with. The action of placing it down was deceptive but might have been remembered had it not been for the pantomime rubbing sequence designed to convince them the card had been genuinely placed there. This, like the previous covering of the card to change it, was a punctuation point, placed in the middle of a sequence, which made it very difficult for them to think back far enough to solve the mystery. Once they believed the card was being secretly retained (because the first unconvincing vanish telegraphed its 'obvious' presence in the hand), they would no longer need to retain a memory of what happened before (and whether or not there had been a way of whisking the card away unseen). A presumption (that the card was there a second before the final vanish) had been created, and presumptions sit very snugly in the unconscious and are not so easily undone.

A magician appears to spirit away presumptions of what is physically possible. In life, there is a deeper, peculiar feeling that comes from realising that a single unquestioned belief, upon which we have built many other understandings, has been a misleading sham. I can chart several such presumptions in my own life that were pulled out from under me and the feelings with which I was left when they vanished like a card believed to be obviously palmed. Ask a person what presumptions they have abandoned in life and you request a fascinating list of private evolutionary steps leading to that individual's current level of maturity. These are important stages which may remain unknown to a biographer and, in the case of one's own forsaken beliefs, would feel trivial if setting out a written chronicle of one's own life. Yet they offer some of the most personal and revealing insights: tiny, seemingly inconsequential points of growth that combine to comprise a person far more fully than descriptions of job, education and hobbies. Here are mine:

Age	Presumption	Experience of enlightenment
7	That my father was the famous British actor Oliver Reed.	Upset and embarrassed at the age of seven to find that my parents had been lying to me for so long, and lying because my father looked a lot like the actor when he was younger and it amused them to pretend that he and

		Reed were one and the same to their impressionable son. I had been insisting on my father's double identity with my cousins when my mother was called in to answer the point of contention. She, no doubt a little embarrassed to be caught out in front of her sister-in-law, laughed and settled the seven-year deceit by flinging a flippant 'Of course not, don't be silly' in my direction. Mortified.
c. 9	That Father Christmas somehow snuck into my parents' house every Christmas Eve and left copies of shop-bought toys at the foot of my bed during the night.	Very moved that my parents were buying me all those toys. Closely followed by a worry there may have been other things I needed to know that I hadn't been told. May have asked for clarification re. the Tooth Fairy at this point.
c. 11	That I would get into trouble for playing irresponsibly and letting a playmate of my toddler brother's fall down the stairs.	Sheer, evil delight at the realisation that they were too young to tell anyone that the accident had been my fault. So I lied and said that either (a) she had fallen while I was working in my room, or (b) my brother had pushed her.
11	That schoolchildren were not allowed to talk during lunch or run in playgrounds.	The shift from the draconian rule of my primary school headmistress to the more contemporary approach of my

secondary school brought with it the newfound freedom of a twentieth-century approach to education. I could not believe my luck. I had been repeatedly 'sent in' at primary school for breaking the monastic code of silence, which was enforced by some of the favoured 'big boys and girls' during lunch. Once, to my outrage, I received this punishment (which amounted to finishing one's packed lunch privately with the headmistress in an adjoining room) for expressing joy and amazement at T—'s discovery of a single, massive, conjoined Monster Munch in her crisp bag. Surely after the unearthing of such an extraordinary object astonished discussion* among eight-year olds would be permitted, but no. I was sent in, again.

---

* The discovery of the mammoth nibble was exciting for three reasons:

1. Any such mutation of a favourite packed-lunch item was bound to be fascinating. In this case, however, a packet's-worth of the chunky snack had seemingly amalgamated into a single savoury tube, with stretched claws running along the full length underneath. Viewed from the front, it looked identical to the maize crisp we knew and loved, but as you turned it to see the side, it became unfamiliarly

25– 30	That God existed.	A delightful sense of a burden lifted, to realise that I could live this life without worrying about a second, imaginary one; a temporary sense of loss of the presence of an objective yardstick (by which I mean a set of prescribed values and a measure by which you were apparently loved and valued even if you didn't feel the

elongated. We passed it carefully around, and only to those whom we trusted not to break it.

2. This was no ordinary crisp: this was a Monster Munch. Monster Munch were, by their nature, monster: their size, more even than their eccentric flavours, was their primary appeal. So to find an unnaturally huge example, monstrously mutated to such freakish proportions, had an ironic appeal that was not lost on us at that age.

3. The single, tubular Munch also offered an insight into the manufacturing process that we had not considered, but were able now to vaguely fathom. Clearly, the crisps were initially made in such a tubular form; a long ur-Munch was then divided by blades into readily edible sections. This conjured up speculative images, which have long since stayed with me whenever I see packets of this particular crisp on shop shelves. I picture a long, thin mould into which a fatty, corn-based, chemically flavoured compound is poured to cool. The metre or-so tube of setting continuous snack is then brought via some conveying mechanism to a place where the mould swings open and delicate robotic grips remove and support the fragile tube, this process having been carefully designed to keep the crispy pipe from breaking under its own weight or the tiniest bit too much pressure from the gripping hands. These clamps lower the revealed yellow shaft of flavoured maize to the cutting surface alongside maybe fifty identical lengths, each held in place with a pre-programmed amount of

same affection from your peers) which eventually gave way to the realisation that my own values, self-image and outward attitude would provide that sense of inner worth and confidence instead. This felt liberating, life-affirming and mature. Finally, a feeling that I must have been excruciating to be around all the years I'd been

pressure which balances zero slippage with the avoidance of breakage. Then, from below – *swish!* – forty-nine fearsomely sharp blades swing up and round and divide each metre length into fifty equal parts. A split second of silver slicing and then, mercilessly, the clamps retreat and the entire line is pushed forward and off the edge of the surface, whereupon the segments drop with a final, beautiful, consistent uniformity on to a conveyor belt, there to jostle and roll with many others on their way to colourful branded packets, held open like gaping mouths by smaller clamps as a dialogue between cleverly designed diagonal re-directing bars on the conveyor belt and a stop–start rotating system of packaging ensures that the correct amount of crisps, agreed by Monster Munch heads and food-marketing experts to be the right and proper number for each customer, drops at the right moment into a perfectly positioned bag. Somehow, against all odds, T—'s anomaly had avoided the slicing part of this automated procedure; seemingly her eight-inch chunk had broken off following a machine malfunction that day, and rolled on to the conveyor belt and into a bag unseen.

I wonder sometimes what caused the mishap, and whether it was human error, in which case the giant undivided example we found that day, which caused me indirectly to be sent in to have lunch with Routy and watch her eat eggs, and years after to record the find in this book, may have been

		claiming I knew for sure that He existed and evangelising to my friends.
30	That I would always be thin.	I weighed in at less than eight stone at the end of my first year at university. I could eat any amount of whatever I wanted without gaining any weight at all, and never involved myself knowingly in any form of physical exercise. I awoke on the morning of my thirtieth birthday to find myself with two handsome pink breasts and a fine round belly. Since then I have experienced a relentless bi-polar swing with regard to my physical health, pulling between boredom in the gym and self-hatred in front of the mirror.
38	That love would be as I expected.	I began some wonderful friendships at university, and imagined that love would come in a similar

the unexpected result of a machinist's momentary daydreaming, as some thought other than tending to the soulless routine of that day's work glimmered across her wandering mind and caused her eyes to glaze and lift, at the exact moment when a discrepant, seceded length of Monster Munch happened to drop unnoticed into a bag, immediately to be heat-sealed, pulled away, packaged up and sent to the shop where T—'s mother chose to buy her groceries.

shape, consisting of a strong intellectual base, bold ideologies and a
hunger for adventure. Now I find
that what binds me most to my
beloved is our ability to make
each other weep with laughter.
Coming to love at a late age, I
was delighted by its surprises: by
the lack of any template and its
emergence from unsuspecting
corners.

Such tiny, private revelations are among the most touchingly human aspects of ourselves, and to enquire of others
as to the nature of their own coming-aware tales, and then
to share such stories, is to enjoy a conversation and insight
far less guarded and more fascinating than those which follow
the usual enquiries. How many people dread being asked,
for example, what they do for a living? Accountants must
groan inside every time that dull and inevitable request is
insincerely put forward at a gathering. As must the man who
works on composing a symphony at weekends, takes time off
from work to snowboard at thrilling speeds down mountain-
tops, or devotes his evenings to answering letters from the
children at the orphanage that he helped build as a travelling
student and now generously funds, but who happens to enjoy
a nine-to-five profession as a loss adjuster, or any other profession which he imagines people are likely to find of no interest.

If we imagine a spectrum of professions, with these hope-
lessly conversation-closing examples at one end, there exists at
the other extreme any number of perfectly fascinating jobs

which the individual in question might equally dread to mention. Not because of embarrassment, but because to answer the party-guest or friend-of-a-friend making the polite enquiry as to what he 'does' would be to commence, yet again, a conversation identical to that which he has endured so many times before. Here, it is not that the fascinating aspects of his character are being missed, but rather that they seem all too predictably appealing, and to admit to them is to engage in a too-familiar conversation about himself in which he has long since lost all interest. An actor friend has come to dread the following compulsory exchange whenever he meets new people:

PERSON: So what do you do?

ACTOR FRIEND: I'm an actor.

PERSON: Oh! You're an *act-orr* [*second syllable inexplicably emphasised and drawn out as if both persons were eighteenth-century powdered wags exchanging bon-mots while waving perfumed hand-kerchiefs at the poor*].

Perhaps this is best viewed as a small tax to pay for having an interesting profession. Yet I, for one, have no idea how to answer the question of what I do if it is asked of me (thankfully, one of the positive aspects of being little known is that the question is posed less and less). A magician? No: my mind fills with images that are not right. A psychological illusionist? This term, once invented out of necessity following journalistic desire for a label, sounds preposterous and I'd only have to explain what I meant, which would then beg the same question. To say that I read minds and/or do so regularly on television casts me as a particular animal I don't wish to be for the purposes of an evening out, and feels a little unfair on the other person too. So, of course, does avoiding the question completely with an evasive answer. Either way, like our fictional loss adjuster, I dread being asked.

And between what might seem like these two extremes, how often does knowing what sort of office people go to every day really help us to get to know them? We may feign interest in what they do, and they may feign enthusiasm in responding to our feigned interest, but would we rather not know that someone loves the thrill of weekend paragliding than that they work in IT? And would they not rather tell us?

Despite my feelings about the limitations of their use, I do have a love of hoary old self-help books, and there's a pile of them next to my lavatory. I am happy to offer advice here gleaned during my toilet-making from one such volume: Leil Lowndes' *How to Talk to Anyone*. Ms Lowndes is good enough to tackle this very problem. Her answer is to change the question: she suggests ridding one's mind of the useless 'What do you do?' and replacing it with 'How do you spend your time?' Thus, the person can interpret the question, and offer an answer according to whichever way they feel best presents themselves: as a hang-glider, a thrill-seeker, or, if they prefer, a mind-reader or accountant. I have adopted this suggestion, and enjoy the flicker of interior dialogue that stammers across people's faces for a second before they smile, repeat the question, then offer an answer they can enjoy giving. Most of us largely bypass talk of their employment, unless we clearly feel a passion for it. I can confidently assure the reader that making this small change in interpersonal chatter, albeit one garnered from my unsavoury reading habits, can hugely improve the pleasure of meeting new people.

Now, there are many who pooh-pooh the idea of reading while toileting, finding the juxtaposition of literature and bottom-tidying an affront to the dignities of both author and reader. For some, the act of expulsion is to be carried out as quickly as is hygienically possible; it's a functional process no more to be dwelt upon than cleaning out drains or removing socks from the tumble drier. I am, however, of the alternative type that quite enjoys the comfy privacy of a loo well stocked with cleansing-papers (scented-moist and quilted-dry) as well as several shelves of books and pleasant things to look at. My small library in that room comprises self-help, humour and essays, all within easy reach, and I find a pleasure in the piecemeal act of reading a book a few pages at a time during trips. Books are placed in this private, frivolous wing of my collection when they can be easily read in small bursts. Particularly well-thumbed favourites include:

Bernard Shaw's Music, Vols I–III,
by George Bernard Shaw. Shaw's reviews of local concerts and scathing opinions of unfortunate talent make for very happy and suitably bite-sized reading. This is a mammoth collection, and one perfect for dipping in and out of when time is brief. Having bought it at a time when I was regularly attending the lunchtime concerts at St George's, Brandon Hill, in Bristol,

reading these volumes immersed me into a private aesthetic that infused my afternoons' attendance at the chamber venue (i.e. St George's, not my toilet), and occasionally evenings at the cathedral, with an inflated sense of status that I'm sure did me no good at all. These are also very thick books, which can be useful for ensuring stability at one end of a row if arranging books upon a cistern.

Roger's Profanisaurus,
by *Viz* magazine. The magazine which for me seemed to miss in so many places made at least two undeniable hits when I occasionally read it as a student: the Top Tips and Profanisaurus features surely stand out as its highlights. For those of you unaware of the latter, this is a separately published collection of brilliantly foul terms helpfully offered for free-floating sexual, cloacal or alcohol-related phenomena in need of a pithy moniker. Many have entered common use, and when I first found my own name included in its lists I felt a surge of pride and excitement which quite turned my mind from the private activities so tersely described elsewhere within those pages.

Boswell's London Diaries,
by James Boswell. One of my very favourite books. I have several editions, the most humidity-friendly of which sits in my bathroom. The man-about-town's brilliantly recorded experiences of the city, its high- and low-life, prostitutes and celebrities, make for an astonishing and hugely funny slice of autobiography, and is required reading for any self-respecting modern dandy. It is difficult to fully immerse oneself into Boswell's

world through spasmic reading-bursts, so it is recommended that the reader have a second copy, or the discipline to keep the book to hand whether in or out of the lavatory, in order to be able to continue reading without the tingling discomfort of numbed legs caused by sitting too long upon a toilet seat.

The Complete Prose,
by Woody Allen. His earlier writings – *Without Feathers, Side Effects* and *Getting Even* – are the best. This collection, which brings them together, constitutes the finest comedy prose ever suited in length to the production of a healthy stool. Essays, scripts and stories are of a comfortable extent to avoid need-lessly extending an evacuation, and as there is no requirement to read them in order, one does not need to dog-ear page corners or improvise bookmarks with toilet paper.

While Benedict displayed his lack of interest, Charlotte and Joel, both leaning forward, turned and looked at each other again with wide eyes. My palm was still upturned following the vanish of the card; as I extended it a little towards them, both he and she touched it, as if to be sure there was nothing there. Connected, I looked from Joel to Charlotte. She looked up at me, as did the American.

They removed their fingers, and Benedict swung himself back round to face us.

'Watch,' I said, and stood, pushing the chair back and taking the deck into my right hand (with the three chosen cards now on top, unbeknown to the group). I showed my left palm empty, and dipped it into my left trouser pocket. I removed it a moment later, as if I had made a mistake. I passed the deck to my left hand, palming Benedict's card from the top in my right as I did so, reached my right hand straight into the right side pocket, and emerged with this card. A second later, my left hand, with the deck held deep, dropped into the jacket pocket on its side and manoeuvred the second chosen card in order to be displayed at fingertips a moment later as I brought it and the deck back out. I took the deck (with the third card remaining on top) in my right hand again, opened the right side of my jacket with the same hand, swivelling this final chosen card away from the top of the deck and behind the lapel, so that my left hand could enter the inside of my jacket, steal the card away en route, and pretend to remove it from my inside pocket.

Card Palm

The reveal of this invisible flight of the cards to three separate pockets brought a small burst of applause from Joel and Charlotte, and peripherally I saw Benedict glance at his partner, across to Joel, and back to her again.

Two other thoughts crossed my mind during the sequence. First, as I palmed the card in my right hand (an action which involves bringing the tip of the little finger down and over the corner of the deck to lift the card into the palm), I could feel that my fingernail needed a cut. I remembered that I had meant to see to it that morning but had not been able to find the scissors. Nail-clippers had been available, but these had never appealed in the same way as a pair of dedicated nail scissors still do, the sickle-shape of their slim silver blades achieving a curvature not unlike the bill of the beautiful but extinct female Huia bird I remembered from a documentary and which once graced the southern part of New Zealand's North Island. However, I concede there are several satisfying aspects to using a clipper on the tough, overgrown nail of the thumb: firstly, swivelling the arm of the handle around, over its knuckle and back upon itself, so that it kicks up, inverted, a model of efficiently produced leverage; secondly, inserting the whitish crescent of the nail firmly into its blades and enjoying the neatness of its fit (while deciding from which side of the nail to slice, as well as anticipating the disappointing fact that the blade will not remove the entire free edge, but rather cut into it halfway, leaving it protruding, necessitating a re-manoeuvring of the tool to the opposite edge to line up and clip once or twice again to complete the job); and thirdly, the clipping itself, feeling the tension and release of pressure as the edge of the nail drops free into the steel mandibles of the clippers, ready to be attentively removed before being discarded, the hard keratin smile examined for a moment with a mixture of curiosity and faint revulsion – *this is a dead piece of me* – then flexed and bent between the trimmed thumb and forefinger before it is dropped into the waste bin and forgotten.

This morbid delight is something I extend to all satisfyingly substantial units of myself that fall dead from my body. As a perpetually self-injuring child, I soon found that after the pain of a grazed knee, a scab would form and eventually be discarded as a by-product of the healing process, and if the temptation of picking at the scab was resisted there came a point when it could be painlessly levered from the kneecap to reveal pink new skin beneath, removed as a single piece and held, turned over, even smelt and placed against the lips in order to appreciate its delicious range of sensory qualities.

As I grew, and grazed my knees less and less, this pleasure was replaced with the joy of quite unexpected appearances of bodily scraps and chaff. The removal of excess thumbnail is anticipated and can be savoured, but it lacks the sudden burst of immense pride that comes, for example, from a finger making an absent-minded excavation into the nostril, and then inadvertently dislodging, and emerging with, a perfect dried mucoid cast of the entire nasal chamber clinging around the fingertip.[*] A similar period of respect is observed before an item like this is tossed away. After this reverential inspection it can be wrapped carefully in tissue before being placed in the bin, or in particularly noteworthy cases it may be photographed from different angles in order for those images then to be electronically shared with partners and close friends.

---

[*] An ENT doctor I spoke to referred kindly to nose-picking as 'having a tidy-up' during a discussion about my lifelong propensity for nose bleeds. This euphemism struck me as a particularly happy one, to be used comfortably in mixed company when needs must.

While the private awe engendered by these superfluous curvatures of fibrous protein falls into the same category as that created by well-formed snot, eyebrow and auxiliary hair of particularly admirable length, imposing stools and other significant effluvia, there is also the microcosmic surge of relief brought about by the belated trimming of a finger- or toenail, which is for me reminiscent of the quiet sense of liberation triggered by a certain class of undervalued activities. These are the minor actions I regularly postpone and forget about for a while before postponing again; until eventually I take the trouble to carry out the niggling task and find myself enjoying a silent 'That's better' before continuing on my noticeably more perky way.

I had made a mental note of the importance of seeing to these activities when finally getting round to changing my shoelaces one day. The breaking of shoelaces leaves me irritated and disappointed both with myself and my footwear. I am forced to carry out the rigmarole of tugging out the lace on the affected shoe in order for a reasonable emergency fastening to be carried out, which involves hooking my finger under any crossing cords that appear slack and pulling upwards to gather enough purchase to even out the ends without inadvertently drawing the frayed, broken end backwards through its eyelet. Once the lengths of exposed lace are roughly even, I must head off with a silly miniature bow atop one shoe, which then, due to the fact that it is now more tightly tied than the other, forces the secondary action of re-tying the other so that each lace applies roughly the same amount of pressure through the leather and across the brow of its corresponding foot. Rarely do I purchase a new lace as intended; indeed the breakage is only remembered when I remove the shoe upon arriving home and change into a slipper.* I may admonish myself at this point and again decide to buy a new set of laces, but then I forget once more to do so, and remember only when I next come to remove the shoe, forgetting quickly again, and so on. It is some while before I buy the much-needed accessory (for aside from the scarcity of places to buy such a thing, I also need to have the shoes with me at the time to count the eyelets and

---

* I cannot comfortably perambulate my apartment without slippers. The feeling of socked feet directly upon the wood of a floor or a carpet has about it the feeling of unsettled transience: somehow I have not arrived; somehow I am not properly home. I have two pairs, for the feeling of slipperlessness is so distressing that I will shuffle unhappily around the place in search of them until a pair has been located, and a second set doubles my chances of finding comfort. I was delighted to find leather travel-slippers for hotel-stays, but having bought them I rarely pack them, having come to quite enjoy the slippers provided by hotel rooms: sanitary-packed, one inverted and slipped inside the other, one-size/one-shape-fits-all, soles cut out of light, fragrant rubber and covered on one side in soft padded towelling stitched around the edge; a slightly stretchy five-inch-wide strip across the front, bearing the name of the hotel in contrasting embroidery, which hugs the upper side of my foot as I walk my toes under it and into its snug elasticised grasp; the slippers proffered, strangely, not in the uncarpeted bathroom where I need them most but in the wardrobe, where I only find them *after* I've had to negotiate swivelling the floor-mat from bath position across to sink position, which is impossible to do without treading on the wet hard cold floor, at which point the slippers would have offered ideal protection.

Identifying the floor-mat can be confusing: the small rectangle of towelling may be distinguishable from the actual towels only by virtue of having a wider pattern of stitching along its short edges, meaning that on

decide whether I need a 60cm or 75cm packet), and by the time I do eventually pride myself in making the effort and replacing the set, I have become so used to the fiddly process of tying that shoe (and each time scolding myself for having forgotten to fix it) that the new-found ease of fastening gives me a warm glow of proud pleasure. This occurs first at the tying, and then later when I notice the new lace again: delighted at my organisational skills, I find that it quite lifts my day.

The relief and pride derived from the trimming of a thickly

---

occasion I have found myself standing on a hand-towel while drying my face with what I suddenly realise is most likely meant for the floor. This initial distaste is quickly followed by the question of whether it should make any difference at all, or whether there is a disparity in the manufacturing (or washing) process that makes the designated face-towels somehow better for or softer on the skin. When this happens, I generally arrive at the conclusion that they are all indeed the same, but pull a fresh face-towel from the heated rail just in case, throwing the suspected floor-mat on to the floor alongside the potential face-towel upon which I am standing.

At this point I remember that 'on the floor' means 'please replace' as far as the housekeeping staff are concerned, and that the instruction coded by two towels cast on the floor in this manner might signify that I do not share the serious commitment to the environment held by the hotel and outlined on a small folded card next to the miniature plastic bottle of hair conditioner. This stirs a tiny bubble of worry in me, but leaves me unsure as to which one I could replace on the rail ('will use again') to leave a better impression of myself: the sodden, trodden face-towel (which may not dry without the aid of the rail and does need replacing) or the barely wet floor-mat which I have used for my face (but which definitely belongs on the floor). I think a little about whether or not the members of the housekeeping staff even bother to form an opinion of guests from such clues, and eventually leave both on the floor along with my pants.

extended fingernail and the insertion of new shoelaces only serve to identify the low-level background irritation that not attending to such minor worries must constantly, residually stimulate. For several years I have taken great delight in the process of seeing to these little things, and enjoying the small surges of relief that are felt somewhere inside me as I realise on each occasion that my life just got a tiny bit easier or tidier. For example, I have many times thrown out all my socks and bought twenty identical pairs. Rather than having to laboriously match them after washing, I can simply bundle them as one into the sock drawer, with a view to later extracting two at random and being assured that both feet will be sheathed in matching cotton.

I had once replaced all my socks with several from the black Marks & Spencers Fresh Feet range, these particular sock-variants being easily identifiable by a patented pocked area on either side of the foot which, as the folded cardboard slip that formed the minimal packaging for the five-pair set assured me, allowed my feet to *breathe*. For a second I considered the unwittingly self-inflicted horror of the many years I had spent torturing my feet with ordinary suffocating socks, before buying as many of the multi-packs as I estimated would fill my drawer. Then, some months later, I was filming for an American series of *Mindcontrol* and managed to step into a swampy area of wetness underneath Brooklyn Bridge across from Manhattan. My foot, ankle and most of my lower leg became suffused with slop and grot. I pulled my leg free, now dripping and foul, whereupon my kind producer, Simon, offered me a pair of his own black socks to wear. If memory serves, he may even have removed them from his own feet;

either way, his generosity combined with the necessity of clean socks for further filming spurred this selfless act. Imagine my surprise and delight when I took the (clean or otherwise) new pair and saw that they were none other than a set from the same Fresh Feet range! Here we were, under a bridge in New York, realising in a moment of minor sartorial crisis that we had both, some time previously, picked out the same socks for ourselves while shopping in Marks. Not only that, but it also transpired that Simon had had the same idea of buying them in bulk and throwing his old ones out: he, like me, had a drawer full exclusively of this precise brand at home. Delighted at our new bond, we speculated excitedly about the need for the patented Fresh Feet system; spoke with mock solemnity of the dangers of socks without such built-in breathing apparatus; lightly alarmed each other with descriptions of the painful toe-fungus and arch-dew that might form in the sealed, moist bacteria-haven of a regular unpocked sock; then cheerily continued with our filming. From time to time one of us might still catch sight of the other's socks and remember to enquire with faux concern as to the ventilatory wellness of the other's feet, whereupon both of us would chuckle a little in respectful acknowledgement of the memory of the joke before getting back to business.

I find that the sense of relief caused by replacing mixed socks with a drawer's worth of identical ones, a new shoelace being threaded into place or a fingernail being trimmed relates to the feeling of relief triggered by:

Replacing a bin-liner
I feel the revulsion of piling scraps and litter too high for the

lid to close; the awareness that the point where the liner was able to tie off with all the contents contained neatly therein and free from slimy obtrusion has long been passed. After the decision to be responsible and pull out and fasten the bag, I note the secondary pleasure that all the contents *do* fit safely inside once the liner has been removed from the metal tube and opened to its full extent, the sloppy detritus dropping to the bag's base. There is the careful lifting of the tied bag, for fear of the plastic breaking at some point on its journey to my hallway ready for the next day's collection; and finally the gratifying removal of a new white bag from the dispensing case. (I use size H Brabantia which fit neatly into the bin of the same brand, but will begrudgingly use black liners when I have no white ones left. The black bag is less appealing: its rim hangs eight inches over the top of the bin, pinned down by the lid, looking like a plastic mini-skirt, and is far less easy to tie. Each white bag, however, contains a fancy drawstring which always feels like it will rip the bag or break under the weight of the kitchen rubbish, but which against all intuition manages to hold the sagging, stinking load every time with confidence.)

Getting my hair cut

Buying a new refill for a favourite pen
The gradual reduction in ink-flow happens over a long enough time to be largely unnoticed until the final stages; until then I tend to imagine that the paper is to blame for any diminution in ease of writing, perhaps by being 'acid-free' or, for all I know, having too much acid in it. Bothering to stop at the relevant

concession while shopping in my local department store and buying a new fibre-tip refill guarantees a private moment of pleasure when I eventually write and see a strong, effortless, moist black line upon the page.

Switching to a fresh pair of earplugs
I favour the firm, cylindrical, beige foam plugs offered by Boots:* the orange conical variants can hurt the ear after long-term use, and wax ones are a sticky and revolting business. Now living in a noisy part of London, extended use of earplugs has resulted in me becoming quite addicted to them. Having become used to drifting off to the sound of my own pounding insides every night, I find it impossible to fall asleep without

---

* Now, sadly, no longer stocked. For many months the ubiquitous high-street chemist sold two very similar types of earplug, identically packaged and both accurately described by two of the adjectives I have used: 'cylindrical' and 'beige'. However, there was an important difference: one type (which I preferred) was made of denser foam than the other, and was therefore far more effective. To buy the correct pair, it was necessary to undo each packet, then remove and feel its contents. As I tend to buy five or so packets at a time, this necessitated a regular in-store exploratory process which I knew must have appeared to other shoppers as if I was in some way mentally ill. I crouched each time in the aisle with ten or so packets undone before me (or lined up on the boxes of own-brand plasters and surgical support stockings), gently squeezing each set of foamy sound-bungs with proctological diligence. As I became better known to the general public through my television work, this was an increasingly self-conscious procedure. Sometimes as I squatted, performing this task in a scruffy coat, surrounded by my shopping bags and glancing shoppers, I wondered what really separates the mentally peculiar from the merely particular.

this womb-like accompaniment and the comfort it affords, even when sleeping somewhere entirely silent. As they are used, they become softer, and sometimes a little discoloured from the inside of my ear. For far too many nights I push them into my ears knowing that they should really be thrown out and replaced, but make no effort to change them. This is because the moment when I think of hunting down the packet from which they came and extracting a firm, sanitary new pair for use comes at the precise instance of maximum reluctance to act: namely, when I am engulfed by quilt, nestled into my pillows and beginning to drift off; the point where night-time conversation has naturally ended and I pretend to be deaf to any sleepy, semi-sentient entreaties or dozy comments from the other side of the bed. Therefore, each pair is used more times than is probably hygienic, and the texture gradually deterio-rates until they become so flimsy they feel like they may become lodged in the inner ear or absorbed by the brain itself. After many weeks of this I am reminded one night of the need to change them *before* getting into bed and do so a little excit-edly, anticipating the pleasure of rolling the firm fresh foam between my fingers, squeezing each to a point and pushing the dense aerated stoppers into my eager ear-holes: one push with the thumb and forefinger to lodge it in, then an immediate second shove/wiggle with the fore-fingertip (while the thumb and second finger rest against the top of the jawbone for stability) to quickly press it deeper into the canal before it expands so much that I would have to remove it and start again.

Starting a new tube of toothpaste

Washing my jeans

Descaling the kettle

The water in London seems to be unnaturally hard, and the modern pleasures of a high-end coffee machine and steaming ironing-system are mitigated by the monthly necessity of carrying out a painstaking descaling or filter-changing process. I have a kettle with a clear stripe of glass up the side, which means that I can see most of the limescale that, disturbed from its chalky bed, rises up in flakes and kicks around in the water when the kettle is filled. I remember learning from an instruction manual for a previous model (one with a removable filter inside, just near the spout) that the common practice of filling such a modern kettle by pouring water in through the stumpy spout was an error, as any calcium deposits would gather on the wrong side of the filter when the vessel was filled from the tap and would then be added to your tea during pouring like wayward grated flecks of Parmesan cheese. This simple piece of logic seems to me to be very much ignored by most kettle-users, for whom the act of filling without lifting the lid is de rigueur. For many years in my kitchen, the build-up of grey flakes would continue until they completely clogged the sink after emptying the kettle, or to the point when I would disgust myself by finding a flake in my teeth. Now I look forward to the descaling, as it means a trip to the ever-useful, ever-reliable, ever-open Robert Dyas situated nearby.

I adore this shop. Downstairs there are gardening tools and broken light-bulbs and electrical goods, and upstairs is a wonder-world of cheap crockery, packs of LED stick-on lights, mousetraps, leather-cleaners, water-filters, mops and tele-phones, as well as USB mice, novel combination pepper/salt-mills, musical cake-slices and the occasional remote-control car around Christmas; their presence on shelves and in piles underscored by the perpetual high-energy background voice-over that accompanies a promotional video designed to insidiously and subliminally persuade me to buy a wonder-tablecloth that repels all stains, or avail myself of the magic duster that works without polish, or the brush that, as I am told repeatedly with the forced, soulless energy of a long-serving provincial radio disc-jockey, thinks it's a mop. The tireless enthusiasm of the sales-pitch generally has me curious to know what ground-breaking new invention has surfaced to save me wear and tear or effort or money. What new knife is this that will never need sharpening? Of what space-substance is this slab that promises to melt my frozen lamb in minutes? From what science-fiction vision of the future comes this improbable method of keeping my wine fresh for so long?

I have bought the magic tablecloth, and the Euro-chopper that takes the hassle out of chopping vegetables, and being a lover of gadgets I would probably buy the magic defrosting-slab and identity-confused brush-mop ('brop'?), were it not for the creeping sensation that I am succumbing to some marketeer's idea of how I can be programmed to purchase. The obvious crassness of the sales script; the shameless 'If you like X, then you'll *love* Y'; the curiously apologetic, uniquely British 'Why not . . .' formula that we hear so often in department stores ('Ladies! Why not step up to our fourth floor, where . . .') but whose very structure has us searching for reasons *not* to step up or buy; the 'Tired of X? How about Y?' cliché that always makes me wonder who that customer is that stops in her tracks and exclaims to herself, 'Me! *I* am tired of that!', and whether she should be shopping without supervision. Yet clearly these techniques work, for the cool, sassy, knowing advertisements we classier folk enjoy are just as cynically targeted to cool, sassy, knowing audiences as these loops of tripe are designed for people mindlessly browsing for storage jars, drain cleaner and travel alarm clocks.*

---

* I like to think that the marketing world will soon undergo a major paradigm shift. Future ideas-people will have no interest in the traditions of technique-obsessed, small-minded marketing as it stands, rooted as it is in another age. Perhaps there will be a move away from the them-and-us model of clever marketing folk v. us dumb, programmable consumer-robots to something more free-flowing, as we accept rather than try to ignore the deep irrationality and unpredictability of our decision-making processes.

This thought, or perhaps the pleasant alternative it points to, reminds me of those science-fiction films that show Earth (by 'Earth' read 'America') according to some futuristic vision. One recurring device in such movies is the frightening intrusion of advertising: virtual sales people and individually targeted ads appear in hologram form when our hero walks by, painting a nightmare picture of a destiny where the annoying sales promotions and pop-ups we now suffer have been ruthlessly developed with new technology into an insidious and perpetually inescapable fact of future existence. This device works well for us now: it is effective and sinister, which is what the director intends. But the most fascinating aspect of these celluloid visions is how effectively they describe only the era in which they were made. We enjoy the mistakes made in eighties films set in some distant future yet-to-be; we recognise the amusing eighties logic that, for example, cassette tapes would get smaller and smaller in the future (rather than being abandoned altogether), or giggle at the fact that for all the production

My wipe-clean cover is folded away in a drawer, to be used once a year on New Year's Eve, when it sits comfortably among the cheap (Dyas-bought) champagne glasses offered to party guests upon arrival and the disposable plates piled high in standard party plate/napkin/plate/napkin formation. At times throughout the year, normally while searching for a lost item that leads me to neglected drawers, I will find it, be repelled by its shiny ugliness and question why I ever bought it. During that moment of self-admonishment I will recall other occasions

---

values and extraordinary set designs of a seventies sci-fi movie set in some century yet to come, we are still looking at scenes populated by actors with seventies hairstyles and make-up. Unable to genuinely see the future, these films unwittingly distil the present-day into essentials that are so rooted in the here and now that writer, director, set- and costume-designers, a part of this era too, may be largely blind to them. (This would be in contrast to the conscious decisions of these writers and directors to purposefully bind the film to their own age by allowing the threats and themes of their screenplays and movies to echo the worries of the time in which they are made: communism, the dawning computer-age, the new millennium, or terrorism, for example.)

For that reason, classic images of UFOs can never really convince: the gleaming, chrome, round-edged flying saucers we see in grainy photographs are clearly objects from the fifties Earth that first spawned them, far more at home on top of a period American refrigerator or the hood of a Chevy than in the space-fleets of a distant star. I once came across a book showing charming Edwardian illustrations of London as imagined several hundred years in the future. In them, the sky was thick with flying automobiles powered by flapping wings; all surfaces resembled a nautical Jules Vernean riot of copper and brass pipes, portholes and rivets; the streets (again!) were dense with advertisements that may have switched Pears Soap for the fancied consumer items of this envisioned future, but which still employed the familiar sentimental designs we associate with the earlier era.

191

when I have bought items knowing full well that I will hardly ever use them, and wonder at my capacity to be fooled into spending my money on known-to-be-useless items purely because they were displayed in appealing packaging on a shelf. Faint memories of other purchases I knew to be misjudged even as I embarked on the transaction at the shop counter flash through my mind in a regrettable slideshow of my own gullibility. Such images include:

(i) *Several packs of electronic, stackable blocks,* each cube bearing on its face an LCD screen showing an animated stick man. This man sleeps, stands up, walks around and so on, and when stacked above, below or next to another similar cube (containing its own figure) will hop across on to the neighbouring screen and interact with its occupant in an amusing series of

---

Ladies in gloves and parachute dresses stepped out of flying cars helped by decidedly Edwardian gentlemen, and the entire effect was one of the distilled, true essence of Edwardiana rather than anything that reflected the (now realised) future.

Cassettes did not get smaller and smaller and the skies will not be filled with flying vehicles according to the vision of that illustrator, or Jean-Luc Godard, or Fritz Lang, because presumably we'll have less need to leave our homes to go about our daily business. Perhaps our grandchildren will smile at the rapacious advertising techniques commonly offered as a fact of future life in our current films and see them as a product of the weariness and paranoia they engendered among us now, and we can look forward meanwhile to a new model of marketing overturning the old. Perhaps. I don't hold my breath, but standing in Robert Dyas listening to an exhausting, pleading pitch for a hand-held spider-trapper, I'd like to be right.

pre-programmed sequences (such as fighting and handshaking). The idea was so simple and entertaining I thought I should buy ten of these packs, each containing two cubes, which I imagined I could give to children of friends if I did not come to use them much myself. The delight of the toy is diluted by the fact that each cube is battery-operated and therefore must not only be switched on but switched off again when the viewer has seen enough and does not wish the batteries to run down. This undermines the whimsical raison d'être of the toy, which should ideally be allowed to run indefinitely in a corner, with ten or more cubes stacked and attached to form a strangely envisioned apartment block, to catch and amuse the casual eye, which while languorously scanning the room for a lost thought might alight upon the plastic architectural caprice and be held for a moment, half-enjoying the voyeuristic glimpse of these repetitive, automated monochrome lives, half-unseeing as the viewer is lost in his own reverie. The consideration of diminishing battery-power renders this untenable.

(ii) *Any number of cheap compact discs* bought at service and petrol stations. I very quickly learnt that compilation CDs offered by such outlets are immediately disappointing, consisting as they do of the cheapest out-of-copyright ersatz recordings lumped ingloriously together to form a charmless anthology of unlistenable quality. The misleading cover designs and confident titles – *The Platinum Collection, The Wonder Years, The Voice of . . ., The Classic Sound of . . .* – suggest a hand-picked omnibus of the artist's finest works. Yet once the disc has been bought, returned to the car and drawn into the sleek slot of the vehicle's CD player upon leaving the forecourt, those first crackling bars betray that a penny short of five pounds has been cruelly wasted. In comparison to the sound quality of these purchases, Edison's pioneering waxed cylinder recordings of his early phonograph seem to resonate with the sparkling transparency of a glass bell rung in a bright, empty ballroom. Yet I still find it almost impossible to resist these compilations, and now own any number of unlovely assemblages of exhumed, prohibition-era recordings wisely disowned by singers who went on to achieve greatness.

My unswerving ability to buy bad CDs, even to find myself consciously pushing from my mind the thought *don't buy this, it will be awful*, reminds me of how some glitch in my nature allows me to eat my way through a bowl of salted nibbles which I am not at all enjoying. I find that after a while the visual appeal of the presented savoury snacks outshines the dismal memory of the last one's disappointing taste; thus another is picked up, put in the mouth and consumed with familiar displeasure, triggering a mental note not to take any more; yet, minutes later, they again appear inexplicably irresistible and a further one is ingested without enjoyment.

Normally, after a minute stood in Robert Dyas watching the sales video in horror and being seduced or amused by the item advertised, I walk away and remind myself of the kettle descaler, or whichever item is the reason for my being in the shop. As I do so, the voice follows me. The pitch for that week's item is played on a loop, and my browsing is distracted by the obsessive act of listening for the point when the tape begins again: the rejuvenated vocal burst of the voice-over starting anew triggers a mildly rewarding, compulsive satisfaction when I hear it. Finally, I wonder what the ongoing experience of this perpetual blabber is for the members of staff: how long it takes them to accustom themselves to it and whether they ever reach the point of stopping hearing it altogether. When on rare occasions I have been irritated by sales staff in the shop, I have taken the opportunity to remind them of it. 'Wow, that tape must become annoying,' I say, and watch their faces for signs of dismay as they suddenly become aware again of its incessant jarring crassness.

To descale the kettle or to take care of any of these minor domestic irritations is to enjoy the unexpected reprieve that accompanies the realisation that some barely noticed, low-level irk has been eliminated. This is rather like the sudden awareness of glorious silence following the automatic switching-off of air-conditioning, the stopping of refrigerator-humming, or guests leaving one's home after turning out to be dull beyond words.

CHAPTER

6

The second thought that crossed my mind during the reveal of the three cards occurred as I displayed the final card just apparently removed from my inside pocket. I held the card in my left hand, and as I displayed it I flicked its right edge with my middle finger. It occurred to me, as Joel and Charlotte applauded and Benedict's alienation from the group became more apparent, that I *always* flicked the card like that at this point, and that the action really served no worthwhile purpose that I could think of. It was a pointless affectation: neither a pretty flourish nor enough of a worthwhile punctuation point to emphasise anything in particular. It had settled into place through muscle-memory, and had remained unconsidered; equally I think I did it only because at some point I had decided that that's what magicians did.

I enjoy noticing similar habitual tics in my behaviour that seem automatically triggered by certain situations. After noticing for the first time my card-flicking habit, an image of myself as a habitual creature flitted across my mind, and the ghost of several other private customs were felt in that instant:

Teeth-cleaning songs

I regularly enjoy loudly humming or aah-ing a tune while brushing my teeth, allowing the warbling acoustic effects created by the toothbrush to mingle amusingly with the violent coloratura I incorporate to assist the melody. The choice to continue with the tune despite the distortion, in fact to increase the volume and persevere more proudly while watching myself in the mirror, makes this twice-daily private chamber performance particularly pleasurable. At times I will even sing, which augments the enjoyment by involving the lips. These try in vain to form certain consonants: they struggle to meet, or to connect correctly with the teeth, as the stem of my Colgate Extra Clean is brandished and agitated between them. A favourite song reserved for this time is 'The Impossible Dream' from *The Man of La Mancha* (lyrics by Joel Darion, music by Mitch Leigh, foamy gurgling embellishments by Derren Brown).

Other personal songs

I have a small repertoire of privately conceived songs which emerge to add a splash of musical theatre magic to otherwise dull, workaday activities. They include:

(i) '*Where's My Glove?*' Upon not being able to find my gloves, I will normally wander through my apartment looking in all the appropriate places, singing the following words to the tune of 'Where is Love?' from Lionel Bart's *Oliver!*: 'Wheeeeere's my glove? / Is it in the drawer above?' At this point I routinely note that 'drawer above' is not a satisfying substitute for 'sky above', making in fact no sense at all, and I abandon the song with a sense of distaste.

(ii) *'Clean My Teeth!'* Not to be confused with songs sung while the teeth are cleaned, this one surfaces during the preparatory act of squeezing toothpaste on to the toothbrush. No particular tune is identifiable, which is why it is best not sung during the act itself, when strong melody is all-important. It's a simple ditty, more akin to a short rhyme, and in place of a discernible melody it is spoken/sung aloud with the enthusiastic tonality of a mother bouncing her baby on her knee and trying to engage and amuse the infant with the simple couplet 'Clean my teeth! Make them clean! / The cleanest teeth I've ever seen!' Occasionally it might continue: 'Make them clean! Make them strong! / Clean my teeth the whole day long!'

Other songs for specific rooms

I find that, much later in the day, I might return to the bath-room for the normal health reasons, and catch myself humming the same teeth-cleaning refrain upon entering, even though I had not given a second thought to the tune all day. In fact, had I been asked what particular air I had warbled that morning while brushing, I would not have been able to supply a certain answer. Yet hours later, upon walking in, the tune returns, and I am humming it before I recognise that I am doing so. This phenomenon is not limited to the bathroom. I might head for the kitchen and immediately begin quietly singing a pop tune upon arrival, one that had been unknow-ingly stored exclusively for kitchen use that day, having been sung that morning during the preparation of breakfast. These trivial occurrences betray the machinations of the unconscious mind: much in the same way we might attach a tune to a room, we might also attach an emotion to a song when we hear it on the radio, and (as with the sight and smell of a gelatinous blob of pink soap lowering itself into a hand from a wall-mounted restaurant dispenser) propel ourselves back into melancholy, bliss, or the state of mind in which we found ourselves when we first heard it and unwittingly bound it to that sentiment.

The top step thing

I had decided, some time during my school years, always to miss out the final step of a flight when ascending: that is, to land upon the upper level having omitted to place either foot upon the step directly beneath.* I am unsure of the original motivation

---

* When I talk about a flight of steps, I can only view a 'step' as consisting of a horizontal plane (upon which we place our feet) and an attendant vertical, but if you wish to include the upper level as a step too (which, in the case of a single step, might be a necessary measure, and therefore confuses the distinction between step and not-step), then you may have to read 'final step' as 'penultimate step'. Clearly, the word 'step', although defined happily in this context by my Microsoft Office for Mac's dictionary as 'a flat surface, esp. one in a series, on which to place one's foot when moving from one level to another', has in its heart an action of moving from A to B, and is therefore impossible to pin down to any one of the flat surfaces involved. In the case of a single step that cuts across a corridor, which flat surface counts as the step? The lower or upper level? Presumably neither and both. The term 'step' calls into being the vertical

for this decision, other than the fact that I was a curious child who spent much time alone. I kept up this private game for many years, and if I ever forgot I had a self-imposed penalty to spice up the game: I had to, after placing my foot on the upper level, tread back one step before continuing. Both the game of omitting the final step and the back-step consequence of forgetting became minor obsessive actions. Although they did not have the dread attached to them that haunts the true obsessive-compulsive, I always made sure I observed the rule.

While a little spring over the last step would not always be noticed when climbing stairs in company, the alternative drop-back-one penalty was odd enough to raise questions. Therefore

———————————————————————————————

interruption to a plane, and alights trickily on the horizontals. But if you asked me to take the teapot that at the moment sits upon the table before me, and place it on the single step in this corridor that we imagine, and I only had this one step to consider, I would be rightly considered a fool to try to adhere it to the vertical surface. Instead, I would place it on the lip of the upper level, which, I suppose, has its concomitant vertical plane attached and is easily thought of as a step in a way the lower level isn't. Certainly, if you asked me to sit on the step, it's clear that my bottom would rest on that upper surface and not on the lower one. If we take the upper-most level to be a step, I suppose it may indeed be more accurate to say that it is the penultimate step that I would omit in the private game described above, and that to 'miss out the final step of a flight' would involve somehow never alighting on the upper level, but rather to remain floating above it, forever in search of another step. (Only when I found one would I be able to safely place my feet on the current level, for that would no longer be the last step, and then I would be obliged to take that next step again, but only to hover once more; and so on, ad infinitum. You can understand that this is not what I mean when I say that I would miss out the top step.)

I developed sensible ways of hiding the ritual when with friends. If I had forgotten to skip the step and required myself to carry out the punishment, I might pretend to hear a noise behind me that would necessitate a casual step back before continuing. On other occasions I would appear suddenly to remember something that would stop me in my tracks at a moment of unsettled equilibrium and have me step back momentarily for balance. These tactics, over time, became tiresome, as did the game itself, so I would allow myself on these occasions merely to step back and forward *mentally* at the very top. This imagining of the stepping back-and-forth, in turn, became reduced to a 'duddle-dum' noise I would make in my head, which described the sound of the rapid one-two-three footfalls I imagined (top level, back to the step, then up again). To this day, as I climb stairs to my apartment on the frequent occasions when the lift is not functioning, I notice that I occasionally still skip a step at the top as I reach my floor, and whenever I do not, 'duddle-dum' quietly to myself as a form of punishment.

Swiping open lift doors
I recently noted that I have developed a private custom when standing alone in a hotel lift holding the plastic key-card for my room, or when I am in the lift of my apartment building and happen to have a credit card or business card in hand. It occurred to me that on such occasions I habitually swipe the long edge of the card down along the millimetre-or-so gap between the closed lift doors just before they open. This allows me to pretend that I have myself caused the throwing wide of

the doors, and in turn that I had gained access to a glittering private penthouse suite,* by the use of the special key-card. I think that the pleasure I derive from this action lies not so much in play-acting the part of the billionaire playboy, but rather the satisfaction of running a card edge along any narrow gap. Malmaison† hotel lifts, for example, have leather walls that appear at first glance to be simply stitched into squares, but on closer inspection it is revealed that the many stitched panels are combined into a few large separate pieces, placed alongside each other. The lines of stitching detract the eye from the narrow gaps between the pieces. To find such a gap is to discover a pleasantly tight slot through which to run the key-card. I let the panel edges guide the card along the wall while I enjoy the feel of the easy glide. It is the near effortlessness that makes this pleasant enough to do absent-mindedly every time I find myself alone in a lift that affords such a card-width slot – a similar satisfaction to that which blossoms gently inside whenever a nicely engineered drawer runs back and forth with a surprising smoothness, or when a writing surface proves to be especially well suited to the pen being used. (For those who do not know it, there is a particularly happy chirographic relationship

---

* Or a secret underground vault, very much like Batman's, but which contains all of my mentalism tools, mind-control devices and general secrets. It depends whether I'm going up or down.

† Which translates, of course, as 'bad house', 'wrong house', or even 'House of Evil'. There is a Napoleonic history to the name, but it always struck me as a strange one for a hotel to choose for itself. French was never my strongest subject at school, but even to my mind Bonnemaison seems a preferable alternative.

between biros and banana-skins that is well worth exploring the next time the reader finds him- or herself with both to hand. Writing with the former upon the latter is in fact so rewarding that I would imagine, should an aeroplane carrying a cargo-load of ballpoints crash-land on a suitably inhabited jungle island, monkeys would soon develop the ability to write simple messages to one another.)*

Swivelling on glass pavement tiles
Because of the satisfaction yielded by actions that prove unexpectedly smooth due to the interaction of two well-suited

---

* Skateboarders, when 'grinding' on marble, tend to report a similar tactile satisfaction. This trick, which involves riding the board with the wheels' trucks up on the edge of a kerb or step, is a move commonly included within the often astonishingly balletic performances given by these slack-trousered, recalcitrant pedestrian-botherers wherever steps and smooth surfaces are juxtaposed in town centres. The more common granite stair does not offer the cool, frictionless feedback of a marble edge, and thus the shiny, veined pedestrian planes of Barcelona, Prague and some other European cities are to many skaters as Bayreuth or Graceland are to lovers of Wagner or Presley. Skateboarding is performance art for the prototypically nonchalant. Aside from the great names of the scene, immortalised in a thousand independently produced DVDs and showcased online, most of these performers seem to present a series of rapid stop/start non-sequiturs: eternal private practice sessions that never culminate in complete performances. As soon as a trick is successfully performed, the skater is likely to stop, or merely try to repeat it. There is some desire for audience approbation, usually in the form of a few supportive sounds and handshake variants from the skater's coevals, but perhaps the lack of showmanship and concentration instead on sheer technical skill is part of the saturnine teenage embarrassment regarding full-blown engagement with society.

surfaces (such as biros and banana-skins), I have also developed a habit of seeking out the small, thick, glass square tiles set into pavements which allow light from above to illuminate a basement below the street. They are normally placed alongside each other to form a large enough window area for their purpose, but for me, walking on this street, a second use arises, which the placing together of so many of these tiles makes very appealing. I like to place the ball of my foot upon the centre of a glass square, lift myself ever so slightly on to it and swivel as I walk forward. The collocation of these squares means that I can replicate the action and recall the same sequence of petty pleasures across a few steps: firstly, the enjoyment of the smooth glass beneath my turning leather sole; secondly, the tantalising risk of slipping and falling backwards on to the hard pavement; thirdly, the peculiar gratification afforded by the publicly spastic walk which arises from the series of violent, staccato semi-revolutions of each planted foot. It is worth noting that the swivel cannot be achieved unless the ball of the foot is planted centrally upon each tile; attempting the move while grating against the metal grid that holds the glass in place is to ensure failure. As the tiles are small, it is impossible to know whether that central point has been correctly engaged, which means that I do not know *until* I twist whether or not it will happen at all. This adds to the enjoyment of the process and introduces an element of challenge: can I achieve three excellent twists in a row?

The sniffing years
Most of my childhood was spent engaged in one or more habitual tics, prone as I was (and still am, only far less so) to

obsessive behaviour. At its worst, I had a teenage period of sniffing loudly and violently for no reason other than that the thought of doing so would be impossible to resist once it had lodged in my mind. One of my more gut-wrenching memories is sitting in the auditorium of the Berliner Philharmonie as a late teen, listening to Alfred Brendel's solo performance of Beethoven's piano sonatas, the concentrated stillness punctuated by my snorting paroxysms. I remember my suffering German neighbour offering me tissues for what she must have suspected was not the commonest of colds, and then having much of the row to myself when I returned for the second half. Truly, deeply, anus-invertingly excruciating.

Bad friend of Dorothy

The obsessive habits took all forms. As a teenager, I performed as part of my school curriculum a duty known oddly as 'General Studies', which consisted of volunteer work. In my case, I visited a lady of a certain age every Tuesday along with R—, for tea, cheese and crackers, to be followed by shopping excursions with Dorothy in her wheelchair. R— was only with us a while, as he found Dorothy to be in essence quite repellent. This was unfair, but some people seem to possess a true horror of old ladies and no amount of encouragement from me would alleviate his nausea. Of course his reluctance to touch or even look directly at her caused me much mirth and I enjoyed cheerily volunteering him for all manner of unsavoury and intimate tasks whenever they arose.

His disinclined personality contributes to my memories of school principally due to a lazy habit he developed when writing short stories for English homework. He was not a keen English student (his greatest talents lay elsewhere, in the realms of music and history, if I recall correctly), and his attempts at fiction were half-hearted at best. The solution he found to the problem of creative writing was to cast himself as the protagonist, lumber through some surreal adventure and then, when the tricky problem of finding an ending became unavoidable, abruptly curtail the narrative with his trademark device: the sudden, final non-sequitur 'Then I woke up, then I died.' Time and time again he employed this stratagem, to the increasing amusement of the English class and the frustration of the teacher. We would call for his stories to be read aloud, and then at the eagerly awaited denouement explode into bounteous laughter, cheering and applauding.

I, however, continued to visit the cackling, immobile Dorothy regularly until I moved away to Bristol. I would wheel her through the leafy dells of Croydon in search of places to picnic on grated cheese sandwiches and Fanta, or seek out post offices from which to collect pensions, and she would pinch the buttocks of girls as we went past so that they would turn around and glare at me with furious incredulity.

Here, too, I developed an obsessive custom that plagued our journeys around her locale. The particular pavement we would follow in order to make our way to the preferred nearby shopping area declined fairly steeply for a hundred yards or so, meaning that rather than push Dorothy in her chair per se, my task was actually to pull back gently against the weight of the chair as we made our way forward, and thus try to keep the chair under control. The habit I came to both enjoy and dread was as follows: once we had begun the decline, I would (a) let go of the handles of the wheelchair and, while it continued freely under its own impetus with me walking behind, (b) *close my eyes*. Dorothy, an exhaustingly verbose woman, would continue to chatter away happily, unaware of the momentum that was gaining beneath her as she began trundling, freely and alone, down the hill. The challenge of this behaviour was to see for how long I could walk behind her, eyes closed, picking up speed myself, continuing to offer casual *oh-yeses* and *reallys* to the unwittingly freewheeling octogenarian in front of me, before being overwhelmed by a gripping fear that one of the following events would occur: Dorothy would turn and see that I was no longer in contact with the wheelchair, but instead walking some way behind her with my eyes closed; or the chair would reach a critical speed, I would be unable to catch up to grab it, and she would instead be propelled further down the hill at a rapidly increasing velocity, her cracked voice rising in pitch and volume as she called and then screamed to anyone for help, as I ran, terrified, behind her, unable to gain ground; panicked pedestrians jumping out of the way as she hurtled towards a turn in the road that she would not be able to navigate; unable with her tiny gnarled fingers to steer the wheels which would by now be whirring like propellers on either side; her long life flashing before her eyes . . .

My eyes would spring open and I would grab the handles of her chair and curse myself for such unforgivable behaviour while simultaneously enjoying the thrill of having got away with it. Her chair steady again, I would resume conversation with an air of relief, and then, after a few seconds, let go again and repeat the procedure.

The obsessive private habits we foster are scandalous revelations that immediately delight or shock others when we describe them: to talk openly of such things is either to miraculously find ourselves in the company of a fellow obsessive, or more likely to have our peers drastically reappraise us to allow for what sounds like a sickness of the brain. Indeed, some of these rituals do seem to knock tentatively at the looming fortified door of the asylum. But before we reach the corridors of the pathological hand-washers and those who spend miserable nights relentlessly and repeatedly arising from the bed to check that all doors and windows of their home are locked, there are those who may, to be sure, not toy inexcusably with the life of an elderly lady but when walking will (a) close their eyes for a few yards, (b) avoid or specifically aim for pavement cracks, or (c) calculate with what frequency they will step evenly across such a crack if they walk at their normal, regular pace. To mention such behaviours in company is immediately to divide a room: some feel the relief of discovering that they are not alone, while others who do not know the bizarre private moments of the occasional obsessive are generally horrified to hear of such routines.

This latter, more common reaction is similar to the incredulity provoked by a person defending, in the face of a room's derision, his or her means of wiping his or her bottom or bottoms. A friend of mine once mentioned to a group of friends, including me, and with the casual deportment of one who believes he is stating something of such everyday banality as to be of no interest to anyone, that he half-stood in order to perform that particular sanitary process; another friend that he wiped back-to-front rather than front-to-back. In each case, a sudden, deafening roar of dismay stopped the individual in mid-sentence and he, taken aback by this emotive abreaction, responded first with dumbfoundedness, then quickly shifted to a passionate defence of the normality and convenience of his preferred method of ensuring cleanliness. These attempts at self-vindication by our friends only increased the room's insistence on how demonstrably preposterous and probably unhygienic their takes on the act were. We stood or tipped sideways on our chairs to illustrate our points, and performed exaggerated, incredulous mimes as clear proof of our friends' insanity. Still they vehemently defended the act to which they were accustomed, having none of it, insulted by our unambiguous conclusions that they self-evidently lacked the basic level of personal hygiene appropriate for a modern adult.

I have since, however, found several other half-standers (no other back-to-fronters, I hasten to add, though I am sure one or two readers must be experiencing a boiling defensiveness similar to that which my friend endured following his blasé admission), so clearly this method at least has a minority following. But of most interest is the horror and disbelief felt by friends when they realise that one in their midst has the mark of an outsider and is therefore not to be trusted. Some deep ancestral fear seems to be triggered: perhaps of discord, possible attack or, even, in this case, infection. To admit to releasing an old lady's wheelchair ensures a not dissimilar response, albeit one mitigated by the discussion that then

follows and the bifurcation of the group into those who understand the tyranny of obsessive acts and those who cannot relate
to the problem on any level.

Of course, had Dorothy been accompanied by more than
one of us on those days, and had we all been chatting as we
went along, the urge to let go would have been easily resisted
had it surfaced at all. Distraction is the key: when the mind is
occupied with real, external things, the compulsion to perform
the taboo act cannot gain ground. Again, this is negative
suggestion, the equivalent of being left to live in a locked room
that is empty save for a large, shiny red button on the wall and
a sign fixed above warning the incarcerated not to press it.
When the mind is not occupied with real concerns, it feeds
upon itself; the thought *I must not . . .* has the capacity to send
one spiralling towards the very action one is determined to
avoid.

Here, though, the negative suggestion is helped along by
muscle-memory: namely, the body's capacity to remember
familiar sequences of physical actions without conscious
thought. This type of memory is invaluable to performers: a
pianist can allow his fingers to play without having to consider
which note comes next; the actor finds himself reaching the
same way every night to pick up a prop without thinking
about it; the dancer does not have to consider each step; I find
myself moving automatically on stage, shifting into emotional
states, even coughing or glancing in certain directions, identically night after night, because habit has set into place a
number of automated sequences that sweep me along and keep
the show moving at pace. Before a show, I warm up my voice

through a series of relaxed hums and aaaahs and ga-ga-gas which make me sound like I am in the grip of a turgid yet flamboyant orgasm, and I know that the muscle-memory of producing sound that way means that on stage I can produce a voice which will remain comfortable despite two hours of projecting to large houses every night. We use muscle-memory when we shake hands: we do not need to reflect upon what comes next in the sequence of actions involved when a person extends his hand to us, instead we simply lift our hand in return, grasp theirs, move up, down, and so on.

This ability to have our bodies lead us effortlessly into automatic actions can also be a curse, for the smoker hoping to quit, for example, or the person plagued by habitual tics. The muscle-memory of facial tics or bizarre tension-release sequences carried out by the sufferer of such things is strong, and due to the localisation of the tic to a particular set of tiny muscles, it is easier to give in repeatedly to the urge than it is to, say, persistently excuse oneself from the table, step outside and smoke a cigarette. As an adult, I have a slight nod which surfaces during times of self-consciousness or unease. This is unfortunate as a performer, as those times tend to be when I'm in front of a couple of thousand people, or before a single jour-nalist. When happily on my own or with friends, I rarely do it. I also notice an odd momentary stammer that occurs when I am asked for my name over the telephone.

The mixture of muscle-memory, the self-consciousness and auto-suggestion that perpetuates the tic (*I'm doing it now, I look odd already, I've crossed that line, I might as well carry on*), its value as a release of tension, and the overarching fact that we are surely creatures of habit more than we are creatures of survival (hence the habitual smoker), all make for a familiar crippling behavioural cocktail for many.

My childhood was marked by a series of such habits, of which the sniffing was probably the worst. As a pre-teen, any feeling of sudden excited anticipation was accompanied by a need to stand up, run around in a circle, and sit down again. This childlike display of excitement was harmless, amusing to all, and did not feel unduly compulsive, but it soon became compacted into a tension in the knees (no doubt the first stir-rings of the previous need to stand) which could then only be abated by knocking the knees together. The painful knee-banging (I naturally developed painful bruises, which made the ritual hurt even more) soon itself took over as the compulsive behaviour, and before long it had become a regular habit: I was unable to avoid it once the thought to do it had let itself be known in my mind. The more I carried out the compulsive act, sat in the front room watching television with my parents, the more that sitting there became a trigger to do it again, like finishing a meal becomes a cue to light up for the smoker. Worse, the negative suggestion from the pressure *not* to do it (my parents, exhausted by these habits and not knowing how best to deal with them, would only tell me to stop, and I would feel awful, not knowing *how* to stop) completed the vicious circle; I would become increasingly tense, inwardly fighting the compulsion, which in turn compounded the desire to carry it out, focusing as I was on the very muscle-groups in question.

My grandfather, whom I adored, was creative enough to suggest a hypnotherapist to rid me of this demon – hence my first taste of this arcane world that would eventually lead to my strange career lay in being treated for debilitating tics. My mother booked an appointment to visit such a practitioner at his suburban home surgery, and we both drove there curious as to what the consultation would entail. He turned out to be a tall, astonishingly hirsute, suitably medical-looking man who stared unnervingly through heavy eyebrows and spoke softly from behind the luxuriant growth of his beard. There was not a hint of the limp, holistic, New Age quackery that would be hard to avoid today. He sat us down and asked me how my bowel movements were (I answered, 'Fine thank you, I pass water regularly'; my mother corrected me with a gentle, prompting 'Other end'), and a number of other questions to gain a sense of my general health and relationship to my family. Then he and I had a private chat, during which he asked me more about my home life, and then it was my turn to sit outside and read the numerous certificates which formally illustrated his authority and authenticity along his hallway – a hallway which, while trying to appear professional and suitable for clients to sit in while their mothers were being told that their sons were not worryingly abnormal, betrayed touching signs of family life: a pair of unclean wellies just by the door, and, under a console table, a toddler's Fisher Price ring-stacking toy comprising several colourful plastic doughnuts of decreasing size atop each other and encircling a white central stem. I must have been entirely unaware of what hypnosis was at the time for I do not remember any sense of apprehension, nor did I amuse myself by searching through the framed credentials issued by the various national medical and hypnotic associations with imposing names, to see if I could spy daunting diplomas boasting 'Most Number of Onions Believed to be Apples' or 'Most Effective X-ray Specs Used Allowing Audience Members to be Seen in the Nuddy'.

Despite the promise of success implied by the hypnotherapist's height, hair and calming manner, he was entirely ineffectual. The once-fortnightly Thursday-afternoon sessions did, however, have the very positive result of getting me out of school sports just as often, and I distinctly remember encouraging the continuation of the process for that very reason. Remedially, though, nothing changed. Once, during a session, I opened my eyes a sliver to peep through my lashes and see what the doctor was doing, and was shocked to see that he had gone from the room entirely; his voice was emanating from a cassette-tape recording into which he had seamlessly segued at some point after my eyes had closed. Even when present in the room he did little else other than give me techniques that did not work, and ask me questions that I could not answer and made me upset.

Instead, I simply grew up, and the tics have almost entirely been left behind. I would forget a particular habit for a long time; the muscle-memory would dwindle and I would no longer be gripped by it. I would sometimes develop another in its place, which would also eventually pass, and soon the tics became almost entirely a relic of my childhood and teenage years. Today I notice minor variations in plenty of people I meet. There is that guttural, sucking 'throat thing' that many will confess to, a noise irritating to long-suffering office colleagues, who will normally spend some time unable to identify its source, sounding as it can like the faint sound of a radio left on in the background. Others with this obsessive streak roll their eyeballs oddly behind closed lids. Stepping into more familiar territory, a larger number bite their nails as the result of a similarly generated compulsion. Many nail-biters, in part enjoying the masochistic pleasure of tearing back at tender finger-tips once the thought comes to mind, occupy one end of a long line that passes through throat-snorters and knee-bangers, continuing on to those poor souls seized by Tourette's.

When I took driving lessons at eighteen I was still not entirely free of these devils: I would close my eyes for as long as I felt I could get away with it while my instructor gazed firmly at the road. Unsurprisingly, I failed my test, and part of the reason why I have not endeavoured to re-take it is the fear, upon realising how commonly such dangerous urges occur among drivers, that I would find myself open to all sorts of terrible temptations. The horror caused by finding out that someone close to you is prone to these enticements when you have no experience of them yourself was never as apparent to me than when discussing such behaviours with a couple I knew well. The fact that I did not drive had arisen, and I had explained the reason (not knowing if I could entirely trust myself on the road), citing Dorothy and her freewheeling chair as an example. The wife, with audible relief, at once declared herself to be plagued by a powerful recurring urge to swerve her car, with both children on board, into oncoming traffic at full speed. The husband was unable to process this news without voicing the most severe distress, clearly fearing genuinely for the safety of his family. Our petitions that the urges were common enough horrors that played on the minds of many, that they all but never resulted in the feared behaviour, and that he should not be so alarmed, rang hollow.

The tics and habits may, I sometimes suspect, be a by-product of the naturally obsessive nature of the solitary creative spirit, and aside from whatever medical intervention may exist, I do not know how they may be effectively stopped in their tracks. Certainly being calm, happy and engrossed in activity for extended periods can in most cases cause them to lose the grip they otherwise maintain through repetition and familiarity.

If an isolated, artistic childhood temperament increases the chances of developing obsessive rituals and twitches, then I was asking for it. My brother was not born until I was nine years old. My mother came into my bedroom and asked, 'How would you feel about having a little brother or sister?' Misunderstanding, I thought the decision was being left to me. My reply: 'I don't know. Let me think about it. When do I have to decide?'

Most of the childhood I remember was spent engrossed in drawing or Lego. I recall at age four or so spending many frustrating hours at my desk trying to reproduce the nose drawn on the cartoon face of Fred Basset's owner in the *Daily Mail*. It was simply an upside down '7', but to me, bewilderingly three-dimensional: I could not understand how the nose seemed to rise from the paper and descend again to meet it.

My mother had brought home from her secretarial work two reams of paper for me, one yellow and one white, and this gift of a thousand shining blank sheets has never been surpassed in terms of the unsullied exhilaration they provoked. I riffled through them and ran my fingernail up the sides of the pile to make long pale lines that would break like a straw refracting in water if you cut a block of paper from the top and placed it beneath. I turned the sheets like pages in a book; even indulged myself by throwing some away with a single line drawn on them, or before they had been used at all, thrilled at the naughtiness of the purposeful wastage.

Several of these sheets were used to practise drawing the nose. I sat at the little writing bureau that I remember as being on the landing but which I presume was actually in a bedroom and tried to draw this befuddling appendage that grew impossibly out of the paper. I started my pencil on the paper; lifted it above the surface of the sheet and drew the length of the nose in the air; then brought the pencil back down again for the final short line that suggested the underside of the nose. I then compared my effort with that of Alex Graham in the newspaper. His unnamed dog-owner still looked out at me with a three-dimensional nose. On my page, two dots. I tried again, this time pressing *into* the paper rather than lifting above it, to see if that worked. I bore down heavily on the page, ripping the sharp graphite point of my pencil right through it, tearing the paper, then bringing it back up to finish back on top of the sheet. This did not work either: again, no nose pointed forth.

I do not remember whether perseverance or parental intervention solved the mystery. Somehow the nose was drawn, and the conflation of illusion (a three-dimensional nose) and reality (a cartoonist's technique; a kind of foreshortening)* brought with it something profoundly satisfying, triggering a passion for drawing, and eventually for painting portraits that play with caricature – a love perhaps born that afternoon on my parents' landing-or-bedroom, trying to learn how a nose could be flat *and* stick out.

The interest in Lego may have come later. Certainly the grown-up Technic variant, with its gears and cogs and motors, fascinated me the most, and presumably some way into

---

* Upon discovering how the nose was drawn, and that it was simply a matter of copying the line rather than thinking of it as a nose, I felt a little of the joy that I like to imagine the artist who first discovered foreshortening may have felt. Until around 700 BC, judging from the art of the time, people stood with their face and feet turned to the side and shoulders square on – an uncomfortable position made fashionable by the Egyptians, and one which took pains to display the clearest view of all limbs (a sensible if contorted measure, as the purpose of art had been to protect the spirits of the departed in the afterlife, and doubtless to show every part so unambiguously was an advantage in making sure that no aspect of the revered ruler or warrior was forgotten). Then, around that time, an early Greek artist working on a vase dared to depict a foot facing directly frontwards: we see a warrior, taking leave of his wife, standing perhaps for the first time with one foot foreshortened. The five little circles of his toe-ends signalled the discovery of depth in art. When I look at that vase, and contemplate that quietly momentous occasion in art history, I am sometimes, self aggrandisingly, reminded of struggling with the Fred Basset nose at such an early age. I wonder whether Euthymedes, the Greek artist, sweated and maddened himself to create the illusion, and whether he threw down his tools and stared in incredulous rapture at the detail on the pot: a small foot, but one which was to constitute such a giant step in art history. We are so accustomed to the idea that an artist can recreate what he sees; had no artist possessed, until that point, an internal representation

adolescence, as I remember constructing a colourful mechanical Wanking Machine during long periods upstairs in my room. The inevitable problem of round pegs and square holes sadly rendered this particular project fruitless, on many levels, but the manufacturers might like to take note of the idea when planning other themed kits for their teenage boy demographic.

Tracing a path from childhood pleasures to adult skills is an exercise in hindsight and pattern-finding similar to the way

---

of a foot drawn from the front? Or alternatively, as the primary focus of art moved towards something less utilitarian and more decorative, perhaps to paint a foot in this way might have only felt like a relaxing of an outdated rule.

If my own naive experience with trying to capture the nose has any relevance, then there is certainly a disorientating perceptual shift in working out for the first time the tricky conflation of three dimensions into two. Remembering my strange experience, I like to imagine that it was a dizzying experience for the artist. I cannot understand why I was not able simply to copy the line on to the page, and why it was so baffling: in other words, I do not know what I was really seeing when I looked at the face printed in that comic-strip panel.

Over a thousand years after the toes appeared on the Greek vase, Brunelleschi was to take this foreshortening to the next stage and change the world by discovering the formal rules of perspective, teaching artists the mathematics of the vanishing point. Again, does that mean that before him, people could not *see* that objects converge in the distance? What did it mean to unearth such a fact? When young Masaccio unveiled his extraordinary painting of the Holy Trinity on a wall of the Santa Maria Novella and tricked the Florentine congregation into thinking they could see a deep recess in the wall, arched in the latest style and seemingly with figures and a tomb placed solidly before it, was it something the pious crowd could easily comprehend? Did it feel like a trifling amusement, as

most of history is made: in the light of the present we pick and choose events which lead most conveniently to the desired end point of the here and now; we then mistake that all-too-convenient narrative for truth. We are always blinkered by a desire to find confirmation of what we already believe. Without this tendency we would doubtless be unable to operate amid the infinite, conflicting data with which we are constantly bombarded. We confirm our suspicions all too readily but need to harness considerable effort to shake them; we bring our pasts darkly before us and then, attempting to answer a question as to why we are how we are, watch certain segments light up like an interactive museum display to provide an answer. Ask a different question and those lights extinguish, and different parts illuminate in their place. My own portrait-painting narrative begins with a basset hound's owner's nose, but that may be wrong: it may in fact have murkier beginnings elsewhere that I do not remember.

An autobiography is a triumph of selective personal stories, which is why unauthorised biographies can be so painful: it is not that they present necessarily harmful information, rather that they present a different story. They compromise a new narrative as seen by a hack or a fan, different from that told by the subject, and therefore create a disturbing, posturing clone: one who walks and talks as you, but who isn't you; who does not hold your memories; who punctured neither paper to draw

---

3D cinema does to us today, or was it an overwhelming assault on their senses? Did they rush forward to touch the wall and assure themselves of its flatness? I like to think so.

noses nor the enrapt stillness of a legendary pianist's concert with sniffing.

This fraction-of-a-second thought process had been triggered when I caught myself flicking a playing card unnecessarily during the trick. It then had me consider for a moment my own incomplete and faulty 'How I became a magician' narrative. As I held the card aloft in a moment of mediocre triumph, it occurred to me that the plot would run along the following lines:

CHAPTER

7

Part One: The Magic Hat

Twice (once when aged four and again when six) I accompanied my mother's side of the family on a Christmas trip to the Water's Edge Hotel in Bournemouth. I have just now carried out a Google search with the aim of finding pictures of the interior of the hotel and to feel, in turn, a sweetly melancholic rising of nostalgia. This has proved to no avail, so I presume it has since been renamed, or pulled down. Perhaps it eventually slipped from its precarious location into the water. I was hoping to see again the regal staircase where I made a friend called Darren; the ballroom where the comedian Mick Miller performed (my parents, aunt and uncle would laugh heartily at his jokes while I asked my mother to repeat them or explain why everyone was laughing); the room in which I played under the table with Nikki, my adored cousin of roughly the same age. I had entered fancy-dress competitions during both these stays, once wrapped entirely in white toilet paper, with the head part painted black. Unable to move my arms or legs in this mummified state, I had to be carried to the stage by my father. Mick Miller, I think, was judging, and asked me exactly what I had come as.

'A match,' I answered, correctly.

I don't remember how I was placed.

The highlight of the stay in the hotel was the unwrapping of presents on Christmas morning. The night before was generally filled with my draining questions about how Father Christmas could know in which hotel I was staying, and then how he would be able to get into the room upon arrival, given the absence of a chimney (did he collect all the door keys from reception? A skeleton key seemed the most likely answer, although the very term 'skeleton key' played on my imagination and made the image of the bearded old man creeping into the room even creepier), and whether he had a list of which children were staying in which rooms. The first year, I awoke in the fold-out bed in the corner to find that a pillowcase* had appeared, as promised, at its foot during the night, stuffed with gifts. I can remember something of the opening, but most vividly I remember the treasure inside. Father Christmas had bought me, among a few other rewards for my year's worth of goodness, a magic set.

This was no ordinary magic set housed in a cardboard box with a plastic insert to hold rings, coin-holders, lengths of rope and cheap cards. The tricks were inside a large plastic *magic hat*. This hat looked like a black top hat – a little too large and uncomfortable to wear, but one which yielded special secrets.

---

* A pillowcase identical to our spare ones kept at home in the airing cupboard. This also provoked concerned requests for clarification. Had Father Christmas been to our house first and helped himself to bed linen? His MO became weirder and weirder.

The label on the bottom surface of the inside lifted up to reveal a secret compartment from which small objects, if previously hidden in there, could be produced, or conversely, into which they could be vanished. A long, thin panel that ran down the inside from rim to base, but which was carefully hidden within the design of the interior, could be pulled open to mysteriously bring into being a wand, right after the hat was shown to be empty. This wand had a sliding white end that allowed the initiated Svengali to create the illusion of it growing longer and shorter. Aside from these built-in gimmicks, the hat was filled with the familiar tricks of the colourful card and plastic variety.

I had never considered magic tricks before. I believe that I was taken aback by the promise of being able to perform impossibilities as described on the outside of the box, not realising that they were mere artifices, relying on secret ways of cheating. My faint memory involves a moment of confused disillusion as it was explained to me that I would not be able to perform *real* magic with the set, despite the contrary rhetoric printed by the manufacturers on their misleading packaging.

I took the hat everywhere with me. I showed Nikki the few self-working tricks I could perform, and immediately, excitedly, explained the secrets to her. In fact, I have no doubt that the explanation of the secret hat-panels and strange reversible handkerchiefs was of far more interest than performing the tricks themselves, and probably preceded them every time. Above all, my memory of the hat is as something huge and unbelievably extravagant. No doubt it would be tiny if I were to see it now, and the memory of the awe I felt upon removing it from the box, pulling it up and out with both hands, mouth agape, looking back and forth between it and my grinning parents, would be permanently diminished. It would shrink in the way that certain things do shrink, most notably your parents' house upon visiting again after a university course has pulled you away for so long, or your own house in between viewing it as a prospective buyer and the day you move in. Size is such a quantifiable, seemingly objective quality; yet even the feet and inches in which it is measured seem themselves to be subject to the whimsy of age and circumstance. I think of those chairs and writing desks at primary school, and the memory of being sprawled across them when struggling with long division (my cheek flat against the cool pine of the desk top, running my fingernail along deep scratches in the wood, sleepily pushing rubber-shavings along the long furrow designed for holding dip-pens and watching them fall through the big ink-well hole and disappear) – pieces of furniture which seemed so imposing at the time yet which years later made my eyes well up when I saw how tiny they were; those living-room shelves and the cupboards on the wall of my bedroom, which shrunk to a third of their size while I was gaining my degree.

I cannot remember if my interest in the hat was sustained long enough to produce any magic performances; nor can I tell you what happened to it. I presume it was broken and eventually thrown away, for I have no memory of it lingering in my bedroom or being left in the bottom of my wardrobe, which became a gloomy graveyard of surplus playthings for many years. I was certainly spared the experience of performing magic for family and friends. The hat and its secrets came and went, and I forgot all about conjuring for many years.

Part Two: After Eight Mints Box

My parents would from time to time throw small dinner parties. Somehow these do not seem to relate to the gatherings my friends and I now host as adults, brimming with hearty intimates, mirth and uncertain wines: these were the dim dinner parties of parents, known only peripherally to our memories through stifled sounds and rare, illegal glimpses.

The memory of such occasions shifted from the barely conscious to a place of focused awareness one evening about eight years ago, in Bath. I was at the house of a friend who had young children, sat talking late after the kids had been packed off to bed, enjoying a Scotch and discussing grown-up things, when we noticed one of his offspring appear at the doorway. Jeff, the boy in question, was perhaps eight years old; he stood in the dim light, clutching his duvet around his colourful pyjamas, rubbing his eyes with a practised pretence of insomnia, asking for a drink of water, clearly hoping to be invited to sit with us (I suspect I was a favourite guest among the kids and Jeff was hoping for further magic tricks or some such). His father leapt up to send him back to bed with a reluctantly poured glass of water and a scolding manner.

I, left alone for a moment in the lounge while the water was begrudgingly secured, had an impulsive flashback to myself at eight years old, a not dissimilar character to Jeff (we were both rather precocious, creative and cheeky), and for the first time, conversely, saw myself, at a distance, as an adult. There I was, eight years old and suddenly at the doorway, having guiltily tiptoed downstairs, knowing I might be in for trouble but excited to eavesdrop and ultimately trespass on the arcane alliance of adults: a private downstairs world, audible only through the grown-up peals of muffled laughter that would permeate the floorboards and mattress which separated us. I stood there, in Jeff's place, seeing these adults sat across from each other, drinking Daddy's drinks in the special glasses, feet up, talking in that manner that adults never do when children are there to be aware of and included. I saw my adult self sat over there, all grown-up and foreign, in the way I knew I had seen Uncle Stuart and my father talking one night after curiosity had snuck me back in, the request for water ready at my lips for when I was caught. At that moment, as a wave of Sartrean nausea found me, I took in the whole of my friend's room through Jeff's eyes: the upturned boxes with books stacked on them, the ethnic CD-tower in the naive folk-shape of a giraffe that years later, amplified in size, would dimly play in his mind as he recollected the house where he grew up (*Did we have a big statue like a giraffe?*). I saw these as future memories, and among them, myself: the murky recollection of a late-night Friend of Dad's, all whisky and jumpers and feet up on footstools, laughing and relaxing in that unfamiliar way.

This adult world was not there to be seen, save for those times when, having changed into my pyjamas, I was allowed to come back down and say goodnight (a time when the mood of the room would already have changed to something unknown; when I would be surplus to requirements rather than the centre of attention), or when at the house of a family friend I would be brought down later, in my sleeping bag and over my father's shoulder, my cheek and jaw bouncing against his shoulder-bone as we descended the stairs. I would clutch the mouth of the sleeping bag a little around me to stay warm (the bottom was always folded up and held in place to stop it from dragging, which allowed me to skim and wriggle my toes against the trough of the silky lining); we would go down into the hallway, past cooing, whispering aunts and rosy grown-ups, through the adult milieu, I pretending to be asleep but burying my head deeper into shirt collar and jumper to hide my face; then out into the sudden brace of cold night air, briskly up the garden path and into the car. My mother would open the doors as my father approached to place me inside. If I had successfully maintained the pretence of sleep, I would not be expected to assist this process and could enjoy being passively bundled in and gently placed on the back seat – a delicate, snoozing son-parcel.

My parents would drive home, and with my face submerged into the crook of the back seat, I would, as I dozed, listen to them talking about someone's new girlfriend or criticising the food from that night, their voices taking on the strange other-world quality that parents' voices adopt in the front seats of cars when you are young and have your eyes closed in the back. I was so aware at that age of this peculiar change in vocal tone that I would enjoy opening my eyes periodically to look up and see the streetlights strobing past the window or the night view swing round as we turned corners, just to close them once more and hear the sound of my parents' conversation change again from that of Mummy and Daddy, who were present and within touching distance, to the strange, detached voices that might have come from a radio, separate from me, indeterminately far away, not quite those of real, nearby people.

This enjoyment has remained with me as an adult: the ease of falling asleep while others talk in the room around me; the soporific nature of background chatter once tiredness closes my eyes; the shift in how those voices are heard and how differently attention is paid once one has cut oneself off and publicly abandoned any chance of contributing. No longer do the sounds impinge; a wall has been built, and in the back of the car I would relish the cosiness of my more immediate sensory world: breathing into the trough of the back seat and feeling the moist warmth on my face as condensed child-breath trickled down the pocked leather; the drool around the corner of my mouth which dampened the sleeping bag still pulled high around my chin; the stretching out of legs to press my feet against the arm-rest of the far door in order to quietly open the ashtray set into it, hooking my big toe under the lip of its pull-open lid and finding the leverage to facilitate the manoeuvre while pushing gently down on it with my other toes to avoid the noisy *pop* when it sprang out.

The love of the bouncing, trundling car gave rise to the game of anticipating when we were about to pull into our driveway, and therefore when the deliciously snug ride would be over. I would aim to recognise the ascent of York Road, a steep hill close to my parents' house, by the pushing and groaning of the car and my rolling deeper into the seat, and the sharp right as we flattened out at the top. I would then feel for the inevitable deceleration, the unmistakable sweep round to turn into the drive, and the *bump-scrape-bump* as the pavement gave way to the steep decline and confirmed, lamentably, that we had arrived home.

All this flooded rapidly through my mind as the brief, rising gurgle of my friend filling a tumbler with water came through from the kitchen. As father reprimanded son in the hallway over a crime that I hoped also touched the former with recognition and love, I made some calculations in my head regarding the age of my mother and father and found myself arriving incredulously at the conclusion that I could remember my parents *at the age I myself was*. I realised that my earliest memories of my mother (two quite alien aspects long since abandoned: long brown hair and a cigarette) were of her around thirty. Thirty! Startled, I considered myself, at that moment the same age – an eternal student in Bristol, full of nonsense, preposterous in many ways – and thought what a travesty it would have been for someone as naive as me to be accountable for a child. Suddenly, my parents were just young people doing their best with a kid, rather like these friends of mine in Bath who had children, one of whom was now being forced to explain to his own child why he could not just sit quietly with us and not say anything.

My parents shrank like those primary-school desks, bedroom cabinets and magic hats. I reconsidered all the frustrations and complaints I'd had as a child and saw this man and woman as I could imagine myself, coping as well as they could with an infant, learning as they went, abandoning their old lives of trips to Brighton in a series of sports cars of which my father still talks so proudly, and taking on the vast responsibility of bringing up a child. And me! How naively had I fought with my father and sided with my mother; how ludicrously could I still nurture the mundane, inevitable grumbles of progeny towards them, decades later, as if this young couple – then the same age as me – had done anything other than their brave and extraordinary best.

This reverie was ended by my friend's return to the room, and we continued our conversation as I swung between absorption in the topics at hand and the imaginary observing of our chatter from the perspective of an unnoticed eight-year-old standing in the doorway.

I imagine there was a point, around nine or ten years old, when I indignantly expected to be allowed to attend these dinner parties of my parents; it was particularly confusing to be told I could not, when the guests were all people who seemed to like me. Either my parents held their ground, or their parties became fewer and further between than I remember, but I have no memory of ever being ushered into these hallowed gatherings. Other than Christmas with my grandparents, or family gatherings on Boxing Day, I cannot remember sitting with adults around our dining-room table. However, I know for sure that these events occurred when I was younger, due firstly to this faint memory of exclusion, and secondly to the seemingly constant presence of empty After Eight mints boxes in the house.

A sickly whiff of mint fondant mixed with dark chocolate clings stickily to many of my early memories at home.

These kitsch slivers of confectionery, with their trademark prescription of the precise hour at which consumption becomes lawful, were the insignia of seventies middle-class suburban life, to be followed in the eighties by Viennetta and Ice Magic (a bland, faux-chocolate topping of unholy fashioning that would harden unnaturally once it came into contact with ice-cream), and, in my mind, inextricably associated with the purchasing and reading of the *Daily Mail*, which I imagined at the time to be one of the posher papers in circulation. I remember a moment at school when I was set straight by a mocking classmate on that account, and complained bitterly to my parents upon coming home that we were using a sub-standard means of keeping up with topical events. My parents, rightly, were annoyed at my precocious indignation, and refused to change papers. To this day it makes me uneasy that this illiberal publication is still their primary source of enlightenment regarding world events.*

The ubiquitous post-prandial square, launched in the early sixties, pioneered the concept of the After Dinner Mint. Before 1962, it seems we were happy with a mug of tea, a healthy

---

* For many people of my age, there is a clear memory of when we first discovered as an adult that our parents were at least a little bit racist. It's up there with hearing about a relative's affair or Nana's first cappuccino. Maybe not seriously racist, but certainly prepared to say things that sound as much by today's standards. A fantastically misjudged comment is made over turkey one Christmas and a tiny piece of us dies. I am sure that a lifetime of reading the *Mail*, with its life-affirming editorials and open celebration of diversity, never once contributed to such lingering views in our household.

constitutional or spanking the kids to round off a meal; today when dining out, due to this one-time piece of forward thinking by Rowntree, we are privately rather pleased when our coffee arrives with a concomitant conflation of mint and formed chocolate. These petits fours seem to accompany coffee as naturally as a cigarette does for so many. The After Eight boxes, either brought by guests as gifts or more likely bought by my mother in anticipation of an imminent dinner party, would be taken the morning after the gathering and placed in the sitting room, next to the record player. I was allowed to help myself to whatever remained.

Each square was slipped into a crisp black paper sleeve, glued along three sides, reminiscent in miniature of the singles covers of that era. The front of each bore a suggestion of a rococo golden clock set to seven minutes past eight, and on the back a crescent of paper was removed along the top edge to aid with the removal of the confectionery, rather like the conven-ient half-moon of access offered on the back of my Bicycle card box. My mother, knowing the value of presentation, would serve about half of the chocolates, still sheathed, spread in a loose fan upon a floral-bordered tea plate. This meant that any little envelopes left in the box would normally, upon removal, cede a chocolate as expected. There were rarely any empties, but a glance along the row from above would normally settle whether any had been left (perhaps my mother had stolen a chocolate herself by removing it from its packet but leaving the latter empty in the box): a neat, evenly spaced series of paper edges, every other one a mint-thin-width apart, promised a full yield from whatever packets remained. I would then upset this regularity (both that of the paper-edge-spacing and of the packet-to-mint-thin ratio) by removing the thins but leaving their paper covers inside.* When only a few had been removed in this way, it was easy enough to tell where the empty wrappers were, but after a crucial tipping point had been reached, the box became a mess of black papers. The visual check was confusing and redundant, and it was very hard to tell when all the chocolates had been eaten. Thus, I was occasionally able to have the pleasure of finding a final chocolate or two when all hope had been abandoned. This belonged to the fond category we might label 'childhood moments of delighted surprise', most typified by the realisation, closely following a morning's resentfully early awakening, that the day in question is a Saturday and that there is no need to get up for school.

The mints were, and still are, delicious, and home experiments showed the gustatory advantages of refrigerating them first; of eating five at a time in a pile; and on occasion, when a mint had been left too long under the lamp and melted messily into its housing, of peeling apart the paper wrapper to scrape, with the teeth, chocolatey fondant from the inside.

However, it was the box that provided the unexpected pleasure and the relevance to our story. Inside the original black-and-green box of my childhood there was a secret flap.

---

* Having recently bought a box of After Eights to compare the old packaging to the new, I offered a friend a chocolate from within. He made a point of removing the little sleeve and discarding it, proclaiming the act of leaving an empty one in the box a 'cunt's trick'. I made a mental note.

(The modern, green Nestlé container has been changed, as all things must be, and now we have a softer, more ergonomic clock design on the front and the flap has sadly been replaced by a secured piece of card that does not hinge.) It sat between the front facet of the box and the black corrugated paper that is still used to hold the mints,* and allowed the lid to close neatly and tuck inside without disturbing the chocolates. This long flap was the width and height of the box, and thus inadvertently created a secret compartment inside the otherwise innocent chocolate container.

This used to fascinate me. Possibly it reminded me at some level of the secret flaps inside my magic hat. As I remember, it could be lowered to rest flat against the bottom of the box, or brought up to sit behind the front side, which meant, as I think about it now, that something flat, placed inside the box, could be vanished or switched by the lowering or lifting of the flap. I was too young to perceive this precise potential for a magical method, but was also unable to understand why the flap was there at all, so I would sit and be gripped by the potential for

---

* The corrugated paper seems to be made of the same crisp substance as the little covers for the mints, which means that the action of removing a mint from the box is quite noisy. While not necessarily being intentional on the part of the manufacturers, this crinkling sound, unchanged over nearly fifty years of production, has become part of the ritual of After Eight eating, as intrinsic and satisfying as removing the square from its wrapper and admiring it before consuming. Immediately recognisable, this crinkling is a sound many of us have unconsciously stored, ready to be rocketed back to the pungent minty-chocolatey moments of our childhoods whenever it is heard.

jiggery-pokery without knowing quite what could be jigged or poked. Occasionally a confused trick of sorts would emerge, where method was all and discernible effect was absent: a piece of paper, for example, was shown to be placed into the flap, which was then openly lowered before closing the box; upon opening the box, the piece of paper could be seen in the expected place. Shazam. My first, entirely unmagical, trick.

Part Three: Cigarette Chopper

This befuddled half-sense of infant conjuring may never have developed had it not been for Hamleys. Not the sprawling giant of a toy-shop on Regent Street, but rather a lesser-known, modest sub-branch of the same in Croydon. I can remember nothing of this particular shop, save that it had a small counter upstairs that stocked magic tricks, most of them plastic-moulded and ready to perform. Neither can I recall at what age I would have visited the shop, but I imagine I was somewhere in my early teens. My memory even of the magic department is faint: I make shady images of a glass counter and of some dark packaging; I remember that the tricks seemed expensive, and I recall saving up to buy the plastic Cigarette Chopper.

On second thoughts, I may not actually have saved up. Around this time I was a budding thief, and while I doubt I would have been able to swipe the trick from Hamleys, I imagine I would have at least acquired most of the coins necessary from the change my father kept in his jeans, which normally lay discarded on the ottoman in my parents' bedroom. I would sometimes creep slowly into that room, which was directly above the sitting room where they were watching television, keeping near the wall, aware that the floor was ready to creak loudly, stopping if it did so and lifting my foot so gradually that the board beneath could silently regain its position, eventually reaching the flung-away trousers in question (usually the jeans but sometimes the grey Farahs), whereupon I would tip the contents from the pocket into my hand. If the bounty was plenty, I would pilfer a couple of pound coins, and perhaps a fifty-pence piece too.

I have heard a few times in my life that shoplifting begins with stealing sweets, and escalates from there. This was certainly true in my case. At some young age I would reach into a shop's open display of Blackjacks or Fruit Salads and remove a handful, then change my mind and seemingly drop them back in, while retaining a couple in what I would now think of as a loose Finger Palm or Thumb Clip. I might then pick up something larger like a Mars Bar with my other hand, place the guilty one with the palmed penny sweets into my pocket to remove some change, leave the purloined confectionery within as I emerged with a few coins, and then, following a pantomime realisation that I did not have enough money, return the chocolate to the display and walk out. Or if I had the cash, I would fairly buy Pineapple Cubes, Aniseed Twirls or Aniseed Balls (which would turn dogs insane, I was once told), but boost my boiled booty with a few illegally acquired soft chews.

The late eighties introduced to the retail shelves a range of gadgets and stylish gizmos without which a teenager such as myself simply could not do. At the age of seventeen I worked on Saturdays in a suit-hire outlet, fitting out gangs of Croydon men with frock-suits, morning coats, cummerbunds and cravats. During lunchtime breaks I would browse the neighbouring shops and frequently help myself to whichever of these new contrivances was accessible and appealing. I would pick up a small object behind a larger one, then sneak the former away into a coat sleeve or inside pocket while remaining apparently fascinated by the latter. I saw my first compact disc while working in the suit-shop: a classical compendium, brought in by an elderly customer, who had asked the manager to pack it in with his suit. I was intrigued, and soon after began to assemble a malfeasant collection of such discs myself, filched from the nearby That's Entertainment! music and video shop on the way to the bus-stop. These were very early days of CDs, and this particular shop did not display the casings separately from the discs, so, being also the era before doorway alarms and security tags, I could help myself to whatever I fancied. A box set of classical composers, and several individual discs were dropped into bags or smuggled out under an overcoat.

I was never caught, though I did once set off the alarms in Harrods by walking out of the music department with a Luther Vandross cassette tape in my pocket. (My co-workers at the suit-shop were soul-lovin' black or mixed-race men whose opinions of what constituted good music entirely moulded my own musical tastes at that age. Before taking this job, I had no interest in music of any sort, but by eighteen, stolen cassettes or CDs of Alexander O'Neal, Luther, Cameo and others joined

245

substandard introductions to Schubert and cheap versions of Beethoven on my bedroom shelf.) I was shopping in the Knightsbridge emporium with P— from school, who was unaware of the fact that I had slipped the cassette into my pocket while we were chatting. I was convinced that my days as a petty shoplifter were about to end in humiliation and criminal action when I realised that the sudden piercing whining that screamed through the air had been caused by my ill-judged exit past the sensors. At that point I noticed peripherally two store detectives heading over to us, so acted out to P— (but really for the detectives' benefit) a display of embarrassed confusion over how a tape I had meant to buy had ended up so closely upon my person. They believed or at least accepted the charade, and I was not apprehended, but this event hastened my decision to end the long spree.

The Cigarette Chopper belonged to the sub-category of magical apparatus designed for the demographic of novice or even child performers, among whose numbers I certainly counted in both instances. Whereas the best magic props should be instantly recognisable and beyond suspicion in their everydayness, these contraptions resembled nothing else on earth. Such things of course remove any sense of real *magic* from a performance (by putting the focus on a childish prop rather than the performer himself) and replace it with the less wondrous sense of being fooled by a shop-bought puzzle. Yet I have a passing fondness for these awful tricks: the design and thought that goes into the cheap, mass-produced box that vanishes a coin, or allows a miniature sword to penetrate a borrowed ring, or indeed the device that cleaves a fag in three and then restores it, do speak warmly of our capacity for whimsical design and a jostling delight in fooling each other through invisible mechanical means. The fact that the Japanese Tenyo company, which makes many of these tricks, not only exists but seems to flourish is a testament to their peculiar appeal; perhaps not so much to a magic-watching public, as these are not the apparata we would expect a professional to use, but to amateur magicians, and the designers who sit, try to sleep, or go for long walks while pondering how a pen might be made to visibly penetrate a plastic sheet or a borrowed, signed penny disappear from one box and appear in another upon a little tray.

I have known such a designer well, and he lives solely for the joy and pride of claiming new innovations in this area. He carries footage on his mobile phone of him demonstrating his inventions, and will show these films at every opportunity. He lives among a mess of card, scissors and glue, constantly building and rebuilding prototypes of some new device to make a box change colour or a deck of cards slowly disappear, and is shy and awkward when not talking about magic. The pleasure he takes in the appreciation of his cleverness means that, after impressing an audience with the footage on his phone, he will eagerly tell his spectators the secrets of the design, and therefore the method of the trick, to secure a second gasp of astonishment and fair recognition of his extraordinary mind. There is undoubtedly a pathological geek-iness about the whole venture, but equally something touching about the capricious silliness of it all, and the fact that this life and so many others could be unapologetically devoted to the seemingly childish act of fooling other people as prettily as possible. It is one of the beautiful whimsies of humanity. I do not know of any appropriate correlative in the rest of the animal kingdom. I have neither observed my pets nor heard of giraffes vanishing small objects to amuse each other.

I must have eyed the Cigarette Chopper trick jealously for some time, as I remember feeling quite excited to buy it. Being expensive, it was all the more wonderful to bring it to the counter and pay for it. I imagine that I had seen the trick performed by a shop assistant first, been fooled by it, and, eager to know the secret as well as handle such a strange contraption, had made the decision to save or steal to acquire the clever piece of plastic.

It was a small rectangular object, a little longer than a cigarette and perhaps three inches wide. The central length of the prop was exposed, so that a cigarette could be pushed vertically into its middle and be seen clearly. A central horizontal section could then be quickly pulled outwards, apparently sliding the central part of the cigarette out with it, a little like the way a magician's assistant's tummy is apparently dislocated sideways in the stage illusion known as the Zig-Zag Lady; similarly, here the cigarette would be visibly sliced into three. Then, by pushing the central section back into place, the cigarette would be impossibly restored, and could be fairly removed for inspection. The spectator, of course, would not be allowed to examine the Cigarette Chopper itself.

One has only to perform the slicing/restoration sequence in slow motion to see how the trick works. At that point one no longer enjoys the illusion, but instead marvels at the beautiful efficiency of the design, and above all the satisfying *action* of what amounts to an invisible, mechanical production of a matching middle section of cigarette from within the workings of the toy, combined with a simultaneous concealment of the actual centre. Performed slowly, it is fascinating to try to follow both aspects of the exchange at the same time.

The delight that is immediately taken in the design of the trick reminds me of the enjoyment provoked by those travel alarm clocks or business-card cases which contain a slow-motion sprung cover that, upon the press of a button, gradually unfolds itself in a beautifully controlled, drawn-out action not only to reveal the timepiece or cards inside but also to elevate the clock or case from the table so that the time display can be read with complete convenience, or cards can be removed at the leisure of a busy executive who may not have time to pick up the case from the table.* I feel a slight frisson of the same

---

* This slow, automated movement concerns me in the example cited here of a business-card case. Any form of card-case, beyond the most battered and unassuming, is surely an aesthetic and social travesty. To withdraw, say, a silver case from the pocket before removing a card is surely to trumpet a ludicrous gaucheness and maladroit pretension. It is impossible for the intended recipient of the card to view the case as anything other than a misjudged piece of peacockery; unfeasible to avoid a brief inner commentary along the lines of *oh, he's bought one of those . . . he decided this would make the act of handing over a card a signal of his success as a businessman and a certain refined elegance as a gentleman . . . probably picked it out himself . . . please God it was a Father's Day gift from a child who knew no better.* Thankfully, by the time one has wondered whether one is obliged to comment politely on the item, it has been returned to the pocket and one is holding a card bearing a number one hopes never to have to call. But imagine the act of

satisfaction when I close some modern drawers. I gently push and begin to let go without thinking, expecting to consider the drawer-closing act no more, but then, a moment before the drawer would otherwise thump into place as anticipated, my attention is suddenly drawn by the engaging absence of that impact: it is as if the drawer unit says, 'That's fine, I'll take it from here,' takes the sliding unit in its own gentle hands and guides it slowly and professionally into place. When these drawers started appearing in the nineties, I would find myself, upon coming across one, repeatedly opening and closing it, as if caught in some obsessive-compulsive ritual, purely for the joy of that denied moment of wood hitting wood. I could attempt to violently slam, but regardless of my intentions, some elegant piece of engineering ensured that the drawer, as if in defiance of my resolute aggression, still closed silently and elegantly. In many ways this action mimicked those doors seen in office blocks and multi-storey car-parks which use some form of air-cushioning to avoid the jarring noise of heavy slamming. But in the case of these drawers, and because the sudden deceleration might happen while the hand is still in contact with the fascia, the action has a pleasing, almost tactile

---

having to place your card-case on the table, in response to a fellow executive asking for a card; having to hold him back while you activate the slow-motion revolving lid; watching it interminably self-open and believing yourself to be making a tremendously positive impression while all potential of future business slips away with the same systematic inevitability demonstrated by the mechanical action of the case; then, most insulting of all, gesturing to the would-be recipient of the card to take it *himself* from the now proffered stack.

quality that such hefty doors do not. I like to imagine that the designer who first included this closing mechanism was surprised by this aspect of his own ingenuity, and stood opening and closing his drawers with the same gratification, wondering at the tiniest element of disappointment that is also engendered by the experience, as he was denied the sound and feel of his applied force impacting as expected. Undoubtedly this lack of resolution is the very feeling that moves one to try again and again, as if looking for some sort of closure, as it were.[*]

The Chopper presented some challenges: firstly, no cigarettes offered themselves at school for marvellous trisection, and secondly, the duplicate pre-sliced cigarette part had a tendency to spill the dried musky flakes of its innards into the mechanism and preclude a smooth operation. Thus, as with so many other magic-trick purchases that would follow this first acquisition, the Chopper soon ended up at the back of a drawer, ignored for years, and eventually simply disappeared.

---

[*] There is a musical equivalent of this drawer-slamming feeling at the start of the Sanctus of Schubert's Mass in E Flat. I first heard this played on a crackly eighties record player belonging to the father of a German friend while we ate unusual cake in the front room of his parents' Franconian farmhouse. Strings build dramatically over a few bars to an anticipated climax that is then cruelly denied us: a choir leaps in but withers rapidly with a 'Sanctus' that fades to nothing. Again the trick is played, and the repeated effect is enormously affecting. 'Jeder Satz eine Entäuschung,' my friend commented – 'Every phrase a disappointment' – and I concurred: the rising passion and consistent denial of satisfaction (until the final explosive resolution) is very stirring, urging the listener towards resolution. It also has an obvious sexual quality, in a way that drawers really do not.

Only recently, long after Hamleys of Croydon had closed and in a sudden burst of nostalgia, did I buy myself a second one. It was a little slimmer and shinier, as were the new Penguin Bars over the old ones of the seventies, and the packaging was different, but I took great pleasure in trying it once quickly (to fool my eyes) and then again slowly to try to follow the beautiful substitution.

If we were to continue this early narrative, such fledgling excursions into trickery would find their natural resolution many years later when, as a student practising extra-curricular hypnosis, I started to learn conjuring from a book entitled *Mark Wilson's Complete Course in Magic*, bought from a remainder bookshop in Bristol. Fascination and dedication led to small local success and a couple of books written for the fraternity, until the comedian and magician Jerry Sadowitz thought my name worthy enough to suggest to a television production company intrigued by the notion of a mind reader – and the rest, as they say, is selective and incomplete history. For there is also a quite different psychological narrative, which I perceive just as clearly and which might follow these lines:

1. Only child until age of nine; precocious and sensitive; spent much time alone.

2. Father key figure in the sports department at school, which was much loathed and avoided by the creative/sensitive son.

3. Friends consisted mainly of other members of ostracised and ridiculed 'Music School Gang' (also known charitably as the

'Poof Gang'), enhancing general sense of alienation from the milieu of a sporty all-boys school.

4. Constant teasing from said sportier boys, who were ungenerously disposed towards scrawny and effete games-dodgers.

5. Sixth Form provides a relief: pupils seem to grow up overnight and friends change. Excited at sudden acceptance, I become an eager showman and comedian. Popular caricatures of teachers get me welcome attention.

6. University provides a completely fresh start. Two related threads run parallel: firstly, a desire to be noticed and different (after many years of being treated as an outsider, there is a now adult urge to not conform at any cost), and secondly a residual fear of ridicule (and presumption of non-acceptance) from the sportier types. Result: a garish and mannered personality, starkly built in contrast to the beery, butch world of fellow students.

7. Hypnosis and magic provide a means of resolving both threads. Performing permits the attention-seeking traits to be validated, meanwhile the tendency for the more laddish students to be quite responsive hypnotic subjects allows for a kind of confidence to be finally enjoyed in their presence.

8. Lack of relationships during and after university (a means of avoiding the awkward confusion of whether I should happily accept the whoopsie within or wait for him to somehow pass)

frees up huge amounts of creative energy to spend practising card-sleights and developing tricks.

I have retained a belief that it is the popular sporty kids at school who grow up to have the least interesting lives, and the unhappy young souls who develop into the most extraordinary adults. Whoever heard of a creative genius being understood as a child and well loved by his classmates? Who likes to imagine an artist who emerged into adulthood content with his lot? And, conversely, how satisfying to hear that almost without exception, the untroubled, popular kids at school have ended up blandly as accountants, solicitors or 'in IT'. Hold on, misfits, your day will come.

CHAPTER

8

After flicking the final card with that unnecessary gesture following the production of the cards from my pockets, I dropped it on to the table alongside the other two. Showing my hands empty brought applause from Joel and Charlotte: the open-handed pose, made while standing, was an applause-cue, silently calling a 'Ta-da!' that naturally provoked a response; at the same time, the showing of my hands empty demonstrated that nothing was concealed, that there was no solution to be found for the appearance of the cards. This latter point is note-worthy, as showing the hands empty after producing cards from pockets proves very little, in fact is an irrelevance; yet by allowing the spectators to see bare palms even when they would not expect to see anything concealed, the impossibility of the flight and the seeming innocence of the magician are somehow, illogically, amplified.

As Joel and Charlotte reacted with delight from either side of the table, they turned their gaze to look at each other in disbelief; both leaning forward, their wide-eyed faces came close together, the cotton-covered stone slab of the table between them. They wordlessly exchanged their shared feelings of incredulity and pleasure, before sitting back: the applause-cue had apparently signalled the end of the trick and it was natural to then relax and allow the feeling of what had just happened to settle into the bones. In doing so, Charlotte found herself again alongside Benedict, who, already leaning far back into the sofa, looked at her and let the tiniest half-laugh move through him – a spasm of amusement that consisted of a sudden contraction of the chest muscles, which in turn forced a tiny expulsion of air up from the lungs and out of the nose in a ripple of movement that tipped the head momentarily backwards and left it rocking slowly back into place like a parcel-shelf dog. It was the mildest half-chuckle the body can produce, the sort of brief, closed-mouth response that might occur when privately watching something only slightly enter-taining on television. It was a detached, mocking response not to my trick, but to the pleasure his girlfriend was taking in it. From his removed position, he was presumably interpreting the enthusiasm of his two companions as a sign of childishness, and the easy rapport they shared in their delight as something to treat with disdain.

I neither liked nor disliked Benedict. His displays of indif-ference were a little tiresome but would be forgotten the moment I left the table to repeat the trick elsewhere. I accepted that I was a threat to his place in the group, as I had seen this disdain many times before, and would many times again, until theatre and television audiences replaced those in close-up situations and such obvious exhibitions of apathy were no longer necessary. I do not presume that people should enjoy

magic, nor, in a case such as this where I was forced to ingratiate myself into their company, that I should find myself
welcome. It is just that where people choose to engage, and are
fascinated, they become more suggestible and my job becomes
easier; otherwise I must rely on the calculated, fixed structure
of my script to ensure that the trick at least works correctly.

There is a grammar to magic which, when followed attentively, ensures the illusion of an impossible event having
occurred. The magician generally wishes the spectator to experience events as a straight line with no flaws or inconsistencies,
from start to impossible finish. Usually this line is based around
the rule-of-three formula:

$$A \longrightarrow B \longrightarrow C$$

Where, for example:

A = card selected and returned to the deck

B = cards spread to show the selected card has disappeared

C = chosen card appears in the spectator's pocket

In reality, the ABC line perceived is misleading: in fact, the
spectator is paying attention to points B, D and F along the
following line:

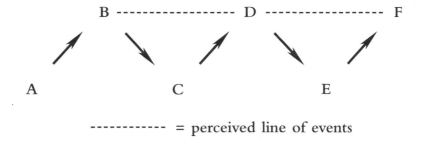

--------- = perceived line of events

Where, for example:

A = card loaded into pocket of spectator some time before the trick

B = card selected (duplicate forced from deck) and returned to the deck (but secured somehow)

C = magician casually shuffles the deck and brings the chosen card to an accessible position, palming it as he asks (misdirects) the spectator if she can remember the identity of the card

D = cards spread to show the selected card has disappeared (in fact still held in palm)

E = while instructing the spectator to check her pockets, the magician casually mimes the action to demonstrate (in fact ditching the palmed card in his pocket)

F = spectator finds card in her own pocket

As long as the BDF line is the one remembered by the spectator as the only noteworthy sequence of action, and is therefore mistaken for an uninterrupted narrative (a false ABC), the illusion will be secured. The cause and effect have been misunderstood, due to a purposeful manipulation of attention, whereby the hidden 'moves' are carried out in a relaxed fashion and are always logically motivated (such as the way the card is ditched in the pocket at the end), in order that the audience does not register them as important and can easily forget them.

Glancing up at the club where I am currently writing, I notice people (important) but not how many chairs are around the empty tables near me (unimportant); looking back at my work, I see the last few words I have written (important, in that I wish to add to them in a way that continues their sense and grammar without disruption) but do not see the rest of the written page (unimportant, at least until I come to review it), the contents of the Microsoft toolbar above it, or the precise arrangement of the letters on my keyboard below. We constantly edit and delete information, for we would be otherwise unable to function. If something is presented as unimportant, and we have no reason to question that status, it will slip by unnoticed, even if it contains the solution to an important riddle.

I observed the same false ABC phenomenon when talking to a psychic healer who had carried out healing on a friend following a scalding of the friend's arm at a party. She was proud of the fact that her intervention had been successful: the poor chap, after having had a boiler explode before him, would have otherwise needed hospital treatment. Her line of understanding ran thus:

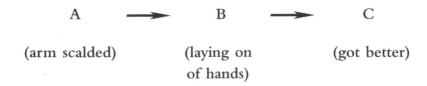

A   ⟶   B   ⟶   C

(arm scalded)   (laying on   (got better)
                of hands)

Whereas upon talking to other guests who had been at the party, a presumably more accurate line of events emerged:

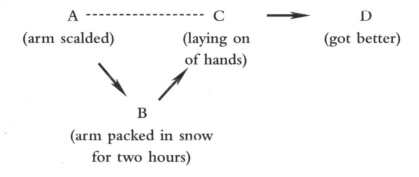

A ----------------- C   ⟶   D
(arm scalded)   (laying on   (got better)
                of hands)

B

(arm packed in snow
for two hours)

This suggested a less miraculous reason for the healing. B, though, in this fuller explanation, was only incidental to the healer, and did not feature along her line of understanding. Conversely, to the other guests at the party, the plot was equally as simple:

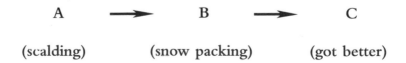

A   ⟶   B   ⟶   C

(scalding)   (snow packing)   (got better)

One way of allowing actions to pass under the spectators' radar is to perform them while physically relaxing, directly after an important revelation. Thus, as I now sat down to resume my position at the table and give my small audience a moment to respond to the appearance of the cards, I was, during this dip in attention, able to set up the next stage of the trick. I found the short card by riffling down the corner of the deck with my thumb, then allowed a further card to spring off the same thumb for each letter that spelt Benedict's card, before casually cutting the deck there with one hand. As my thumb counted to the letters being spelt in my head, my other hand brushed away imaginary crumbs from the taut, crumbless tablecloth. I then pulled my seat forward with both hands (apparently: the counting hand merely dipped under the seat and appeared to pull it forward while my foot did the job on that side, and the momentary disappearance of the deck allowed for an unseen, one-handed cut to be performed at the side of the chair). I also smiled and looked at Joel, Benedict and Charlotte, each in turn, as I carried out these moves, to keep their eye-line away from my hands and level with mine.

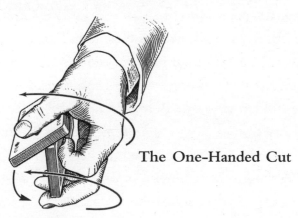

The One-Handed Cut

I took each of their three cards and had them call 'stop' as I riffled openly down the side of the deck and placed them into the centre at their chosen points. Through a series of one-ahead mathematical ruses and calculations, the relative final placements of the cards in the deck could be engineered, despite the apparent randomness. A final, open cut of the deck at that short card brought all the cards into their required positions.

Benedict's card was the last to be inserted. Whereas the other two, enjoying the game, were happy to call 'stop', Benedict, resentful of his enforced participation, had raised his eyebrows nonchalantly and, looking at the back of his hand, mumbled a loath, almost inaudible, 'There' instead.

I inserted his card at the reluctantly chosen point, and then, just as I was performing the final cut, and just as the bottom half, lifted a little into the air, was starting to be lowered on to the tabled top half, Charlotte looked at Benedict and said, 'Hey. Stop being an arse.'

The two halves slapped together and lay there, one on top of the other, a little misaligned.

I removed my hands.

I glanced up at Benedict, then looked back at the cards.

Just as I was about to neaten the piles and bring the broken edges of the deck into a smooth, flush formation, I was halted by the sudden rising of Benedict from his sofa. He stood up, patted his trouser pockets, and picked up his mobile phone from the table. He murmured under his breath, something about having to call somebody, and in order to let him out I had to shift my chair a little to my right.

'Oop,' I said, lightly, as if entirely oblivious to the tension his sudden departure had left in the air.

'Don't worry about him,' Charlotte said a moment later, and looked back at me, her eyes fixing on mine from behind her tortoiseshell frames, before glancing up to note his path to the front porch from where he was presumably going to make his call.

Joel, across the table from her, looked at neither of us, but silently squared his cocktail napkin to be precisely parallel to and equidistant from both sides of his corner of the table, and then picked up his wineglass and set it neatly and exactly upon the napkin's centre.

My polite 'Oop' had been a message to Benedict and the group that the statement made by his abrupt leaving had gone unheard, as if I were dim enough not to sense his displeasure or respond to it. It was rather like the light obliviousness I had feigned some time before when talking to an opinionated drunk at a party. As is not uncommon, she was an ex-girlfriend of the host who had not made her peace with her former paramour and was only able to communicate to guests via barbed comments and bizarre left-field hostility. Real conversation was impossible, yet dialogue with her was uncomfortably sustained by the fact that no exit point was offered; instead I busied myself with not appearing at all offensive to one so unusually ready to be offended (an offence I might have committed by walking away). Conversely, I was suffering the pangs of normal social commitment, and feeling faintly obliged to respect the level of frank ingenuousness at which I was being addressed: a duty to remain in private conversation with the imposing confidante, while simultaneously being desperate to flee. My response was to appear blindly insensitive to any barbs or digs being made, to treat everything as a light joke, and to agree flaccidly with all comments without committal. My cheeks and mouth soon suffered a dull ache from sustaining the necessary smile, as did my arm from being crossed so long between us with its drink. The situation was worsened by the inebriated guest muttering everything under her breath while frequently looking away to take in the room, and with an unevenness of timbre that made it very hard even to *hear* the acerbic non-sequiturs that comprised these dark glimpses of her toxic mental state.

Thus I agreed banally with spiteful snippets I could barely hear, and did myself another in a series of injustices that constitute much of the average party experience. There is a sliding scale of insincerity that includes most conversations held at such gatherings. Even when we warm hugely to a fellow guest, this affection is more commonly a reflection of the easy flow of conversation and his warm enthusiasm for our interests than any sense of honest or truly open exchange.

The party experience has become more pleasant since arriving as part of a couple. For many years I would find excuses to avoid such events, and where I did attend, I would sustain pleasant chatter for an hour or so before yielding to a kind of dissociated exhaustion that would find me sunk deep in a sofa, watching the guests chatter and laugh, with me feeling grossly incapable of normal human interaction. This rapid detachment was largely caused by being unable to talk for long about any subject other than my own interests: confusing likeability with being a 'fascinating character', I would try too hard to force the impression of the latter while undoubtedly failing grandly at the former. Also, without the accompaniment of a partner, there were only the harshly contrasting alternatives of sustained social engagement and detached observation of the group, and it did not take long in this removed mode before I started to feel that my attendance was a terrible mistake. I learnt quickly to leave once I had reached this point, rather than remain staring at the chatting guests in a heavy-hearted slump.

The 'Oop', therefore, was delivered with the forced lightness we might assume when we are eager to show that we are not experiencing the embarrassment we might be presumed to feel.

I live currently on the first floor of a small East London apartment building, whose floors are served, unsurprisingly, by a lift. I ride it down to the ground level if, when walking past the electronic display situated to the right of the doors, I see that the car is waiting on, or descending from, a floor no higher than the third; any higher and I consider it an indulgence to wait for the lift to arrive.* A common occurrence is for the lift

---

* The lift read-out causes me several minor concerns:

   1. It shows a series of animated 'down' arrows to signify a descending car, interspersed with a display of the number of the floor that it is at that moment passing, or perhaps only merely approaching. It is difficult to tell which is the case. It shows the '1', for example, followed by further arrows, well *before* the doors open at the first floor, but it is not possible to tell how long the car stands stationary before entry is made possible

to open and contain someone who, having pressed the 'G' button higher up on their own floor, and having watched the numerical display count down slowly from their number to '1', has mistaken the first floor for their destination, and is intending to step out. At which point they tend to:

1. Notice me, and in stepping forward make half a step to the side, with a view to circumnavigating the obstruction I present to their exit. I, expecting them to remain in the lift and

---

This would not matter, save for the fact that I like to imagine the lift descending past the various floors as I wait, and am unsure as to exactly how to do that. For example, as the red '2' appears, is the lift *at that moment* speeding past the second floor? Is the hard metal-lined edge of that higher level sweeping up past the descending lift at precisely that point? I imagine a glimpse of the hallway's red carpet and fire-hose and a helpfully placed sign pointing out in which direction one might head to reach one's desired door number; and even, as I like to do, the lives of a hundred residents, caught in a snapshot of laughing and arguing (I try to hear an unlikely split-second of cacophony as each floor is thrown past the door) as well as cooking (to walk the corridors is sometimes to be stifled by an osmic irruption of a hundred assimilated aromas from Europe and the East which hang thick in the air in a heady, unpalatable blend). It is impossible to know, and this makes it frustrating to try to imagine with any accuracy the descent of the lift as I await its arrival.

2. There is a repetitive *tock* sound which can be heard echoing from inside the shaft as the cables raise and lower the metal box through seven floors without ever killing anyone (an astonishing feat, of which I remind myself whenever I find myself grumbling at the machine's frequent indisposition for maintenance reasons), but this sound, though metronomically paced, I feel in my gut to be irritatingly asynchronous with the animation of arrows and the numbers on the

270

continue their ride down to the ground floor, am stood quite close to the door, and do not make the expected, courteous gesture of stepping to one side in order to let them out. Thus, in the split-second before they realise their mistake, they experience surprise (at finding they have to sidestep me) and annoyance (at my immobility).

2. Understand that they have arrived not on the ground floor, but have been stopped at the floor above (by my pressing the

---

display. It is roughly three *tocks* to a floor, and my suspicion is that the read-out moves at a slightly faster pace than the internal machinery; but if there is a discrepancy, it is too small to identify by merely looking and listening while the lift drops a few floors. It is not even quite possible to tell when waiting on the ground floor and following its descent from the very top (when I have shopping with me to justify the ride and break the third-floor rule), a rare situation which gives me the maximum number of *tocks* and floor numbers upon which to base my calculations. Possibly the noises happen simply a fraction of a second *after* the display changes, or alternatively they occur at a slightly slower rate. This latter option confuses me, as I know that the floors are of equal height and that the regular noise means that the car has not been interrupted: somehow I cannot make sense of the fact that the noises from the lift can occur at a slightly different pace from the appearance of each floor's number. Presumably they can, but some limitation to my internal faculties precludes any audio–visual representation of how that might work; instead my head becomes jumbled and I am unable to think it through. This mental block is something I experience from time to time, and rarely do others understand my confusion. I consider myself reasonably adept at mathematics, and am not intimidated by the subject, but occasionally I find myself utterly unable to assemble the relevant mental images or edit the necessary imaginary film that might allow me to understand

button and interrupting their private descent to the foyer). Therefore they step back into the car, sometimes muttering an apology, embarrassed at their clumsy and ill-judged attempt to exit the lift.

3. Suffer for the remaining ride the double awkwardness of (a) sharing the confined space with someone unknown to them, and (b) that 'someone' having just seen them make an inelegant and faintly amusing error.

---

something that strikes me as counter-intuitive. Most recently, I was measuring the cubic volume of my bedroom in order to see whether or not a portable air-conditioning unit would suffice for the job. The unit, I was assured, would happily serve a room of up to eighty cubic metres. I measured the room, mistakenly, in feet, and recorded dimensions of eighteen by eleven by eleven feet. The volume was therefore 2,178 cubic feet. I converted this figure to metres, by multiplying by 0.3048, and arrived at a room with a volume of about 664 cubic metres. An absurdly high amount, and *over eight times* that which could be managed by the air-conditioner. I was dumbfounded and checked my calculations, to no avail. After considering the conundrum for some time, I found out by accident that I had to convert each measurement to metres *first*, before multiplying. Then, dazzlingly, the product of the numbers was sixty-something, and made complete sense. I was shocked to have made what I presumed was a fundamental schoolboy error, and more dismayed to find that none of my friends shared my surprise at the inconsistency of results.

3. Sometimes I am in a hurry to leave the building, and am impatient to see whether or not the lift is close enough to be worth taking. When in a rush, I know that I can walk briskly down the stairs in the same time it takes the lift to travel from my floor to the foyer, so I only take the lift on those occasions if it is already waiting, or if its approach to my floor coincides with my flustered arrival in that part of the

There is an undeniable pleasure to be felt in this situation, which comes from a number of sources:

1. I have become used to people making this mistake, and now often, a split-second before the door opens, wonder if someone will be in the lift (probability: 30%), and if so, whether they will make this mistake on this occasion (probability, given that there is someone in the lift: 70%).

---

corridor. As I hasten round the corner to the lift area, I first check to see if it is descending by looking for whether the scrolling arrows signify 'up' or 'down', and if it is, I do not have the patience to stop, look and wait for the arrows to then change to a floor number in order to learn its location. Instead, I keep walking, eyes on the display, until a number appears, at which point I can decide whether to continue into the neighbouring stairwell, or stop, return and have the relative pleasure of the brief lift-ride. However, the three or so descending arrows which separate the appearances of each floor number seem to be interminable in these cases; I hover, leaning forward in mid-stride, as if tugging at the lift myself, urging it to hurry, eyes fixed on the display, my sense of time somehow altered to the point that the arrows seem to lower themselves impossibly grad-ually, like stalactites forming on a cave roof, while I, frozen, fume at my improbable ability to arrive reliably at the precise moment that means having to wait for the full three arrows before the appearance of a floor number. Although the time period in question is only a handful of seconds, at the time this is always disproportionately frus-trating (following, as it generally does, my furious attempts to leave the apartment and find my pen, as outlined previously), as if a few wasted moments could impinge at all upon the already suffering time-management of my day. Upon cooler reflection, however, it reminds me of our similar capacity to glance at a watch and believe

2. If they do, I enjoy their little dance. (Combined probability: 21%.)

3. There is a power to be felt in knowing that they will be mentally reviewing the event as we descend together, slightly embarrassed with the whole thing. Particularly so, for some reason, if they are dressed in expensive designer clothes (probability: 50%): somehow the ease with which their efforts to

---

that the second hand, and therefore the watch, has completely stopped. Somehow, because we have happened to look at the ticking hand at the conception of a fresh second and therefore have to wait the entire duration before the hand in question judders forward again and we see movement (waiting time which here only amounts to a *single second*), this unusually maximal hand-viewing period quickly strikes us as unnatural, and we even have the opportunity, before it finally steps forward, to process the uncommonly extended stasis and decide that the timepiece has stopped. This illusion of immobility is similar to the game played with the flashing colon that divides hours from minutes on an oven-clock or clock-radio display – a game that has entertained me to the point of minor obsession since childhood. Here, the aim is to negate the flashing, and to create the illusion of a constantly illuminated colon, by closing the eyes for the duration of the symbol's intermittent absences, and to time the opening and closing of the eyes as precisely as possible in order to sustain the trick perfectly for the maximum length of time, until ocular discomfort or the risk of epilepsy dictate cessation. The process can be altered, of course, to produce the contrasting mirage of no colon at all.

4. On occasions when I am in a hurry, and impediments such as heavy baggage *require* me to use the lift, I find myself attempting after summoning it to hasten the car's descent by pressing the 'call' button repeatedly in the interim, even though I am fully aware that such an

attain elegance can be reduced to nothing before even leaving the building leave me smiling to myself on these rare occasions when all these events combine (probability: 10.5%) and we are lowered together for the remaining short distance to the lobby.[†]

'Oop' is also the interjection of choice for the brief and uncomfortable exchange at the lift door. It is said to ease the tension: delivered with a gentle smile, it acknowledges the mistake but without embarrassment or annoyance on my part. Yes, they have stepped out at the wrong floor, but it is an easy

---

action will not accelerate its arrival. It is as if I have decided that my next action is to ride in the lift, and, being poised to do so with nothing else to consider or do in between, any extended period of inactivity between now (not being in lift) and then (being in lift) is intolerable. Thus I find myself making pointless gestures to hurry along an indifferent world, rather than being able to wait. Similarly, when at a cash machine, I will find myself unable to pause calmly while the cash is counted. Having requested the money to appear, I will drum my fingers or make grabbing gestures at the money slot until the notes are handed to me. I appear to carry out these gestures in order to make the money arrive more quickly. I am shocked at the fact that I seem to feel I have the ability to make such things as lifts and cash machines operate with greater speed, and that a few seconds' wait seems to stretch far beyond the reaches of my patience.

[†] The pleasure taken from seeing balloons of pretension publicly burst has never been stronger for me than when walking to my flat on one occasion, during my years in Bristol. There lived on my street a middle-aged man with an air of high status that was immediately obvious in his sartorial impeccability and the look of faint disapproval with which he greeted most people and things. Certainly this included me, for I dressed in flamboyantly bohemian tatters and frequently had to pass him on our very long street. Having once nodded a hello in passing and not finding the gesture

slip-up to make. Sometimes I extend it to the cheery 'Oop, sorry – one more!' as I step in to press the 'G' button myself. Very rarely, and normally when the passengers in question belong to the community of American women who live in the building, they reply with a self-deprecating chuckle, or 'Oh, I always do that', which, in openly accepting that the minor blunder was entirely their fault, removes any possibility of residual tension from the brief balance of the journey.

The friendly way I try to step into the lift on these occa-

---

returned, I had taken to ignoring him each time we approached each other on the pavement. Even here his evident, effortless authority was irritating: he would be able to appear quite unperturbed by my presence as we walked towards each other, whereas I would find myself patting pockets, checking my mobile phone or gazing with affected dreaminess into the basement flats of the houses I passed. (This kind of busying-oneself activity, frequently employed in lifts when one finds oneself with an unfamiliar travelling companion, is related to the even stranger gestures we must revert to after making the mistake of greeting a friend who is heading towards us from some distance. The level of awkwardness is cruelly and directly in proportion to the length of street that must be covered. After the initial, enthusiastic wave or gesture of recognition has been made and returned, we must then hold eye contact and smile for a second or two longer while we wonder what to do next, before making gestures of open-armed embrace, jumping daftly in the air or miming to amuse the other, until both parties are just about close enough to each other to talk. The alternative to this promenade pantomime involves, after seeing the approaching friend at a distance, feigning apathy with pocket-checks and extended pavement/scenery inspection until the later acknowledgement of his or her existence. This latter operation means that during the awkward period preceding the eventual greeting, one has been in the unusual position of displaying a lack of interest in a loved one, perhaps long missed.)

On the morning in question, I was about to turn into this same long

sions reminds me of the way in which, upon walking away from people after they have made an amusing remark to end a conversation, I will often retain an artificially held smile on my face and allow them to see it by turning my head a little to render the raised cheeks and upturned mouth-corner visible in the quarter-profile. This came from my own tendency when younger to turn and watch people when they walked away from me to see if they were still smiling at a comment I had made, or whether the smile dropped from their face the second

---

road when this gentleman emerged a few feet ahead of me from a bank, which was situated directly on the corner. It immediately became clear to both of us that we were about to embark on the long stretch of road to our respective houses with me walking awkwardly close behind him. He had an irritatingly languid gait, which meant I could not comfortably solve the proximity issue by slowing down and putting more space between us. Equally, he was not strolling so slowly that overtaking would have been straightforward: to have done so would have involved an exertion of effort which would either have had to be maintained (but which would have then propelled me down the street at an unnatural pace), or alternatively, were I to have quickly passed him but then slowed down to a normal speed, may have read as obsessive and belligerent in its abruptness.

The third option was to overtake and then *slowly* resume a natural speed, in such a way that would not be obvious to him as he walked behind me. I use this technique when faced with the same problem in the corridor of the apartment building where I now live. There are many sets of double doors which I need to open in order to walk the length of the hallway to my flat, and it is not uncommon to hear a resident enter the same corridor a little way behind me, near enough for me to feel I should hold open the doors as I pass through them, but (given the large number of such doors) wanting to gain distance so that I can open the remaining ones further down the corridor for myself without repeating the chivalrous gesture each time (an action which quickly becomes embarrassing for both parties). My

277

they presumed they had left my sight. I would be so delighted to see that a smile had lingered, and that I was genuinely being found witty rather than just politely tolerated, and I still find myself on occasion looking back at a person I have just walked away from to see if he or she has genuinely enjoyed some comment I have uttered. Thus, I do the same for others: a person on the street calls out a remark I have heard many times before, and I will laugh heartily as if I have just heard it for the first time; continuing on my route, I will retain a grin and turn

---

answer is to get ahead not by walking quicker (which, I worry, would be obvious to the person behind), but by taking *longer* steps at the same speed, so that I can be seen to apparently maintain the same pace but deftly move further ahead without the other resident knowing how. I figure that with the foreshortening effect of viewing from behind, the lengthier strides are not at all obvious. These efforts are, however, undermined by the doors themselves: until I gain the necessary distance, I am still required to hold open the doors for the other resident, and the necessary pause each time on my part enables my follower to catch up with me, thus rendering pointless my intermittent attempts to gain distance. I then have to double my efforts in the longer stretches of unbroken corridor in order to try to put myself safely enough ahead. This does sometimes work, but it would be an odd sight to anyone who happened to open their door and catch a glimpse from the side. Caught between the twin fears of being seen to not hold doors open for neighbours on the one hand and of obviously running from them on the other, I would be seen taking these exaggerated steps, striding like Hoffmann's gory tailor towards my door.

I was considering which of these three options to take as I began to walk down my road behind this man, already furious at his impossible sense of self-worth that dictated he walk at a pace uncomfortably slow for anyone caught behind him.

And then a fortuitous event happened. He sneezed.

He sneezed, and instinctively brought his right hand up to contain the

a little to make its edges visible, in case it is normal for other people to glance back in the same hopeful way.

'Oop' (or, for that matter, 'Oops'), when said as a reaction to someone else's mistake (such as an ill-timed exit from a lift), also shows an empathy with the person: after all, the 'Oop' should really come from *them*. For us to offer it first is to diminish their embarrassment: if we are happy to share in it and accept some of the blame, then there is less reason for them to be concerned. It is interesting that we have learnt to offer this

---

germy blast from his thin moustachioed mouth. A second later he withdrew his hand, not realising that a long, thick snake of mucus had attached itself to the back of it. A yard of snot, unusually dense and catching the sunlight of a bright spring morning, was clearly visible to me, so close behind him, as it hung heavily from his face to his dropped hand. Knowing that he was well aware of my uncomfortable proximity, I felt the rush of pleasure of finding our normal roles reversed: his authority had now been expelled at high speed in a gummy rope of face-gag, and I had the privilege of being able to grin happily at his misfortune.

Even from behind, I saw his composure dissolve. Continuing to walk, he flicked his hand at one of the street's decorative cement plant troughs as he passed it, but this did not rid him of the viscous swag: instead, a second line somehow separated itself from the main strand, swung under and around with undeniable panache, and formed an auxiliary festoon connecting his slimy hand to the council-maintained municipal pot. By this point I was stifling actual laughter, which only became more difficult to control as he was forced to involve his left hand and detach the foul, adhesive length from himself in a messy procedure reminiscent of a clown battling with a plate of spaghetti.

I did not overtake him, but remained close behind and making my footfall asynchronous to his own, to ensure I was audible. And so we walked almost the entire length of the street: I, behind, never having felt happier, and he, I hoped, dying slowly inside with every step.

friendly little sound as a way of mitigating the awkward impact of these moments, and that it sounds natural for us to make the sound – which says, in essence, 'Silly me!' – when it is they, not we, who have been silly. In Germany they say 'Hoppla!', which sounds odder still: an 'Oop' slipping out at least feels so close to an 'Oh' to seem quite a normal little noise to make; this German word feels entirely contrived in comparison. When I lived in that country I took great pleasure in using it. I would step on to a bus and let it spring from my mouth in a flourish as I circumvented a native. The word leaps high and then somersaults on the tongue, finishing with arms wide open in a classic applause-cue. It is a verbal circus-call, used for making lions do tricks, yet can also be helpful when sidestepping elderly Bavarian ladies descending from public transport.

I did not want the group before me to feel any discomfort on my account; hence the mumbled 'Oop' communicated only ease and fellowship from my side. Neither did I feel any genuine discomfort. My only concern was how easily the trick could continue with one participant missing.

Participant. The accepted word in magical literature describing the person taking part in a trick is a *spectator.* This is an interesting symptom of much of what is wrong with magic, at least in my eyes. A *spectator* watches, passively. She may be described in the tomes of thaumaturgy as picking cards and handling objects when asked, but that label consistently casts her as one of a series of props designed to act according to the magician's whims. As a spectator, she is detached, an accidental part of the process, a passer-by, and the magic seems designed with her involvement as a peripheral adjunct, an afterthought.

This is at the heart of the non-magic of the tiresome type of conjuror, the pattering, prattling devotee of an eccentric and childish craft. He performs, ultimately, for himself. People pick cards on cue, but they are neither transported nor feel wonder; if they are impressed it is entirely for the benefit of the performer. They are disposable, a mere convenience when practice mirrors are unavailable. The magician speaks with rehearsed spiel but does not engage; he does not reach those in his audience because he has not learnt to care about them. His starting point for a new trick is a sleight that excites him in its ingenuity, and the finished trick barely moves beyond that point; he does not begin with a peculiar experience in mind for the participant.

Participant. A participant is active, a *part* of the process, and a necessary component of the magical experience. This is how it should be. No magic happens unless the participant perceives it as magical, so she can never be a mere spectator. The entire escapade fails unless she is held in mind from the very conception of the trick, her thoughts and desires anticipated from the first stage, and the waters of her ongoing experience (her interest, her boredom, her delight, her scepticism) navigated at every move. She must be transported, entertained, and should experience the elements of childlike wonder and grown-up intellectual astonishment, as well as the mixture of belief and disbelief, that can combine to produce *magic*.

My three-card trick, performed with some diners in a restaurant, was not a realistic vehicle for this kind of involvement. Finding cards in pockets did not easily engender other-worldly wonder. It did not fit my ideal for magic. Yet it allowed for unthreatening fun, and the impression of skill and professionalism, which, if my little groups found themselves engaged, might serve as the start of a journey towards greater depths as I continued my performance. Mistaking mere solemnity for seriousness is an equally disastrous error commonly made by those who search for meaning in magic.

Magic *means* nothing. It has the potential to connect us to something wonderful, as does any performance, but it is not wonderful in itself, for it is inseparable from the particular performance in which it is experienced. A magician who is too fast, too slow, mumbles, shouts, smells, is unlikeable or incomprehensible will unavoidably taint his magic with his personal failings.

As a conjuror of tricks and a reader of minds, I have sometimes found people quite moved by a performance I have given. Some have told me that they have taken real value from it. These are good moments, for my worries about the childishness of it all are momentarily alleviated. But I do not fool myself that meaningfulness is intrinsic to what I do. I would love it to be, but I imagine that the necessary fraud gets in the way of its integrity. Many within magic talk of it as an art, but do not really understand the differences between good and bad art, or art and craft. Art is a narrative that turns and twists through history, and means different things at each new divergence. A pretty and accomplished oil painting of a country scene may be beautiful, and may indeed be art, but it is no longer likely to be *good* art if painted today, for it does not fit on to the end of that ever-changing narrative that once valued lifelike representation of nature, but now scoffs at such bland aims. Art now makes us see the world differently, it slaps us and challenges us, and to produce good art that is relevant today we have to consider such factors. I imagine that a true artist using magic would be quite a different animal from a magician trying to perform 'artistically'.

Magic can, when performed well, be *theatre*, and rise above its usual confines of the 'speciality act'. This is easier to aim for, and undoubtedly a more honest and useful aim than trying to force something into being art, purely for the sake of the label. To work as a piece of theatre, the magician needs to see beyond the reaction of 'Wow!' that magic aims to provoke and look at a more varied, richer experience for the audience as well as an overall arc or narrative for the show. He is also well advised to look at his own role in the proceedings, for most magicians are not human characters we can warm to, or empathise with in their efforts. The great magician and magical thinker Teller – the silent half of the Penn & Teller duo – has highlighted the need for drama in magic, and for drama to exist, we must understand the struggle of a hero. Magicians often substitute showmanship or self-inflicted jeopardy for drama, but the spectacle of a restrained Las Vegas performer hanging over flames, trying to make his escape, is quite empty unless we *feel* for him. Even done well, this sort of stunt tends to be a very thin and bawdy slice of what real drama might mean.

Charlotte and Joel's level of involvement in the performance had just altered a little. Charlotte was clearly a little embarrassed by Benedict's sudden departure, as well as being pleased that he was out of the way. Joel was keeping quiet and revealing little. It was now up to me as to whether they would remain distracted by Benedict's moody exit, or whether I could utilise it to draw them in further. So I leant forward and spoke a little softer, adopting a conspiratorial 'We're better off without him' tone.

I picked up the deck. Following the apparently random cutting procedure, I knew the first card I needed had arrived eighth from the top. 'Watch,' I said to Charlotte, and started to count slowly from the top into a face-down pile. At the fifth card, I said, with just a practised hint of irritation in my voice, 'Just stop me wherever you like.' I was counting on her thinking she may have missed an instruction, distracted as she had been by the exit of her boyfriend, and sure enough, she let me deal a couple more down before calling 'Stop', right on her chosen card. She had shaken herself of the distraction caused by Benedict and was engaging herself entirely once again.

I turned the Two of Hearts over to show her.

'Omigod!' she squealed, laughing, and I noticed that Joel's eyes quickly left the card and lingered on her face.

Riding the reaction, I continued, 'Joel, I'll spell to your card.' Dealing a card for each letter, I spelt 'Jack of Hearts' out loud, turning over the final card to reveal his choice.

They both giggled with surprise, though I did not allow them to react for more than a second.

'Give me a number between one and twenty for Benedict's card,' I requested, looking at both of them in turn.

Joel looked across at Charlotte for an answer.

'Oh, er – twelve,' she said.

They leant forward together as I commenced counting. I produced the Ten of Diamonds by a ruse on the count of the twelfth card, and flung it face-up on the table.

Now I wanted them to react. Joel did so well: his feline face lit up and he laughed loudly, this muscular contraction propelling the upper half of his body into the back of the sofa. I noticed that Charlotte shot back as well, in easy rapport with him, her eyes darting between the upturned cards and the rest of the deck.

'How do you do that?' she asked, not really wanting to know.

Whenever I am asked this question, I imagine trotting out a detailed answer, explaining every piece of duplicity and undoing every meticulously created presumption. The disappointment of having the bubble of mystery burst! This is largely why people do not like to believe that paranormal phenomena have everyday explanations, and why a playwright friend found himself in tears after walking in on Whoopi Goldberg taking a shower at the opening night of his first successful play on Broadway: if we are unprepared, the bubble (of the mysterious unknown/of the world of celebrity) can burst so cruelly.

I laughed, swept up the three cards into my right hand and picked up the deck in my left. With my left little finger, I secretly pulled down on the corner of the deck and let three cards spring up, naturally holding a break beneath them. I had purposefully withheld Joel and Charlotte's reaction until this moment, as I wanted them now to *relax* as much as was feasible to cover a series of sleights.

Newton's Third Law of Motion states that for every action there is an equal and opposite reaction. This basis for classical mechanics has its use within conjuring. In order to create a window for a piece of sleight-of-hand, it is common first to encourage the participant to concentrate as much as possible on the trick. Then, when a magical event has happened (the card has been produced or the coin vanished), the once-attentive witness will relax his concentration for a few moments, his mind distracted with amazement or searching for explanations. He can only hold intense concentration for so long; eventually he must let up, and a magical climax is a cue for him to do so, as well as an ideal opportunity for some piece of legerdemain to occur, which will for the reason of its timing most likely be missed. Hence, the magician creates 'off-beats' in a magic trick, cleverly designed moments when the participant will release his attention, loosening the valve for a few seconds, and the principle is illustrated that the more a person is paying attention to a trick, the more he will need to relax in those instances, and the more likely he is to be fooled.

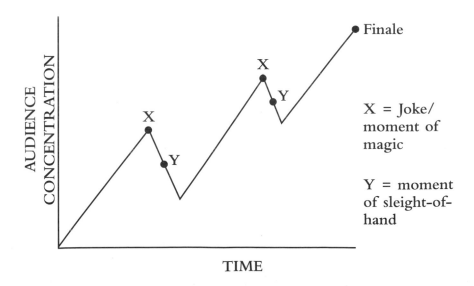

I am reminded of the Newtonian Law every time a new Prime Minister is elected in my country. After vague memories of a bumbling, rural Callaghan, the first Prime Minister I remember clearly is Thatcher: a strong, domineering character. If she became too much so, then the safer, more lacklustre character of Major followed her. After a while, the bespectacled, leporine leader was replaced by another with a high level of charisma: Blair. At last, he seemed a relief from Major's greyness. And after Blair we reverted to a blander figure with the premiership of Brown – another comparatively unprepossessing character. Brown was heavily criticised, perhaps unfairly, for being boring; then, lit by the golden glow of Barack Obama, we looked again for a shiny-faced leader from among the paltry bunch on offer in the next round. And got two. And so on we will most likely continue, undulating between a desire for dominance and blandness in our leaders, criticising both for being what we sought once the desired effect of personality wears off.

This back-and-forth preference for weak or strong personalities as leaders is quite different from the way we choose romantic partners, though we might wish the political context could be similar; sadly, the limited choice of political candidates means we can rarely choose those to lead us with a personality 'type' in mind, honed from previous mistakes. To swing back and forth between strong and weak partners in life would be a very confusing way to go about such things. Where we may try to refine what we're looking for in life, learning lessons from previous relationships gone awry, we are in politics simply offered 'same or different', and thus we remain dissatisfied, constantly choosing 'different', bothered that they are largely the same, swinging to and fro without eventually coming to rest or gaining wisdom. Doubtless this artificiality is in great part due to the fact that each side in politics is required to accept the ludicrous notion that there is only one worthy viewpoint to an argument. If anything stops me from ever entering politics, it is my total inability to have such faith in my opinions.

Attendant to my unsuitability for Westminster cowers another listless failing caused by an indecisive nature: the inability to order food from a menu without confusion, time-wasting and distress. As a child I was an immensely fussy eater: I would touch very few vegetables, and many foods made me squeamish. I retain a lingering distrust of runner beans, parsnips and a few others, and experience a strong repulsion in the face of mushrooms that seems to madden most of my friends who insist that the repugnant fungus is the most versatile of nature's blossoms, and that to eat one covered in breadcrumbs or sautéed with garlic is to taste the substance of Heaven itself. To me they're just slugs, and at best should be salted and left to die.

As a schoolboy, I dreaded being cooked for by the parents of classmates when visiting their homes. As well as those food-stuffs already mentioned I did not like fish, beans, cabbage, peas, carrots, tomatoes, nuts, cream, coconut, salami, new potatoes, blue cheese, eggs or coffee. These are but examples which spring unbidden to mind – I'm sure there were many more.

It took an accident as a university student to bring me out of the paralysing mental block that constitutes fussy-eating. I was in a friend's car returning to halls at the end of a long evening and was hungry. We stopped at a take-away pizza place and one of my fellow passengers went in to order. Being so fussy, I was not prepared to let them choose a group pizza to share without my sanction, as mushrooms have a habit of creeping unannounced on to the base and hiding beneath the cheese. I insisted on having my own one. One pizza on the menu promised 'sausage' and, expecting pieces of British Pork Sausage, I asked for that, already embarrassed at my handicap and how it separated me from the simple bohemian pleasure of a shared late-night undergraduate take-away. The meal arrived, however, bearing *Italian* sausage: thin slices of the kind of spiced salami I had never been able to consume. They, like the unexpected mushrooms that make the mycophobes among us shudder and start, had insinuated themselves between strata of cheap melted mozzarella/cheddar mix and were impossible to disconnect from the filling without ruining the whole thing. So instead I played a trick on myself, which was to lead to a hugely rewarding process of reacquainting myself with erstwhile rejected foods, and to the discovery of many new favourites from their ranks.

I decided that much of fussy-eating was a result of *expecting* not to like something, and presuming that certain tastes were going to be unpleasant. Thus, a process of anticipating the disliked taste, as if awaiting confirmation that the food cannot be enjoyed, maintains the childish, finicky response to food. It is rather like deciding one does not like a particular musical instrument and training one's ears to pick it up during a symphony; then, the moment it is faintly detected, announcing that the piece is unlistenable. I knew I had to block that process, and that the most effective way to do such a thing would be to fill my mind with the pleasurable noises I might make when eating something I was really enjoying. So, rather than search for the salami taste I knew I did not (historically at least) like, I took a bite and made enthusiastic 'Mmmm, that is *gorgeous*' sounds both out loud and to myself. It worked very well. I actually found myself enjoying the slice of pizza, and with each new slice it took less effort to block my practised reinforcing response of old, so that by the time the pizza was consumed, my loathing of the peppered sausage had passed entirely.

Shocked by how easily I had undone years of loudly professed hatred, I began a personal project of undoing all my dislikes, one by one. Coffee came next, for I had always enjoyed the *idea* of coffee-drinking and related paraphernalia quite disproportionately to my uneasy tolerance of the drink itself. I drank espresso and filter variants, playing the 'Mmmm!' trick for the first cup or two until I found I was genuinely enjoying the taste. By playing this game with every food I had loathed, I was able to distinguish between foods I genuinely could not eat and those towards which I had unnecessarily built up a negative response. Today, I still gag at Gorgonzola and fetch up at all things fungal, but a more enthusiastic and eager dinner guest you could not find.

When scrutinising a menu, a lingering aversion towards a few offered items does sometimes limit my choices a little, but this is only a partial cause of the rabbit-in-headlights dithering and vacillation that beset me when handed the *carte du jour*. This infuriating lack of resolve over such a simple decision as what to eat for dinner stems more from a reluctance to choose between items that sound equally appetising. Barring a small handful that have been ruined by the unholy inclusion of *trompettes* or Dolcelatte, many of the descriptions fill me with such pleasure that I find it extremely hard to step back and choose any one over the others.

There is also the quandary, in a familiar restaurant, of whether to return to a regularly ordered favourite or try something new. There are pros and cons to both options, which cause further impediment:

	Eat a familiar favourite	Try something new
Pro	It will be very good, and I know it. I like the idea of visiting different restaurants for particular meals. That appeals. It helps develop a relationship with the staff who might one day ask me if I would like my 'usual'. I dream of such things.	It is likely that the other meals will be at least as good as the favourite. I should always try to explore new opportunities, even with food. I can gain a better appreciation of the restaurant by trying different meals.
Con	I am avoiding new opportunities. There may be even better meals on the menu not being sampled. To always stick to what you know is not a good mantra for life. I have a safe choice to fall back on at any time. I'm not exploiting that. I'm equally denying myself the pleasure of returning to the familiar meal	If the new meal is not as good, the comparison with the better, favourite meal that I *could* have had will make the disappointment even harsher. I'll kick myself. I would be experiencing regret with my meal, and it is an unhappy thing to eat food reluctantly, especially when one is paying for it.

at a later date and enjoying it even more.	It is unusual to find something that is immensely enjoyed, and arguably perverse to deny oneself that pleasure for the sake of variety.
The staff might be laughing at me for always ordering the same thing.	
If I keep ordering the same meal, I'm likely to get bored of it, and therefore deny myself the pleasure of that particular meal.	

This inability to surge unquestioningly forward with a decision or opinion makes expressing sceptical opinions about pseudo-science and the paranormal rather tricky. As an erstwhile believer in God, a discussion with an enthusiastic Christian apologist on the street or over dinner involves the oddly schizophrenic experience of both vocalising my reservations while simultaneously annotating them with imagined objections and counter-arguments by the believer, before the latter has even uttered a word. When I was a Christian, I was fed many pat responses to the sorts of quite sensible objections people usually came out with. For example, when asked 'Why is there so much evil in the world?' one could offer an answer along such dizzyingly inadequate lines as 'Because what's the alternative? That God would make us like a bunch of robots unable to do wrong?' For that reason, I know not to bother with raising such familiar objections nowadays. Equally, I can hear how I must sound from the position of a believer who is likely to have his own clear and very specific filter in place,* and am aware when what feel like watertight and irrefutable statements to me sound like the worst forms of reductionist, narrow-minded scientism to him. Quickly it feels pointless to engage. It seems silly and churlish to attack others for their private beliefs, unless one is entirely convinced of the greater view that harm is caused by the persistence of that belief in society; but when pressed into engaging on the matter, I recall the question I asked myself many times until I found my own faith breaking down:

---

* Being an atheist is merely *not* happening to believe, and is not a filter in the way that a specific belief is. The trouble is, the word 'atheist' *sounds like* it implies a belief, but this is only because it unfairly defines itself in terms of the very thing it has no interest in: the belief in God. As A. C. Grayling has pointed out, being labelled an 'atheist' is a little like being labelled an 'aphilatelist', or a 'non-stamp-collector'. Most of us are aphilatelists, but that says nothing about us or what we are like. We would probably find it odd to be called one, and it would be presumptuous and wrong of the stamp-collectors to insist that by not collecting stamps we were bound by a specific agenda. Likewise, we may of course choose to believe in anything that makes an inherent strong or supernatural claim (such as that God exists, or even that Elvis is still alive), but to insist that those who do not share that belief (atheists, or people who do say that Elvis is dead) are adhering to a belief system as narrow and specific as our own is plain wrong. Of course there are some atheists (or Elvis deniers) who may take umbrage at believers, and choose to attack in one form or another. They hold themselves up for criticism: are they raising important social awareness or just ranting maniacally? Both certainly occur, and ultimately history will judge these individuals. But the *condition* of being an atheist is by definition quite without any binding belief behind it, nor does it suggest any inherent attitude, any more than not believing that Elvis is alive or not collecting stamps dictates anyone's agenda.

Bearing in mind we can all utterly convince ourselves of things that are not true – and that therefore important truths about the universe must surely always be based on more solid foundations than what my easily fooled, fickle feelings tell me – what is it that supports this belief other than my own already-existing conviction?

Clearly an answer that reverts to 'I believe ultimately because I *know* my belief to be true' is no argument: such a statement is merely another indication of how deeply the believer believes, which is already accepted as a given. There may, however, exist a good reason to privately believe that stands up perfectly well, and which could run as follows: 'It may not ultimately be *true*, but to be honest it gives me enormous pleasure and confidence to believe, and that's enough for me.' This is one perfectly valid and sensible argument, although one that is rarely heard.

I used to suggest, in these conversations, a comparison with some of the most transparently daft excesses of New Ageism as an example of beliefs that could be just as sincerely held while being patently false. It was comparing my religious belief with more obviously silly, hippy nonsenses that played a large part in undoing my own conviction. Yet I hesitate to use this comparison now. It is an unfortunate by-product of much of modern Christianity that congregations in many churches are led to demonise – literally – much of the New Age movement rather than expose it as the nonsense that it is. Labelling a threat as evil is, of course, a very familiar technique for rallying dedicated forces to a cause (and distracting from smaller, internal tensions), an age-old ploy famously used in recent times by the West during the Iraq War. The most cursory look at cold-reading and suggestion tells us that Tarot cards are *not* evil; psychics do not 'usher in' the Devil or his minions; and even the creepy old Ouija board can be shown to operate via quite everyday, natural, physical forces. It is a shame that so many evangelical preachers feel the need persistently to reinforce a medieval fear of magic rather than help reveal the Devil's new clothes for what they are. But as long as we teach God, we also need Satan: for all the Church's fighting talk of defeating him, she re-creates and empowers him every day through keeping the fear alive and well in her ranks. How curious it is to consider that the grip of the great enemy could be greatly reduced by exposing his supposed handiwork as the irrelevant charlatanism and self-deception that it is. Yet should Satan disappear, so presumably would God without His nemesis to define Him; in this way Old Nick would arise elsewhere, stronger than ever, in order to revive the myth and save the Church. Conflict, and therefore *drama*, and therefore a *good story*, persistently shine through.

As Joel and Charlotte reacted to the appearance of the three cards, and the Newtonian Third Law as applied to conjuring created the vital 'off-beat' that caused them to pay less attention, I picked up their three chosen cards and switched them unseen for the top three cards on the deck. I scattered the three new cards face-down on the table, then sat back in a clear display of relaxation and of having proudly finished the trick. This larger movement signified that I was no longer worth paying close attention to, that I was not about to do anything of importance, and that now was a good time for the other two either to discuss the trick or at least switch off from what was happening with the cards. Therefore, knowing full well that I had a safe moment for a bold ploy, I palmed off the three chosen cards from the top of the deck and slipped them under the card box, which had been placed to my right into the perfect position at the very start of the trick. The balance of the deck, meanwhile, I placed back on the table, further towards them and off to the *left*, drawing their peripheral eye away from the box at the vital moment.

This was all done as I sat back in the chair. My two participants were not paying attention, according to the Law, and had they seen anything they would have noticed only the placing of the deck towards them, for this was the largest of any of the movements that occurred during those three seconds. Perhaps they had a peripheral sense of me 'tidying up', but no more would have been noticed.

The chosen cards were now under the box to my right; on the table were the deck and three random cards face-down, believed to be the selected three.

Had I let this off-beat linger for too long, it might have been seen in hindsight as somewhat orchestrated, so I leant forward again and reinstated the momentum and concentration. The trick about to happen was already done (the cards were in place). Being so ahead of oneself is a very effective place to be when conjuring.

Now, to cut straight to the climax and merely point out that the cards were no longer the ones on the table but were in fact under the box would not have been remotely magical. Without context or drama, there is, again, only bewilderment. So as I leant forward, I instructed Joel and Charlotte to watch carefully.

I pulled the deck a little towards me, picked up the first of the three face-down cards, and held it close to the deck. 'Call stop,' I said to Charlotte, and with my left hand I picked up the pack and let the cards dribble down one at a time on to the table.

'Stop,' she said, about halfway through this action, and I inserted the card at that point.

I neatened the pile, and picked up the next card as if to repeat the instruction. I hesitated with the card, openly peeked at its face, then changed it for the final card on the table. I did this as if I had lost track of whose was whose, and had first picked up the wrong one – Benedict's. Here was another 'convincer': that is, the switching of the two cards here convinces the participants that the cards being used are indeed the important ones. If they were *not* the cards (as indeed they were not), such an exchange would be pointless: thus it reinforces the notion that they must still be the cards we have been using. This was another false presumption, to make the part that was to follow far harder to fathom.

I told Joel to choose in the same way a place in the deck for his own card, and I riffled rather too slowly, forcing him to tell me to stop somewhere in the bottom twenty-six. This pointless restriction was a purposeful ruse, and was designed not only as another convincer that I must still be dealing with their cards, but also to create a little tension. The fact that the choice of stopping point had not seemed entirely fair encouraged Joel and Charlotte to pay more attention: they felt they had *noticed* something they shouldn't have, and this set up an anticipation of a pay-off – *Aha! Will the card be located somewhere in the bottom half of the deck? What use could that have been to him?* – which was soon to be greatly surpassed by the appearance of the cards in such an unexpected place as under the card box.

I squared the deck again. 'And Benedict's?' I enquired, gesturing at the last card on the table. 'Charlotte, would you?'

I dribbled the cards a final time. When Charlotte called for me to stop, I hesitated and let a few more drop before inserting the card believed to be Benedict's. Another red herring.

I picked up the deck, squeezed and riffled it in my hands, performed a meaningless sleight to suggest some subterfuge had taken place, and then declared the three cards to be vanished.

Fairly and slowly, I spread the cards again in a crescent, this time face-up, showing each of the forty-nine indices that remained. I showed my hands empty in a display gesture, so that they would not be led to wonder if I had somehow removed the cards at that point. I kept both of my palms in view. 'Gone!' I exclaimed.

Charlotte let out a 'No!', and both leant forward, checking to see if the cards announced themselves anywhere in the spread. Of course, none of them did. While they ran their eyes over the sweep of cards, I watched to ensure that neither of them spotted the cards under the box: to draw out the mystery before both solving and compounding it with the remote revelation of the cards was part of the fun.

Fun. For them. I am not sure if it was fun for me, in any obvious sense. Yet there is the experience, described by Mihaly Csikszentmihalyi (pronounced 'cheeks sent me high'), of 'flow':

a kind of retrospective happiness we can look forward to when we are in our 'zones'; when our skills match the ongoing challenges of the moment in such a way that we lose ourselves and our sense of time, and experience the kind of focused reverie, the unhindered creative flux, that chess-players achieve when they play chess, surfers feel when they surf, painters when they paint, and magicians, perhaps, experience when they do magic. It is not pleasure that one feels at the time, in fact one may not feel anything easily describable during the experience, but we later record these occasions as our finest and most blissful times. They are the ones to explore, value and build upon, according to Csikszentmihalyi's research.

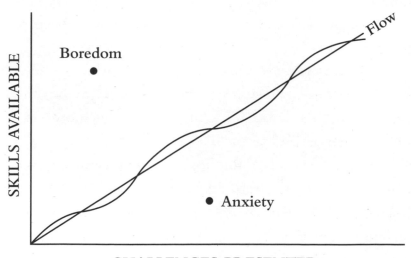

CHALLENGES PRESENTED

Perhaps the reasons for performing at the restaurant every Thursday night resided in the experience of this 'flow'. Of doing what I did well, and enjoying the challenges of each intimate situation in which I found myself having to perform. Of having managed the participants to experience a particular thing that is not just bewilderment or the intellectual challenge of a puzzle, but something deeper and less obvious. Something lost.

Or maybe it was the cheap, childish pleasure of seeming extraordinary, forced through the easiest route available to me: cheating.

After they had a moment to check that the cards were not in the spread, I pointed to the Bicycle box and, beneath it, the face-down chosen cards that had been there throughout the charade, and the mounting rhythm of the revelation caused both Joel and Charlotte to gasp together with pleasure and disbelief. Charlotte's gasp was louder: a little scream, then a movement of her hand to mouth and then her breasts. Joel dropped his head, exhausted for a moment, clearly spent.

While they were looking at these cards, which were over to my right, I had palmed another three cards from the deck in my right hand, unnoticed. I then dropped that hand beneath the table with its cards as my left came across and removed the tabled cards from under the box, bringing them forward to turn them over. Joel and Charlotte's gazes were fixed upon these cards as they travelled towards them and away from the box, and this allowed me to place the three palmed cards face-down under the box, in the place just occupied by the previous three, as their attention was drawn away.

All attention was now on the cards in the centre of the table as they were turned over to confirm their improbable flight. Unknown to Joel and Charlotte, this happened to be the precise moment that the other three were loaded beneath the box, in the dead area of the forgotten corner. Again, the placing of the significant action had been heralded through the designation of space.

A comparable technique of misdirection had been systematically employed by my mother between the years 1979 and 1981 to convince me that a soft toy I owned was able to move around of its own accord. Billy was a limp soldier-doll. I remember a red and blue felt uniform on soft padded limbs, each stuffed white hand fashioned into a mitten shape with a small protruding thumb and three fused, rounded fingers with stitching to suggest the separation between them. My mother would secretly remove Billy from my bedroom and leave him in places around the upstairs of the house; when I asked why he was on a stair, or standing dumbly in the airing cupboard, she would casually tell me that he had walked there. Being of that age when one cannot believe a parent could simply lie, I would listen, shocked, to her offhand assurances that she had, from time to time, seen him strolling (or even marching) unaided across the landing while she was cleaning the bathroom. Then she would occupy me with a task, such as taking towels into the spare room, and when I returned Billy would have moved again; never so far as to suggest that she had exploited my distraction, but just enough to suggest that there was elusive, sentient life within the thin, cotton-wool stuffing of this blank-eyed private.

Billy's curious bedside battalion comprised a bunch of assorted animals that were swept or kicked from the bed on to my floor every night. They were known as the 'Bunnies', although in truth there was only one rabbit among them: Mr

Bunny, a yellow rabbit-creature of sorts, which bore a similarly questionable level of physical resemblance to a rabbit as Mickey does to a mouse. He had been my favourite for many years, and his tail had once squeaked.* An early collector's instinct, which still fills my house with clutter to this day, coupled with the then only-child's need of synthetic companionship, ensured that a dozen or so teddies and puppets and unlikely beasts lined the bed for far too long. My father eventually grew sick of their lingering presence until one cruel day, when I was aged about

---

* It had apparently squeaked when I first owned the toy as an infant, although any memories of this early sound are very faint, and may be conjured up more from my mother's assurances that the tail functioned in this way than from actual recollections. Certainly as I grew up, I heard no such squeak: the mechanism in the white tuft of fur must have worn out, or been damaged when I was too young to remember.

Then, once, as a student, I returned to my parents' home for the Christmas break and found Mr Bunny on the bed in the guest room. My young brother's eagerness for stuffed playthings had probably led to this toy being kept – that and my parents' reluctance, I presume, to throw it away while I was away studying. It had become one of the unloved ornaments relegated to this room, along with any number of misjudged and ugly gifts I had brought back over the years from school exchange trips in Europe. I had not seen Mr Bunny for some time, and had probably not picked him up in ten years. His limbs hung limply from the torso, and I could see the stitching along one leg where my mother had repaired it, following a tug-of-war game I had once goaded our elderly golden retriever into playing from her bed. As I parted the fur to trace the homespun line of matching yellow cotton, I remembered the dog, Tammy, long since dead (put down and carried discreetly from the house in a bin-bag so as not to disturb me on my birthday); my mother's sewing kit; the Tom and Jerry teddies I had also owned and not thought of for a decade; and the repeating brown-and-white geometric pattern of the old bedspread on which they had once so

ten, I returned home from school to find all but Mr Bunny gone. My mother kindly pretended they had been given to charity until, after my outrage, hate and distress towards his unannounced and brutal act had subsided, she admitted he had, in a fury at his son's unmanliness, bagged them up while she was out and shoved them into the dustbin for collection. Mr Bunny had been saved, in a curious, generous aside from my father, but among the names of those who were not so lucky was Charlie, an expensive ventriloquist's doll in the form of a doe-eyed tramp with bright knee-patches and heavy stubble of black wool tufts. He was on loan from my cousin Claire at the time and was ditched with all the others. We had to lie to her family about the loss of the doll. I'm not sure exactly what tale was fabricated that would have convincingly explained Charlie's disappearance, but let this volume now declare the disturbing truth to all.

It was an irascible but understandable act of frustration on his part: the destruction of the Bunnies was a symptom of our two worlds colliding. The world of the Father was different from mine. His consisted of the following:

Bedtime ultimata
The most frequently used was the terrifying count from one to

---

proudly sat. I suddenly recalled the non-functioning tail and, purely to feel what sort of sound-producing device might be stored in it to have once produced the squeak, gave it a squeeze. A single, clear, soprano hoot peeped as I pressed. Mr Bunny squeaked. Just once. He did not squeak again when I pressed the tail a second time, nor to my knowledge has he since.

three. I was always reluctant to go to bed, and even at a young age was able to form precociously solid arguments as to why an extension of my time spent before the television would be both logical and prudent. I would begin to calmly explain my reasons for staying up, upon which my father, having none of it, would look fiercely upon me and start counting: 'ONE . . .' My voice would become high-pitched and rapid as I begged him to stop the count and listen, fully aware that if I were not well on my way when the final number was reached, I would be smacked hard and carried to bed. 'TWO . . .' He was oblivious to the whining crescendo of my pedantic whinges, which made me more frustrated, and thus I would hysterically dispute until the last nano-second, at which point he would make to leap from the sofa, all red face and comb-over, no last-warning two-and-a-halves expected or offered, and I would dart from the room in tears screaming that no one ever listened to me.

Cigar smells

He has always taken comfort and respite from a quiet cigar smoked in the car during craftily engineered private journeys, and my mother has always found distress and disgust in the resultant lingering whiff of stale Castella. He always carried a Gold Spot mouth-freshener spray (which, when rifling through his pockets for change, I would always stop to use), and this covered the musky, musty, leafy smell in the same inadequate way that air-freshener masks toilet-smells ('Flowers on vocals, shit on bass and drums', as someone once put it).

Proximity, hot breath and fat fingers,
when removing splinters from his son's toes with a needle. Father: stocky and very close; densely hairy arms; red T-shirt; smells of cigar, Gold Spot and shaving soap; squeezing the toe to bring the tiny black head of a splinter into view at the surface of the skin while poking and scraping the red sore part with the vicious point. Son: long white legs and blue pants; perched precariously on side of bath, nervous of the needle; complaints unheard, eyes welled up with girly tears. I would tell him to leave it, or insist that Mummy should get it out (which would probably mean cooing words and the comforting smell of pink Germolene), but he always insisted, presumably because he had an army technique that wouldn't hurt as long as I would KEEP STILL.

Old war films
My or anyone's father can be placed in front of a television set showing an endless loop of lamentable, long-forgotten fifties war films, or garish Technicolor tales of men on horses among the orange rocks of old California, and, with a pillow for his head and biscuits to hand, he will happily live out his days and nights, intermittently sleeping and waking until death comes and he snores no more.

The world of the Son was very different, rather delicate in comparison to these things that felt at the time so ungentle. I was a sensitive only child for some time, prone to crying, while he had been one of six siblings whose family had to make do with markedly less than we had. The row of teddies, still arranged along my bed when I was a lily-livered and mannered eight-year-old, must have seemed to quietly mock him.

Yet amid this common enough story of son and father, I retain the memory of some surprising areas where we would connect:

Wrestles

Squealing hyper-excitement in our old house (and therefore until the age of six) as we found our way to bond by playing, on all fours, on the hallway floor. Here I was allowed to attack and leap and climb on his big back until he called something like 'fain-lights' – a strange word, which I have now learnt was his or my mishearing of 'Feignites', a London schoolboy call for a truce.*
This meant I had to immediately cease all assaults and fall panting and shrieking and wide-eyed to the floor while my adrenalin subsided and my father slowly brought himself up to standing.

Draughts

He taught me the game, which I loved, and we would play occasionally in the evenings. I knew vaguely of chess only as some esoteric grown-up version of our game, with strange pieces, and which could be played on the same board by those

---

* I only now know the meaning of the once-popular playground word (and its true spelling) from having just this moment Googled this odd, tiny fragment of my early years. It has remained until this point a surreal un-answered question from my childhood: what were fain-lights, and why did my father evoke them to curtail our wrestling? I was directed to an online forum and all but leapt from my seat to read that some other London user, searching for the meaning, had routinely heard his father call the same word to stop play-fights when they became too rough.

who knew how. Years later I did learn the more difficult game, but do not play well. The sight of draughts pieces fills me with a nostalgia for our games in the front room, sat around one of the smaller pull-out nesting tables.

Drawing

At age six I would hand him my homework book and a pencil for him to sketch Achilles, or a church, or a sea-monster in the designated quarter-page marked out by my wobbly, intersecting pencil lines, and faintly he would begin to sketch light lines or faces or steeples from his imagination with a soft, deft, whispering touch that astonished me. Many years later, after he retired, I bought him art supplies and a course to attend, still touched as I was by the warm memory of being sat with him on the sofa, transfixed by the emerging miniature grey-and-white scenes that I would next day pass off to my teacher as my own.

If I grew up unable to comprehend much of his world, I found my peace with it when, as an adult, I reconsidered my judgement of such things and saw both my parents as fallible, fellow grown-ups. I grew fond of my dad's Dadness; I understood him, enjoyed his less obvious ways of showing affection, as well as his stories, bad jokes and funny behaviour. He still checks cutlery for dirt in each restaurant we visit and makes awkward jokes with the staff, and I love him all the more for his reliable, worn-in deportment. He also still, at seventy, with the comb-over long gone, wanders the house in his pants of a Sunday morning with a tea cosy on his head and, posing like a ballerina with arms extended, daintily lifts a leg to fart.

CHAPTER

9

I only had a few moments to keep Joel and Charlotte focused on the chosen cards in the centre of the table before they would most likely look back to the box (wondering how they could have found their way there) and prematurely spot the other three cards slipped underneath it. So I leant forward, signifying that they should pay attention to my actions, and picked up the three cards from the table. I placed them into the centre of the deck but slid them unseen as one through the deck and a little out the other side so that, as I leant back and relaxed, I was able to remove them unnoticed and retain them in my right hand.

I held the deck high in my left hand, keeping their eyes far from the box to my right, and performed a one-handed shuffle. This is a pretty move, which had taken me many months to perfect. I had, some years before, seen another magician at a stall in Camden Market perform this shuffle and it had immediately lodged in my mind as something I *had* to learn.

The obsessive trait of latching on to something I see others do and not resting until I have acquired the same skill is a pattern I can trace back to being sat on the stairs in my house as a child of seven or eight with my taller, older cousin Martin. Martin, whom I admired greatly, was able to sit with his feet comfortably on the stair two below the one on which his backside was perched, his knees comfortably positioned at a right angle over the middle stair, which was not touched at all. I thought this impossibly cool and grown up and impressive. My own seven-year-old legs would only let me plant my feet on the step directly below where I was sat, but to be more like Martin I would lean back on my stair and reach down with my toes as far as I could, so that the balls of my feet were just in contact with the step two down from mine. I wanted *so* badly to be able to sit effortlessly across three steps like my cousin. When I had grown enough to do so, I remembered being delighted with my success, and I still sometimes proudly note my ability to casually traverse several steps with my legs on the occasions when I find myself sat on stairs, which are now rare, having left university some time ago.

Perhaps a year after first attempting to copy Martin, I became aware that some friends of mine at school could make themselves burp at will. This I found impossible to accomplish, and it seemed to me to be the most fun-filled and praiseworthy talent that I might set myself to the business of acquiring. Petitioning such friends and my mother for instructions as to how to achieve the envied feat was a lengthy and frustrating process, as I soon found my desire to learn pitched against the problems of private language as these people tried to explain the sequence of very specific muscular contractions necessary to first correctly trap and then expel air using the throat. The initial stumbling block was the instruction to 'swallow air', which to my ears amounted to taking a breath in and gulping, which was not the same thing at all. I remember walking in the local park with my mother and our dogs, attempting to under-stand what she meant by holding air in the throat, begging for more clarity, until she bade me stop trying for fear that I would make myself ill with my disturbing and strident efforts.

I have of late found myself experiencing a similar annoy-ance: at the age of thirty-nine, I am still racked with jealousy when I hear a particular friend affect a very convincing child's voice. This is not merely a question of talking in a silly falsetto: it is a perfectly convincing replication of a child of about three years old. Over the telephone it is quite unnerving. I enjoy impersonation and have put many hours into honing a small number of recognisable voices that I occasionally might use to lift an anecdote, but seem unable to create this very specific sound that he can adopt so effortlessly. This frustration is exac-erbated by his attempts to express what he is doing, which of course relies primarily upon the inexpressible machinations of muscle-memory and the unconscious. I listen to what he says and attempt to emulate the voice, but the concentrated effort is thwarted by the laughter my high-pitched squealing provokes in us both. The ludicrous facial expressions that accompany my efforts provoke further giggles and force me continually to stop and start, which in turn means I tend to repeat the same syllable or phrase and quickly sound even more ridiculous, and thus the laughter is augmented and my sincere desire to acquire a skill descends into convulsion and open weeping from us both at my endeavours.

Long after I learnt a one-handed shuffle, I found that my most burning adult determination was to learn how to poach eggs perfectly. In the same way that my rage at not being able to find my pen before leaving the house far outweighs the anger I feel towards social injustices more worthy of my fury, the obsessive ambition I have felt around learning to burp or correctly poach eggs far outweighs any drive I have ever had regarding my career.

I had discovered good poached eggs after ordering breakfast in a hotel* the morning after a terrible gig. The joy of sitting alone on a sunny morning in a half-decent hotel† with

---

* Something about the environment of a hotel and the open invitation of a sprawling breakfast buffet gives one permission to try the most unlikely breakfast combinations. It does not seem untoward to assemble at the communal buffet a salmagundi of smoked salmon, hash browns and pineapple to undergird one's order of Eggs Benedict; then to return a little later for a fruit salad and, as an afterthought, an experimental union of Shreddies and Coco Pops in the same bowl. (Mixing cereals is an innovative move quite foreign to adult domestic life, but somehow irresistible when we are faced with such old favourites offered side by side in large open-mouthed serving jars. I watch guest after guest combine cereals in this way, and I hope that beneath their casual deportment they are each at that moment enjoying the slightest stirring of delinquent delight that connects them pleasantly with childhood. This I consider to be a valuable service offered by the hotel, unmentioned in the brochure.)

† By 'half-decent', I mean hotels with any character and warmth, however shabby. I am bemused by the supposed 'corporate' style of many hotels, and wonder which corporations specifically look to entertain their staff or clients in purposefully insipid, soulless environments with foam-tiled ceilings and blank bars with nauseating names like 'Choices'. Or rather 'choices', because Heaven forfend we should ever begin such a name with

a book and an indecent smorgasbord of buffet treats outweighs the pain of any difficulties encountered in the performance the night before, and clears the mind after a sleepless night of mentally replaying every excruciating moment and endlessly berating oneself in a hot, airless fluster under restrictive bed linen.‡ I have a real fondness for Eggs Benedict and tend to order this whenever I see it on a menu. Many hotels make the classic error of smothering the plate and all upon it with a lake of thick shop-bought Hollandaise; few realise that the key to

_____

a capital letter when we want to capture the cool, casual, contemporary chic of these sophisticated brasseries. I have seen a photograph of one of these unpalatable hotels being constructed, and the ghastly snapshot depicted the room-units being lowered into place by a crane, each one pre-decorated and with furniture assembled, right down to the galling landscape prints on the wall. Everything was in place, save perhaps the miniature kettle and two-pack of stem ginger biscuits, to be added at a later date.

‡ I have spent many nights in such hotels while touring, all of them preceded by the infuriating ritual of gaining entry to the bed. If, in my years as a sceptic, I have found one phenomenon that defies rational explanation, it is the habit of these hotels to *tuck in* their duvets around the sides and base, meaning that I have to walk round the bed releasing the quilt from its pointless restraint. In doing so I invariably bring the undersheet out with it, meaning that I must then walk one more time round the three sides tucking the sheet back under the mattress and therefore in essence making the bed myself – an extraordinarily annoying process to have to carry out when one is tired and perhaps a little woolly from a double-shot of thin Glenfiddich which formed the length and breadth of the entire single-malt range downstairs at Choices (sorry, choices). Sometimes I am too tired to bother with untucking all sides of the duvet and yank out only one long side. This is a mistake, as within moments of entering the partially

the success of this glorious antemeridian concoction lies primarily in the interplay between perfectly poached fresh eggs, a strong-flavoured cured ham and the texture of the bread base. My own preference is for a smoked Black Forest ham on one half of an unbuttered sliced white muffin, or even an Irish potato farl, with two eggs piled on top and only a generous teaspoonful of the home-made sauce between them. The ham should send a sharp savoury sting through the dairy-mildness of the eggs and tangy, buttery slop of the Hollandaise; the bread

---

unlocked bed I find myself attempting to kick or lift the duvet out at its far end with my feet. Not only is this a difficult action by virtue of the fact that leverage is at a minimum, but the fight is also partially against myself, lying as I am on the same heavy mattress, out from under which I am hoping to pull the bedclothes. Thus I become hotter and angrier in the process until, giving up, I fumble around the wall and headboard, blindly flick on the nearest light-switch, leap fuming from the bed, manually rip the duvet free, tuck in the sheet's edge that I have just inadvertently removed, then get back into bed wide awake and, my temper already irretrievable, reach for the switch again. But this proves as maddening as the duvet procedure, for there is a row of three switches that offers neither labelling nor logic to indicate which operates which lamp in the room, and upon pressing one now at random, the room is thrown into harsh, white light as all lamps are flung on as one. I then wildly move through all possible binary sequences with the switches, lighting different parts of the room and vestibule but never achieving the darkness I had seconds ago. Exhausted, I look to the other side of the bed and see more switches there, the up/down status of which must somehow reverse the on/off condition of their corresponding partners over on my side, thus opening up the possible number of sequences that may have to be explored before darkness is achieved, to numbers immeasurable. In a misjudged, exhausted moment, believing that the involvement of these switches might be of help, I hoist myself over to the other side to reach them. However, in the

should give substance and allow for yolk-and-sauce mopping, but any more than a half-muffin or the equivalent thereof makes for too heavy a meal for the morning. The Lanesborough in London did a superlative Benedict several years ago but now offer a bland blend involving uninteresting ham and the predictable thick sauce that seems very far from the obviously home-made emulsion they once served. The finest Eggs Benedict I have ever been served were made by a very gifted chef called Dan Savage who at the time of writing

---

case of fancier hotels, this involves the surmounting of a mound of cushions of mixed furs and fabrics which I had, shortly before, pushed across to allow access to the bed; cushions which had been arranged upon the bedclothes in an act as bafflingly pointless as the tucking-in of the duvet itself. Stifling the desire to scream, I throw the cushions to the floor and try to push my way to the other side of the bed, but the fact that the duvet's top edge extends much further up the bed than is necessary means that in pulling back at the covers I also lift and drag the far pillow from its place – a tiny further hindrance but one which by now feels impossibly infuriating as I strain to reach the far light switches with my fingertips and resume my cryptanalysis of their coded functions, throwing the room into repeating, confused combinations of light and semi-light before suddenly and randomly achieving blackness and I collapse, hot, febrile and pumping adrenalin, to begin a fitful night in a room with ineffective air-conditioning, kicking back at heavy bedding until the eventual dawn chorus of rotten families crunching their way across the gravel to the car park stirs me from my misery, lifts me from the bed and sends me off to loathe all humankind under a tepid, dribbling shower.

I have for many years found it impossible to sleep at night in a warm room. At home, even through the winter months, I will throw the windows open and spend the night in numbingly glacial conditions; in the hotter summers I have constructed air-guiding systems out of clothes-horses and cardboard packaging to direct a chilly flow from a noisy

still runs the kitchen of St Giles' Hotel in Norwich.

After having experimented much with poaching techniques and any number of specialised pans, moulds, spoons and
other aids, I would offer the following advice to a would-be
poacher. Firstly, the eggs must be fresh. If you are lucky enough
to have the contacts, secure your eggs from the source. I had
a brief period of farm-fresh eggs being supplied weekly by a
chicken-breeding crew-member of a theatre where I once
performed, and to switch to poaching eggs that are at most a

---

portable air conditioner towards the bed and force it to circulate around
me. The balance required is that of sleeping inside a warm and toasty bed
but to have a freezing room without. I do not require to feel cold in the
length of my body, just a bracing freshness around my face and, should I
choose to expose it, an arm. Because of this ludicrous sensitivity on my
part, I have devised a way of sleeping when in a hot room which is particularly useful when staying in hotels, where neither partially opening,
suicide-safe window nor abortive cooling system allows for a tolerably
arctic temperature to be achieved during the night. The trick I have developed is to turn the duvet by a hundred and eighty degrees, untucking the
open end (hotel duvet covers are not equipped with press studs or buttons
to allow for fastening) from its already bemoaned under-mattress position
to the head end of the bed. Then I sleep *inside* the duvet, directly upon the
quilt and with just the upper cover over me. The first and most obvious
advantage to this position is that I have the equivalent of a single sheet
covering me, which immediately makes things cooler. But there is a second
benefit of this system. During the night, it is possible that I will grow
uncomfortably cold. If this happens, which it usually does, I can reach back
and grab the far edge of the duvet (presuming I am touring and therefore
on my own) and pull it across to *partially* cover me. Now I am still inside
and under the thin top cover, but I also have a toasty duvet warming me
across my back.

Normally, of course, it would not be tolerable to sleep when only semi-

day old is to discover the kind of joyful, effortless ease that one experiences when exchanging shoes for slippers after a long day, or when switching from a PC to a Mac. Fresh eggs are far user-friendlier.

Secondly, use a wide, shallow pan, and start boiling six or so centimetres of water in it. While it heats, crack your first egg into a tea-cup. When the water is boiling, turn the heat down so that columns of tiny bubbles rise to the surface and keep the water gently moving. If you are only poaching a single egg, swirl the water with a wooden spoon to create a whirlpool; lower the cup into the centre of the water and tip the egg slowly into the eye of the vortex. Sometimes a second egg can be added this way, but if several are being poached, forgo the whirling and add plenty of white distilled vinegar (not malt!) to the water instead. Then carefully pour in each egg from the cup, and if those eggs are fresh, the vinegar will stop the whites from billowing out into the water like Constable's clouds.

Once that hurdle has been overcome, the difficult part is

---

covered in this way. But being already under the thin cover, there is no sense of being annoyingly half-in and half-out. The dual play of duvet proper (shielding the back and side) and thin upper cover (under which the knees and arms find themselves able to move without restriction) achieves a surprising uniformity of temperature; the thick quilty bundle can even be pulled further over or pushed back to raise or lower body heat and state of cosiness respectively. It works very well. The only disadvantages to using this system in a hotel are as follows: the duvet itself can feel a little rough, it won't always look very clean, and Housekeeping will return it to its original position every morning while you're downstairs eccentrically combining breakfast ingredients.

over. Now cover the pan and leave for exactly three minutes. Prepare kitchen towel for drying, then when your timer beeps, trings or trumps, bring the eggs out with a slotted spoon in the order in which they were added and let them sit upon the towel for a moment before piling them on your toasted muffin.

'Would you catch me if I did that again?' I asked Joel and Charlotte, and looked across at the box. Under it were three face-down cards, just placed there under cover of misdirection.

Their attention now directed, the two saw what they presumed to be a reappearance of the three cards. Ahead of themselves, they roared with disbelief. Their conviction that these must be the actual chosen cards (which in reality were still palmed at the time in my right hand) earned me enough of a slip in their attention to (after lifting the box with my left hand) place the three palmed cards from my right on top of the three now exposed on the table. In the action of scooping up the cards, I let the three indifferent cards neatly and invisibly drop to my lap as I displayed the faces of the correct three, retained in the hand. Again, an impossible flight was confirmed.

The surprise of the double appearance of the cards under the box triggered a large enough reaction, and therefore a fulsome Newtonian off-beat for the final bold stratagem that would finish the trick. The three cards were still in my hands; Joel and Charlotte had turned to each other to excitedly share their feelings of befuddlement. I sat back, again to cue a sense that I was doing nothing of interest, and once more switched the three cards in my hand for an indifferent three from the top of the deck. I placed these, face-down of course, on the table. Meanwhile I dropped my hand with the remainder of the deck under the table to my lap and collected the three cards I had discarded there moments before, bringing them just up to below the level of the table. Taking the box in my other hand, I brought it and the deck together momentarily and slipped the top three, chosen cards into the case. It was a perfectly visible move for anyone who may have been watching, but I performed it as confidently, casually and efficiently as I had a thousand times before, knowing as I placed the box back in its position on the table that my participants, distracted by their own enthusiasm, had missed the load.

As I put down the box, Joel had turned back to me and was offering a kind, unabashed verdict on my skills, as he perceived them. Charlotte had her hand over her mouth and was looking at me in shocked silence. A wave of warmth for the two of them passed over me: I thought I would like to know them in private life. But for now I could not break the spell, as there was one more climax to come.

I raised my hand to stop Joel in his tracks. 'Wait! Now you know what to look for. Back under the box. Watch . . .'

I picked up the three face-down cards, slipped them into the deck together and gave it a couple of cuts. Joel and Charlotte were moving their eyes between the deck and the box, waiting to catch the moment of arrival of the cards. I enjoyed their determination to catch me out. A flick of my little finger sent a random card flying from the middle of the deck, which then skimmed across the table towards them, with enough force for it to fall to the floor on their side.

'Would you mind?' I said, gesturing for them to retrieve it, as if the expulsion of the pasteboard had been an accident.

Neither of them moved, knowing I was forcing at least one of them to look away. 'You watch the cards, I'll watch the box,' was Joel's solution to Charlotte, and he lowered himself slowly sideways, eyes locked on the box, while he felt around blindly on the floor for the card. He came back up with it, still looking at the box, and extended his hand towards me with the card without moving his gaze. I reached across to take it and purposefully blocked Charlotte's view of the box for an instant, causing her to sit up straight to peer over the top of my arm.

I wanted them later to ascribe the moment of method to this charade of misdirection. Therefore, I now needed to move straight to the finale, as if I had just invisibly loaded the box at that moment. I took the recovered card from Joel and slid it back in the deck, then clicked my fingers over it. 'Gone!' I exclaimed, and spread the cards in a wide arc once again to show that the indices of the three chosen cards were absent. Joel's eyes were still locked on the card-case, though he clearly wanted to look at the card spread. I sat right back, far from both cards and box, and lifted my hands in a gesture of open honesty, which cued Joel to relax his scrutiny of the box and check the spread instead. He and Charlotte saw that the cards were not there, and that they were clearly also not under the box. I waited for them to look up.

'Are they not under the box?' I asked, and looked back and forth between Charlotte and the box, prompting her to pick it up and see.

She hesitated, then followed the silent command, leaning

over to lift the red and white carton. Nothing there. She put it back down and looked at me, uncertain where this was heading.

'Pick it up again,' I said.

She did.

I gestured for her to shake it.

She shook the case, and as she did so, the rattling sound of the three cards inside announced at long last the denouement of the trick to the three of us.

Charlotte flung herself back into the seat and turned to face Joel, holding the box close to her face, her eyes wide. She started to open the flap and he came in close in order to be able to peer down inside, their faces almost touching as she, a little nervously, opened the box and he reached up to help. They both saw the top edges of three cards inside, and now both were holding the cheap box as if it were something precious, and pulling the cards out together. The cards were facing Joel as they were removed, so he saw each first before it was turned towards Charlotte. They brought them out slowly, almost tenderly.

I gathered together the cards from the table and held out my hand to take back the props. They both still held cards; Joel had in his hands his Jack of Hearts along with the Bicycle box. He and Charlotte turned to face me and speak. She started to, but her gaze was quickly pulled up to a place behind me, and Joel's followed to the same place a half-second later.

A moving presence at my left side . . . Benedict was pushing past, a glass of red wine in each hand. Joel and Charlotte separated quickly and guiltily. A fat arm swung across and dumped one glass on the table in front of her; the other was retained by Benedict, who remained too close, peripherally huge, his colossal white shirt and flapping suit jacket right by my left side, the sweet smell of fresh cigarette smoke caught in their fibres, and his face, when I turned to look, a little flushed from having recently come back into the restaurant from the cool evening air.

I rose to let Benedict in, but he remained stock-still, forcing me to lean back a little as I stood. I saw his wallet was in his right trouser pocket, nearest me. If he sat down, his right hip and my left knee could brush. I thought of the powerful nickel-cadmium-coated rare-earth magnet strapped to my leg.

'Thank you so much,' Charlotte said, handing me the cards, tilting her head to look up, her hair following buoyantly.

Joel stood to shake my hand. I shifted my chair to gain comfortable distance from Benedict, keeping him within reach of my knee, and took Joel's hand. 'Hey, amazing,' he offered, shaking his head to express his happy bewilderment. He did not look at Benedict.

I smiled at the two, placed the deck of cards into the box, and clapped my hands together, quickly throwing the box high into my jacket where I caught it under my left arm. I opened my hands to show the box vanished and bowed a little towards Joel and Charlotte.

I turned and bowed in the same way to Benedict, taking the opportunity to release my grip on the cards and let them drop into my hand at the base of the jacket on that side. A tiny movement slipped them into my trouser pocket.

I left the trio; Benedict was saying something and laughing

loudly and alone behind me. At the table to my side, from which I had taken a chair before the trick, the family were now watching with delight. The boy was absorbed in my movements.

'Here he is!' the tall woman said over-eagerly to her son.

I smiled and stepped across, bringing the borrowed chair with me and retrieving the deck in order to repeat the performance. I turned my body to ensure that the three behind me could not see me take the cards from my pocket, so as to preserve the effect of the disappearance.

The woman continued to speak with a feigned excitement entirely for the benefit of her quiet son. Wide-eyed and possessed of a large, grinning mouth that showed her ample teeth, she assured the boy that I would be able to show him something 'wonderfully amazing!' Her thin husband, in a brown corduroy jacket and green jumper, lifted his eyes to me from behind his glasses and faintly smiled before dropping his gaze to the large brandy before him.

As she instructed me loudly to sit, I gazed through her, and my eyes caught a movement at the far end of the lounge: the grey mass of the fat man finding his way back to his table from the toilets, through the warm light, navigating other tables as he went, hitching at the sides of his trousers. The muted roar of the sibilant cistern followed him until it was again cut short as the door to the toilets swung shut.

I sat down to speak to the son, asking him if he liked magic, letting him answer, while I looked back and forth between him and the fat man, who was reaching his friends and now picking past them to his seat.

Just before he sank out of view and settled back into the distant, warm jumble of conversations emanating from that dim corner, the man looked up for a moment and out across the tables and diners, around at the scattered, ludicrous interpretations of the Eastern Orthodox Empire, and for a moment, it seemed, right at me. Then, across the wide lounge, he nodded. He nodded in that male acknowledging style where the head tips up and back rather than down, in a display of recognition rather than affirmation, and I, a beat later from my side, returned the same movement. But as I did so I instinctively blinked and looked away, embarrassed and thrown; glancing across the walls and windows of the interior for a second, the corners of my mouth lifting as an afterthought, so as not to seem rude, in the way I would keep smiling after walking away from someone's joke, in case I was still being watched.

I turned my attention back to the boy, who had by then already finished speaking. I removed the deck from its case, dropped the empty box in its precise place to my right, cut the deck to bring the shortened Queen to the top and spread the cards in an arc across the table. I instructed them to pick a card each, and turned aside to let them do so.

I looked away, as my profession demands that I do so often, and my eyes alighted on a small window just to the right of the door; the grey woollen hat of a young man passing quickly outside, momentarily backlit by the bright patch of yellow from a streetlamp on the other side of the car park; the lamp haloed by spitting rain, one of several haloed yellow smudges that formed two dotted lines of dwindling size along the route of the main road, lines which (as the family mumbled that their cards were chosen and what should they do next) finally merged into the distant white and red points of the car-lights that were now slowly circling a fat, wet Bristol roundabout in the night rain.

(Then I woke up, then I died.)

Acknowledgements

My fondest thanks to my wonderful friend Iain Sharkey, for reading the manuscript and offering his inspired thoughts for the price of a couple of dinners. Also to Tom Mullica, for inventing such a great card trick, to my editor Doug Young, and to Jennie, and to Joe.